SHIPWRECKED

A Peoples' History of the

Seattle Mariners

Jon Wells

EPICENTER PRESS

Epicenter Press is a regional publisher of nonfiction books about the arts, history, environment, and cultures and lifestyles of Alaska and the Pacific Northwest.

Publisher: Kent Sturgis
Acquisitions Editor: Lael Morgan
Developmental editor: Dan Levant
Proofreaders: Katrina Pearson, Patrick Lagreid
Indexer: Sherrill Carlson
Cover design: Elizabeth Watson, Watson Design
Text design: Stephanie Martindale
Printer: McNaughton & Gunn

Library of Congress Control Number: 20129324477

ISBN 978-1-935347-18-7

10 9 8 7 6 5 4 3 2 1

Printed in the United States of America

To order single copies of SHIPWRECKED, mail $15.95 plus $6 for shipping (WA residents add $1.90 state sales tax) to Epicenter Press, PO Box 82368, Kenmore, WA 98028; call us day or night at 800-950-6663, or visit www.epicenterpress.com. Find us on Facebook.

CONTENTS

This book is dedicated to the two most supportive people in my life, my mom and my wife Michele, and also to Dave Niehaus for inspiring me to write about baseball.

PREFACE

This book is the culmination of sixteen years spent covering the Seattle Mariners baseball team professionally and watching their games as a fan.

I moved to Seattle in September 1994, during the baseball strike that canceled that year's World Series. When the strike was settled and baseball returned in 1995, I began attending Mariners games at the Kingdome on a daily basis.

I quickly realized something incredible — that unlike the cities I'd lived in for much of my first thirty-three years, in Seattle you could actually go to every single game. Getting to and from a game in cities such as New York and Los Angeles was an ordeal that might take up to six hours. Before I moved to Seattle, I would typically get to one or two games a month.

In Seattle, there wasn't as much traffic heading to the games and I found that if I timed things just right, I could park for free two blocks from the Kingdome.

Even better, because the Mariners at the time had one of the best-hitting teams in the league and some of the worst pitching known to man, their games were typically slugfests. While the baseball purists surely hated it, if you liked the long ball and enjoyed high scoring games, this was an intoxicating place to be.

And 1995 was a very special season. The Mariners had never made the playoffs before — and in fact had only finished above .500 twice in the team's eighteen-year history. But there were other forces at work that year, as the team's owners declared that they would put the team up for sale if they didn't get a commitment for a new outdoor stadium. If they didn't get that stadium, in all likelihood the team would move out of Seattle.

The possibility of the Mariners moving was a foreign concept for me. I'd never before had to think about the threat of my hometown team moving out of town. The Yankees and Dodgers had been entrenched in their cities for decades, each with a large following of fans who had grown up rooting for those teams.

What I found incredible in my first year in the Northwest was the opposition the Mariners faced trying to get a new stadium. I found it unfathomable that there was a well-funded group, Citizens for More Important Things, that existed solely to oppose using public funds to build a baseball stadium. Not only that, but a significant number of people in the area were of the mindset that "we don't need baseball" and "let them pay for their own stadium."

This was shocking to me. In the cities I'd lived in before coming to Seattle, it was a given that the teams would remain forever. Yet here I was, in my first year in a new city, going to every game of my new favorite team, but realizing that if the Mariners moved, I'd probably have to move too. I wasn't going to remain in a city that didn't have a major-league team.

In August and September that year, as the Mariners were closing in on the California Angels in the American League West, I was at the Kingdome for every single game. Night after night the Mariners won and night after night, or so it seemed, the Kingdome scoreboard would inform us that the Angels had lost yet again and that the M's had pulled a game closer to first place.

It was the greatest experience in my life as a baseball fan. Support for the stadium, which had been lukewarm earlier in the year, increased significantly as the M's kept winning. On the night of the stadium election, September 19, the Mariners came back from two runs down in the ninth inning to tie the score against the Texas Rangers on an improbable home run by Doug Strange, a player who'd hit just one home run the first five months of the season. The M's won the game in the eleventh inning and with that kind of momentum, it seemed the stadium vote was destined to pass.

The vote narrowly failed, but after the Mariners won the A.L. West in an exciting one-game playoff over the Angels and then defeated the Yankees in the first round of the playoffs, there was finally enough political support locally for the team to get their new stadium.

While I had spent the '95 season as a fan, I decided shortly after that season ended that I wanted to get more involved and set about to create a game program that would be sold outside the Kingdome before all Mariner games.

My reasons for publishing the game-day program, which we called *The Grand Salami,* named after the signature call of the Mariners' legendary broadcaster, Dave Niehaus, were numerous.

First, the Mariners were putting out their own game program just three times a year. Because I went to more than three games a year and figured other fans did too, I saw a need for a program that came out more frequently. Second, the Mariners' program provided no information of substance on the opposing teams. Unlike teams with more baseball tradition, the only information the M's provided about players on the visiting teams was a list of names and uniform numbers on their scorecard. Seattle baseball fans deserved better.

Most important, I believed there was a need for an outside voice, someone to question what the Mariners were doing, whether it be commentary about the players or the team, or about whether management was doing right by the team's fans. I was shocked after the '95 season when the Mariners traded one of their best players, Tino Martinez, to the team they had just beaten in the playoffs — the New York Yankees.

While Mariner fans were understandably angry that the team would trade Martinez to the Yankees since attendance was on the rise and a new stadium was being built for the team, the M's said they couldn't afford to pay Martinez. It was an outrage, yet the media covering the team went along as if it was just business as usual, that the Mariners were always going to operate as a farm team for other teams in baseball, trading away their best players when they became good enough to earn a large contract. Baseball fans in Seattle had proven in 1995 that they'd support a team that won; the local politicians had done their part to get the Mariners a new stadium. But it didn't seem like the team was keeping its end of the bargain.

Our publication has met with significant resistance from the Mariners over the years because the team's PR staff likes to control the message that goes out to the public. One of my favorite anecdotes from our early years of publishing occurred when one of our columnists, Mike Gastineau from KJR Sportsradio, related to me that he had told Randy Adamack, the Mariners' director of communications, that we were putting out a good publication and that the team should get behind us. Adamack's response went something like this, "These things come and go. If we don't support it, it will just go away." Sixteen years later we're still here.

❀ ❀ ❀

The need for a book detailing the trials and tribulations of the Mariners has grown over the past decade as the team sank so low as to become irrelevant in the baseball world, if not in its own home city. Through one misstep after another, the team's ownership has managed to cement the M's position as one of the worst run yet highly profitable franchises in all of professional sports.

While the team seems to have a long-term lease on last place, Mariners ownership has made profits totaling over $100 million in the last decade. The path chosen by the team has been one of relentlessly placing a much higher priority on corporate profits than on putting a winning team on the field. Heading into 2012, the Mariners, who had last made the postseason in 2001, were the only team in the American League and one of just two teams in all of baseball never to have played in the World Series.

The M's record of futility is littered with one bad personnel decision after another, amid persistent examples of meddling by the finance guys in the business of the team's baseball people. Both of those finance guys, Mariners Chairman Howard Lincoln and team President Chuck Armstrong, were contacted and declined to be interviewed for this book.

There's hope for the future, though, as the Mariners have in place a baseball architect, Jack Zduriencik, who has both the foresight and talent-evaluation skills to take the team to the next level. Additionally, Lincoln and Armstrong have advanced into their seventies and seem unlikely to remain in power for more than three or four more seasons. Against all odds, we might see a World Series in Seattle yet.

Chapter 1

THE FIRST FIFTEEN SEASONS

The Seattle Mariners have had a contentious history since beginning play in 1977, which is somewhat fitting because the team was born from a breach-of-contract lawsuit after Seattle's first major-league team, the Pilots, moved to Milwaukee after just one season, 1969.

The lawsuit was settled when the American League awarded Seattle a new expansion franchise on January 31, 1976. The team's original ownership group consisted of six partners, headed up by entertainer Danny Kaye. The others were Lester Smith, Kaye's partner in the radio business; Jim Walsh, president of the Bon Marche department store; Stan Golub, a wholesale jeweler and civic activist; Walter Schoenfeld, a clothing manufacturer; and James Stillwell, a road contractor.

Given the team's origins, it shouldn't have come as a surprise that of the six hundred names suggested by fifteen thousand entrants in a name-the-team contest, "Litigants" was a popular one. Other suggestions included the Saboteurs, Shoo-Ins, Scavengers, Saps, Clamdiggers, Hydrofoils, and Albatrosses.

While expansion teams typically take a few years to become competitive, the Mariners went a decade and a half before having a season in which they won more games than they lost — the longest stretch of futility for an expansion franchise in any major sport. In comparison, their expansion brethren, the Toronto Blue Jays, had their first winning season in their seventh season, 1983. That marked the beginning of a stretch in which Toronto finished over .500 in eleven straight seasons, winning five division titles and capturing World Series titles in 1992 and 1993.

Because they lost so often and played in a mausoleum-like indoor stadium, the Kingdome, the Mariners didn't draw many people to their games during this long stretch of sub-.500 seasons. In fact, they didn't average as many as nineteen thousand fans per game until their fifteenth season, 1991, when they finally finished above .500 at 83-79.

It's not hard to see why the two expansion clubs came away with markedly different results. Toronto had a wealthy ownership that put money into scouting and developing young talent, with the Blue Jays' original architect, Pat Gillick, establishing an academy for Latin players in the Dominican Republic. Meanwhile, in Seattle, Danny Kaye, who put up most of the $6.5 million expansion fee, was the only original Mariner owner considered to be wealthy. The organization was so underfunded it had cut back to just five scouts and three minor-league teams by the time the first ownership group sold the team early in 1981.

When California real-estate developer George Argyros bought the team from the original owners, he was seen as the savior of the franchise. He talked a good game, said he intended to take the Mariners to the World Series, and he even had a personal motto — "Patience is for Losers." Early on, he won over Seattle fans with his enthusiasm, helped Bill the Beer Man lead fans at the Kingdome to a rousing version of "Take Me Out to the Ballgame" and walked through the outfield bleachers meeting M's fans.

It was a short honeymoon. It became clear within a few months that while Argyros had the money to turn the Mariners into a winner, he knew little about baseball and had no intention of spending to improve the team. The team's farm system, led by longtime former Senators and Rangers farm director Hal Keller, drafted and developed many talented players, but with Argyros running the club on a shoestring budget, the Mariners repeatedly traded their best players or lost them as free agents once they became established enough to demand significant dollars.

After his first season of ownership, Argyros refused to give the team's best hitter, Tom Paciorek, who'd hit .326 and led the team in RBI in 1981, the multi-year deal sought by the player. Argyros quipped to the media, "If Tom Paciorek can guarantee his performance, we will guarantee his contract."

After a lengthy impasse, Paciorek was traded to the White Sox for three players of little use. Reportedly the team's policy at the time was to offer multi-year contracts only to free agents from other teams, which was strange because the M's rarely signed free agents in those early years.

The team's best 1982 hitter, outfielder Bruce Bochte, retired at the end of that season at age thirty-two rather than play another year for Argyros. Bochte, who returned to play for Oakland in 1984, had been Seattle's player representative and reportedly, was angered by threats made by Argyros during the players' strike in 1981. Argyros also engaged in a nasty salary dispute with M's closer Bill Caudill prior to the '83 season and traded him after that season. Caudill was the first client of Scott Boras, a young player agent who'd been a minor-league teammate of Caudill's in the St. Louis organization.

THE FIRST FIFTEEN SEASONS

It wasn't just the players who Argyros chased away. Prior to the '83 season he refused to give pitching coach Dave Duncan a $5,000 raise from his salary of $30,000, so Duncan left to accept a two-year, $100,000 deal to become Tony LaRussa's pitching coach with the White Sox. Duncan spent the next three decades with LaRussa, helping the third-winningest manager in history lead fourteen teams to the postseason in Chicago, Oakland, and St. Louis. In 1982, Duncan's first year on Seattle's coaching staff, M's pitchers led the league in strikeouts and finished second in shutouts and saves. That season the club had its best record (76-86) and finish (fourth place in the A.L. West) to date despite having the second-lowest payroll in baseball.

The manager of that overachieving team, Rene Lachemann, would receive calls from Argyros in the dugout mid-game and was fired less than halfway into the '83 season, a move described in an editorial in the *Seattle Post-Intelligencer* as "the most unpopular decision in the seven-year history of the Seattle franchise." Fans at the Dome in the days after Lachemann's firing wore T-shirts that proclaimed "Lachemann Loyal" on the back and "Argyros the Fool" on the front. Members of the Seattle Mariners Women's Club showed up at a game wearing buttons showing a picture of Argyros with a red line through it.

"George was a very impatient person," Lachemann told *The Grand Salami* years later. "He wanted to run a baseball operation like he ran his apartment-management business, but he didn't know baseball. He had good people in the organization, but he didn't want to spend the money to keep them."

The Mariners lost several young stars during Argyros' nine-year run as the team's owner, among them Mark Langston, Danny Tartabull, Mike Moore, Floyd Bannister, Ivan Calderon, and Dave Henderson. Fortunately for the team, M's scout Bob Harrison didn't allow Argyros to screw up the drafting of Ken Griffey Jr., selected as the first overall pick in the 1987 amateur draft. Argyros wanted to select a college pitcher, Mike Harkey, with the pick, but was persuaded otherwise when Harrison rigged the ratings of the two players so that Argyros would not be tempted to select Harkey, who some thought might reach the majors sooner than the seventeen-year-old Griffey.

In October 1989, Argyros sold the Mariners for $76 million to a group from Indianapolis headed by forty-two-year-old Jeff Smulyan. More than twenty years after Argyros sold the team, his legacy lives on in Chuck Armstrong, Mariners president and chief operating officer. Armstrong, who'd worked for Argyros' real-estate operation in California, had no experience in baseball when hired by the M's in 1983, and he didn't want the job, but Argyros made him team president anyway. And while Argyros repeatedly claimed that he couldn't make money operating the team in Seattle, he earned a tidy $63 million profit when he sold the franchise.

Smulyan promised "more promotions, more fun, and a better team." The Mariners improved in the two years he owned the team, culminating in the franchise's first winning season in 1991. But Smulyan soon realized that making the M's financially viable was much more difficult than he had thought. Despite a franchise record 2.1 million in attendance in 1991, six-hundred thousand more fans than the team had drawn in any previous season, the team's revenues were still last among all major-league teams. With Smulyan complaining publicly that he was "throwing money down a rat hole," he decided his best bet to make the Mariners work was to move the team. He secretly hatched a plan to relocate the team to Tampa — as soon as he could figure out a way to get the M's out of Seattle.

Fortunately for Seattle baseball fans, the Mariners' lease at the King-dome contained a clause stipulating that before Smulyan could move the team or sell the club to an out-of-town owner, he had to offer the team to local buyers. That clause came in handy when, in August of 1991, Security Pacific Bank said it didn't believe baseball was viable in Seattle and demanded that Smulyan pay off a $39.5 million loan four years early. The bank's decision to call the loan early was set off by Smulyan's attempt to borrow an additional $4.5 million to help pay off the Mariners' $11 million share of a collusion award Major League Baseball players had won against the team owners for agreeing among themselves not to sign free agents after the '85 season. In an ironic twist, Smulyan wound up having to sell the team because of collusion that had occurred years before he bought the team and that likely did not involve the M's. To that point in its history, the team had never signed a marquee free agent.

On December 6, 1991, Smulyan, unable to find alternate financing to pay off the Security Pacific Loan, announced he was triggering the escape clause in the team's lease with King County and offered to sell the team to a local buyer for $100 million. Under terms of the lease, if no local buyer stepped forward within 120 days then Smulyan would be free to sell the team to out-of-town interests or move it himself to another city.

Chapter 2

HIGHLIGHTS AND LOWLIGHTS, 1977 TO 1991

HIGHLIGHTS

1. The hiring of broadcaster Dave Niehaus

On December 18, 1976, the M's hired the forty-one-year-old Niehaus, who'd called California Angels' games the previous eight seasons.

While initially there was skepticism over the hiring of an outsider as the team's lead broadcaster instead of voices familiar to the region such as Bob Robertson or Bill Schonely (who had broadcast the Pilots games in 1969), Niehaus became a Seattle institution who called the team's games for thirty-four years until his death in November 2010.

2. First game in Mariners history

A total of 57,762 jammed into the Kingdome for the team's first-ever game, a 7-0 loss to the California Angels. The man who would become known as the Ancient Mariner, thirty-eight-year-old Diego Segui, who had pitched for the '69 Pilots, started for Seattle and took the loss. Rookie second-baseman Jose Baez recorded the team's first hit, which was also his first hit in the big leagues.

Two nights later, the M's recorded their first victory, a 7-6 win over the Angels on run-scoring doubles in the ninth inning by Bob Stinson and Larry Milbourne. Two days after that, Juan Bernhardt hit the first home run in franchise history in a 12-5 loss to California.

Earning a salary of $100,000, left-fielder Steve Braun was the highest-paid player in the M's Opening-Night lineup, and the combined salary of the four starting infielders was $104,000. First-baseman Dan Meyer and third-baseman Bill Stein each made $30,000 that year, while shortstop Craig Reynolds was paid $25,000 and Baez just $19,000. Center-fielder Ruppert Jones, who became the Mariners' first All-Star that year, made

$40,000 while right-fielder Lee Stanton's salary was $75,000. Segui was paid $50,000.

3. 1979 All-Star Game at the Kingdome

On July 17, 1979, the fiftieth annual All-Star Game was played at the Kingdome before a crowd of 58,905. The National League won for the ninth consecutive time, 7-6, as Yankee ace Ron Guidry walked Lee Mazzilli of the Mets in the ninth inning to force in the winning run. Much to the crowd's delight, Bruce Bochte, Seattle's lone All-Star representative, knocked in a run in the sixth inning with a chopper over shortstop.

4. Paciorek beats the Yankees — twice

On May 9, 1981, in just the fourth game of Rene Lachemann's managerial tenure with the M's, a Bat Night crowd of 51,903 witnessed a thrilling Mariner victory over the Yankees. Tom Paciorek, who the night before had hit a game-winning home run in the ninth inning to beat New York, hit a three-run homer in the ninth to beat the Yankees again. Upon seeing a second game-winner from Paciorek, the fans went wild at the Dome.

According to pitcher Glenn Abbott, an original Mariner, "There has never been a crowd at a Mariner game that acted like that. I don't care whatever happened before; they never got this excited, never, never, never."

5. Gaylord Perry wins 300th game

On May 6, 1982, forty-three-year-old Gaylord Perry won his 300th career game in a 7-3 Seattle win over the Yankees at the Kingdome. The hoopla brought national attention to the Mariners for the first time in club history. One year later, Perry went 3-10 and was released after becoming a disruptive influence in the M's clubhouse.

The 300th career home run of slugger Willie Horton three years earlier was met with significantly less fanfare despite Horton having to hit his milestone home run twice. The first time, the ball collided with a Kingdome loudspeaker and Horton only got a single, but he made sure the ball found the seats the next night.

6. Opening Night 1986

A crowd of 42,121 was on hand at the Kingdome on April 8, 1986, to see an Opening Night they would not soon forget. The M's trailed the California Angels 4-2 in the ninth when Jim Presley hit a game-tying home run. But Presley wasn't done. Batting in the tenth inning with the bases loaded, he hammered a 1-2 pitch deep into the left field seats for a walk-off grand slam.

7. Griffey's Kingdome debut

On April 10, 1989, a crowd of 33,866 came out for the M's '89 home opener and saw Ken Griffey Jr., playing in his first game in Seattle, hit the first pitch he saw from Chicago's Eric King on a line over the left-field wall for his first major-league home run. The crowd at the Kingdome demanded a curtain call and got one from the rookie.

8. Randy Johnson's no-hitter

On June 2, 1990, 20,014 watched the M's beat Detroit 2-0 as Randy Johnson pitched the first no-hitter in Mariners history. It was just the third complete game and first shutout of Johnson's career with Seattle. Johnson struck out eight batters, but was wild, walking six Tigers batters. He finished off the no-hitter by striking out Mike Heath on a ninety-seven-mile-per-hour fastball, then thrust his arms skyward while being mobbed by his teammates.

9. The Griffeys go deep

On August 29, 1990 the Mariners signed Ken Griffey Sr., who'd been released by the Cincinnati Reds. Two nights later, father and son made history when they both started in the Mariners' outfield with Senior hitting second, Junior hitting third.

The pair made history again on September 14, when they hit back-to-back home runs in the first inning of Seattle's game against the Angels in Anaheim. M's Manager Jim Lefebvre made history possible by giving Junior the green light on a 3-0 count after Senior had gone deep.

10. A winning season at last!

The M's beat Texas 4-3 on October 2, 1991, to win their eighty-first game of the season, ensuring at least a .500 season for the first time in the history of the franchise.

Equipment manager Henry Genzale, who had been with the M's since their inception in 1977, said "This is my proudest day to be part of the Mariners. This is for all those players who ever put on a Mariner uniform. We're winners and we'll continue to be from now on."

LOWLIGHTS

1. Mariners acquire shortstop Mario Mendoza

On December 5, 1978, the M's traded closer Enrique Romo to Pittsburgh in a six-player deal that netted Seattle shortstop Mario Mendoza and two other players. While Mendoza was a flashy defender, he achieved notoriety because of a batting average that was usually on the wrong side of .200.

Two of Mendoza's Seattle teammates, Paciorek and Bochte, began making fun of the shortstop by telling other players, including Kansas City's George Brett, that they would sink below "the Mendoza Line" if they weren't careful. The phrase was popularized after Brett mentioned it to ESPN's Chris Berman and the Mendoza Line has lived on in baseball lore since.

2. The Maury Wills' weeks

On August 4, 1980, the first manager in M's history, Darrell Johnson, was fired and replaced by Maury Wills, a former shortstop with the LA Dodgers. M's owner Danny Kaye, a lifelong Dodger fan, was said to have pushed for the hiring of Wills.

Wills would last just eighty-two games, fired the following May after the Mariners got off to a horrendous 6-18 start in 1981. After Wills' firing, *Seattle Post Intelligencer* columnist Steve Rudman chronicled "The Blunders of Maury Wills," including such "third-grade mistakes" as putting outfielder Willie Norwood on waivers before a game and then using him in the game.

Rudman also reported how Wills would chase kids who caught balls hit over the fence during spring training, demanding return of the balls. Poor Maury probably thought he could last a little longer on the job if he saved the penny-pinching Argyros a few bucks. Wills admitted in his 1991 autobiography, *On the Run*, that he had a cocaine problem during the time he was managing the Mariners.

3. Mariners uniforms stolen

During a May 1981 series in Texas, thieves broke into the visiting clubhouse at Arlington Stadium and stole twenty-two Mariners uniform jerseys and caps, all the M's batting helmets, and gloves belonging to catchers Jerry Narron and Bud Bulling.

Trainer Gary Nicholson said, "We've lost a shirt here or there, but those have been *laundry losses.* We must have come of age — somebody wants our uniforms."

4. Kearney's one-punch knockout

On August 4, 1984, M's catcher Bob Kearney and pitching coach Frank Funk got into it before a game in Oakland. The fun started when Kearney, angry about not being in the starting lineup, ripped the lineup card off the dugout wall and then refused to warm up one of the team's pitchers.

Funk's response was to throw Kearney's catcher's mitt into the clubhouse toilet. Upon discovering the wet glove, Kearney decked Funk with one punch. Funk was fired less than a month later. Kearney played three more seasons in Seattle.

5. M's trade for a washed-up Steve Yeager

In December, 1985, desperate for a solid catcher, the M's traded one of their best relief pitchers, Ed Vande Berg, to the Dodgers for thirty-seven-year-old Steve Yeager, who'd played in just fifty-three games the previous year and hit .207.

Chuck Armstrong was ecstatic about the deal, telling the media, "We think he (Yeager) will lift more than our pitching staff. We think our whole team will get a lift when he walks into our clubhouse."

Yeager hit .209 in 50 games with the M's in 1986 while earning one of the highest salaries on the team, and never played again.

6. Clemens strikes out twenty Mariners

On April 29, 1986, Boston's Roger Clemens struck out twenty Mariner batters at Fenway Park, setting a new major-league record for strikeouts in a nine-inning game. The M's would set a record of their own that year, striking out 1,148 times, most ever in American League history at the time.

7. Mariners trade Henderson and Owen to Boston

On August 17, 1986, the M's made a six-player trade with the Boston Red Sox, leaders in the A.L. East. Jim Street in the *Seattle P-I* termed the deal "perhaps the biggest trade in franchise history."

Perhaps Street meant the biggest trade in *Red Sox* franchise history; one of the two players who went to Boston, Dave Henderson, would go on to hit the home run that put the Red Sox into the World Series that October, while none of the four players Seattle received amounted to much. The other player sent to the Red Sox was shortstop Spike Owen, who four months before the trade had been named the first captain in Mariners history — by a manager, Chuck Cottier, who was fired a month into the '86 season.

8. M's trade Danny Tartabull to Kansas City

While outfielder Danny Tartabull hit twenty-five home runs and drove in ninety-six runs as a rookie in 1986, the M's were upset when Tartabull said he was too tired to play winter ball and traded him to the Royals for three players, including pitchers Scott Bankhead and Steve Shields.

Unfortunately they weren't David Cone and Mark Gubicza, two young pitchers reported by the *Seattle Times* the day before to be on their way to Seattle. Cone and Gubicza combined to win 326 big-league games; Bankhead and Shields won just sixty-five.

9. Griffey shuns fans

Hundreds of Mariner fans were upset in June 1989 when Ken Griffey Jr. left an autograph session at Winners Restaurant at Southcenter Mall in Tukwila, Washington. Griffey tried to explain that he had another appointment, but fans called him names, including "jerk" and "minor-leaguer." Griffey reported later that someone had put "five scratches" on his car while he was signing autographs.

10. Mariners bring in a moose

The M's held a contest prior to the '90 season to select the team's first mascot, with a moose selected over a sea monster. Bellingham's Ammon Spiller cast the winning entry, which read, "I choose a moose because no other team has a moose." Early in the '90 season, Minnesota pitcher Roy Smith called the Moose "The worst mascot I've ever seen."

As it turned out, there were certain perks of being the Moose that neither fans nor players knew about. The Moose would work the early innings, going from section to section entertaining young children, and take the middle innings off and return to work late in the game.

One of the young men who wore the moose suit in the early 1990s boasted years later that he'd spent the middle innings of many games having sex with a female Mariner employee in an empty Kingdome suite.

Chapter 3

NINTENDO STEPS TO THE PLATE

Those in Seattle familiar with the Mariners' struggles in the first fifteen seasons seriously doubted that there was an "angel" willing and able to buy the team and keep it in Seattle. Even though the team was improving and attendance was on the rise, Jeff Smulyan had claimed losses of $20 million in the two years he'd owned the team.

City officials in Tampa, who had met in private with Smulyan about having the Mariners move to their city, were ecstatic. They believed it was only a matter of time before Smulyan would be free to move the M's into their completed, but then-empty stadium, the Thunderdome. Some even thought that the team could be moved in time for the '92 season. All three Tampa-area TV stations broke into scheduled network programming to carry Smulyan's press conference announcing that the M's were for sale.

Business leader Herman Sarkowsky, a former owner of the Seattle Seahawks football team and the Portland Trailblazers basketball team, was appointed by Seattle Mayor Norm Rice to help keep the Mariners in Seattle. He raised a significant amount of money from the business community in advertising and season-ticket commitments, but he wasn't able to find a person or entity willing to put up the money to buy a majority interest in the team. Microsoft founder Bill Gates was approached, but declined to get involved.

Ironically, one of the only people who thought a local buyer might step forward was the man who'd sold the team to Smulyan, George Argyros. He told the *Seattle Times:* "It can happen. There's a lot of wealth in the Northwest — Microsoft, McCaw, a lot of people who can put up the equity it needs to make it work."

Argyros would be proven correct, as executives from both Microsoft (Chris Larson, Jeff Raikes, Rob Glaser, and Carl Stork) and McCaw Communications (John McCaw, Wayne Perry, Craig Watjen, and Rufus Lumry) would become involved in a group known as The Baseball Club of Seattle that offered to buy the team from Smulyan in January, 1992. But most of the purchase price of $100 million was put up by Hiroshi Yamauchi, longtime patriarch of the Nintendo Corporation, whose American division was based in Redmond, Washington.

Yamauchi had been approached by U.S. Senator Slade Gorton, who asked the Japanese executive to help save baseball in Seattle. Yamauchi agreed to do so as "a gift" to the community.

Chapter 4

THE BOYS OF PLUMMER

In addition to new ownership, the Mariners had a new field manager for the '92 season, forty-year-old Bill Plummer. Plummer replaced Jim Lefebvre, who was fired at the end of the '91 season.

The firing of Lefebvre was puzzling, as he had just led the team to its first winning record in the franchise's fifteen-year history. Years later, the reason for Lefebvre's firing was finally revealed; it seems that Jeff Smulyan had told the team's general manager, Woody Woodward, in confidence that he planned to move the team to Tampa. Woodward didn't believe that Lefebvre could be trusted to keep quiet about the team's impending move. Lefebvre was a bit of a loose cannon, having complained repeatedly to the media during the '91 season about ownership's refusal to increase payroll to add a hitter to the lineup.

The M's made a trade for the power hitter they were seeking in December of 1991, sending pitchers Bill Swift, Mike Jackson, and Dave Burba to the San Francisco Giants for twenty-nine-year-old Kevin Mitchell, minor-league pitcher Mike Remlinger, and $500,000 in cash. Mitchell had been MVP of the National League in 1989, when he hit forty-seven homers and drove in 125 runs. Mitchell's numbers had declined in the two seasons afterward, but he had still hit twenty-seven homers in 1991 despite playing in just 113 games.

Woodward, who announced the deal at the annual winter meetings in Miami Beach, Florida, said Mitchell was the right-handed slugger the M's had sought for years. "We know this man comes to play," he said. "He wants to play. He's a gamer." Reached for comment, Mitchell admitted he didn't know much about the Mariners, but said "It's going to be fun. Maybe we can get a winner up there ... I'll go out there and give the fans what they deserve."

The media reaction in Seattle was overwhelmingly in favor of the trade for Mitchell, who only weeks before had been arrested on rape charges. The charges were dropped a few days before the trade, making the deal acceptable, according to Woodward.

The day after the trade, the M's set a new one-day record for season-ticket sales, with thirty new orders, which brought the team's season ticket total to a modest 2,500.

M's spokesman Peter Vanderwarker told the *Seattle P-I*, "Without question, the trade had a big impact. People are saying the Mariners went out and got a marquee player in the prime of his career."

Randy Adamack, the M's vice president of communications, told the *Seattle Times*, "This is the first marquee player we've ever obtained who can be expected to make years of contributions."

The trade for Mitchell would turn out to be a disaster for the Mariners. The loss of the three pitchers had a devastating impact on Seattle's pitching staff, while one of those pitchers, Bill Swift, won twenty-one games for San Francisco in 1993. Mitchell hit just nine home runs in his only season with the M's.

On April 6 an Opening Night crowd of 55,918, the second-largest crowd in Kingdome history, saw the M's lose 12-10 to Texas. The Rangers scored nine times in the eighth inning, with all the runs scoring with two outs. Closer Mike Schooler retired just one of the six batters he faced. Lame-duck owner Jeff Smulyan was not in attendance that night. Three nights later, Texas beat the M's 9-1 to finish off a four-game sweep that left the Boys of Plummer 0-4.

On April 16, in his tenth game as a big-league manager, Plummer wrote in the names of both Tino Martinez and Pete O'Brien on the official lineup card at first base without listing a player at designated hitter. Plummer's gaffe cost the M's their DH for the game. When the error was discovered, the M's were forced by baseball rules to insert their pitcher into the batting order. Plummer didn't actually allow any of the Seattle pitchers to hit, instead pinch-hitting each time the pitcher's spot in the order came up.

On May 7 Toronto's Dave Winfield hit a grand slam off Schooler in the ninth inning to erase what had been a 7-4 lead for Seattle. The next night the same scenario repeated itself, as Detroit's Lou Whitaker hit a three-run homer off Schooler, again with two outs in the ninth. The Tigers, who had trailed 6-2 entering the ninth, won 7-6.

"It's like a nightmare that keeps repeating itself," an emotional Plummer said after the game.

Questioned about his use of Schooler, who was booed by much of the Kingdome crowd, Plummer said, "I still have to go with one of the best. You tell me who I'm supposed to go to in that situation, because nobody has been able to get the job done except Schools."

1992 TOP PERFORMERS

Ken Griffey Jr., .308, 27 HR, 103 RBI

Edgar Martinez, .343, 18 HR, 73 RBI

Jay Buhner, .243, 25 HR, 79 RBI

Dave Fleming, 17-10, 3.39 ERA, 228.1 IP

Randy Johnson, 12-14, 3.77 ERA, 210.1 IP

On June 9 Major League Baseball's ownership committee officially approved the sale of the Mariners to The Baseball Club of Seattle. The very next day, with baseball fans in Seattle rejoicing that the Mariners were "safe at home," General Manager Woody Woodward told the *Seattle Times* that the change in ownership wouldn't necessarily improve the M's chances on the field.

"I think fans are making a mistake thinking that a change in the ownership will allow them to do things right away," Woodward said.

On June 28 Chuck Armstrong was named team president and chief operating officer. Armstrong had held those titles under George Argyros, but was summarily dismissed when Jeff Smulyan took over the club. Media speculation centered on Woodward, who had clashed with Armstrong when the two had worked together in 1988, but that notion was scuttled when Armstrong called Woodward "the best general manager in the business."

In a July 16 Q & A piece in the *Seattle P-I*, John Ellis, chairman and CEO of the group that now owned the Mariners, was asked if he believed player salaries had peaked.

"My gut tells me they have to," Ellis responded. "The finances of the game are rapidly going downhill." But he added that the M's new ownership group had "financial staying power that very few teams have."

On July 16, 52,711 came to the Dome for what the new ownership group called "Opening Night II," but just like Opening Night in April, the M's collapsed in the eighth inning, this time surrendering five runs in the eighth to Toronto, losing 7-2.

On August 14 the Mariners announced that Edgar Martinez, who would win the A.L. batting title that year, hitting .343, had been signed to a three-year contract extension. It was the first major move under the M's new ownership. That same day Ellis gave Woodward a vote of confidence, saying "It just doesn't make sense to jump in and make changes. I don't believe in the sledgehammer approach."

Ellis, who acknowledged that the team had received letters from disgruntled fans calling for the dismissal of Woodward and Plummer, offered a qualifier, saying "But if the team goes into the sewer the rest of the season, who knows what action we will take?"

On September 6, Schooler tied a major-league record by giving up his fourth grand slam of the season, a game-winning, twelfth-inning blow by Cleveland's Carlos Martinez, as the M's lost 12-9. The homer also helped the M's set a big-league record they didn't want: most grand slams given up by a team in one season — ten.

On September 16 the M's lost their thirteenth game in a row, at the time the longest such streak in franchise history, despite a brilliant performance by Randy Johnson. The 6-foot-10 Johnson, nicknamed "The Big Unit," pitched nine innings of one-hit ball, surrendered just one unearned run and struck out fifteen Angels. The M's lost 2-1 in thirteen innings on a single by California's Luis Sojo. On September 27 Johnson struck out eighteen Texas Rangers, tying an A.L. record for a left-handed pitcher, but came away with a no-decision in a game Seattle lost 3-2. Johnson threw 160 pitches in his eight innings that night. No major-league pitcher has thrown as many pitches in a game since.

On October 4, the M's beat Chicago 4-3 to finish the season with a 64-98 record, worst in the American League and second worst in all of baseball.

Chapter 5

LOU PINIELLA TO THE RESCUE

On October 12, 1992, eight days after the '92 season ended, the Mariners fired Plummer and his coaching staff. Ellis said he had agonized over the decision, but said it came down to "the need to change, to keep turning this team into 'Our M's.' We couldn't go to the fans and business community and ask for their support and simply offer the same thing."

Seattle Times columnist Steve Kelley was adamant that the M's hadn't made enough changes. Under the headline, "M's Should Also Sweep Upstairs," Kelley wrote:

"Firing Plummer is only part of the solution. What about Woody? What has General Manager Woody Woodward done to deserve his continued employment? Didn't Woodward hire Plummer? Didn't Woodward conspire with former owner Jeff Smulyan to strip the Mariners of Bill Swift, Mike Jackson, Scott Bankhead, Bill Krueger, and other pitchers? Didn't Woodward fire Jim Lefebvre, the only winner among nine former Mariner managers? Why should Woodward, who has already fired two managers, get the chance to hire and fire a third? This is the time to completely clean house."

The day after Plummer's dismissal, Woodward said that his initial list of managerial candidates included fifty to sixty names. Among the prime candidates were former Rangers Manager Bobby Valentine, former Reds skipper Lou Piniella, and former Brewers Manager Tom Treblehorn.

Piniella, who had resigned his job in Cincinnati just two years after leading the Reds to the 1990 World Series title, quickly emerged as the frontrunner. Woodward had wanted to hire his good friend Piniella after the '88 season, but Piniella could see that the organization, with George Argyros still in charge, was not stable at the time and he hadn't seriously considered taking the M's job. While the Mariners situation had changed since '88, with solid local ownership now in place, Piniella was still reluctant, telling Woodward, "It's just not going to work ... Everything I hear is 'Don't go. Seattle is a place where managers go to see their careers end.'" But ultimately, Piniella found appealing the challenge of taking over a team that had never won anything and accepted Seattle's offer to manage the Mariners. It didn't hurt that the M's had some talented young players like Griffey, Johnson, Martinez, and right-fielder Jay Buhner to build around.

One obstacle that had to be overcome was that Griffey, the Mariners' best player, wasn't thrilled with the prospect of Piniella managing the team. Junior believed that Piniella had mishandled a situation with Ken Griffey Sr. when Senior was playing for Piniella's Reds. "It would be an interesting scenario if Piniella were hired in Seattle," said Griffey Sr. "It might or might not cause a problem, but I'd rather have Junior continue to play in Seattle."

Senior ended up convincing Junior that he didn't have hard feelings towards Piniella and neither should Junior.

Yet, on October 26, while working out at the Kingdome with other members of an All-Star touring team set to play in Japan, Griffey, who'd made the A.L. All-Star team in each of the previous three seasons, told the *Seattle Times* "I think I may only play with Seattle about two-hundred more games. I think if I don't sign a multi-year deal at some time next year, they (will) trade me early in the '94 season, about twenty games in."

"If I don't sign a long-term contract this winter or halfway through next season, I'd play out my option anyway" Griffey said. "At that point, so close to free agency, I'd just be curious to see what I'd be worth on the free-agent market. I'm not trying to be a tough guy. It's just baseball."

The hiring of the forty-nine-year-old Piniella became official on November 9 when he and the Mariners agreed to a three-year contract. At a press conference to introduce the new manager, it was also announced that Ken Griffey Sr. had been hired to be Piniella's hitting coach. Presumably the hiring of Senior would help persuade Junior to sign the five-year contract the M's new ownership had been offering him.

Piniella told the media that pitching would be a key to turning the team around. "It all starts with pitching and that will be our main focus." Piniella added that the '93 M's would be an aggressive team. "One of the trademarks of the teams I have managed," he said, "is they will play hard, get dirty and have fun."

Piniella said he believed he could turn Seattle into a winning team, telling the media, "Winning is the only thing you can build on and when a team feels good about itself, it goes onto the field confident, not cocky."

On November 17 the M's traded Kevin Mitchell, who had hit just nine home runs in his only season in Seattle, to Cincinnati for left-handed relief-pitcher Norm Charlton. Charlton had been Piniella's closer in Cincinnati and was one of the famed "Nasty Boys" who ruled the Reds' bullpen. On December 3 the Mariners signed free-agent pitcher Chris Bosio, who had gone 16-6 with Milwaukee in 1992, to a four-year, $15.25 million deal. Woodward commented that "Bosio and Norm Charlton give us a couple of guys with a little grit. They're not afraid to claim their piece of the plate. We've needed that."

Griffey's agent, Brian Goldberg, told the *Seattle P-I* in early December that the Mariners' new acquisitions had enhanced the club's chances of resigning Junior to a long-term deal. "In my mind and in Junior's mind," the agent said, "seeing those moves indicates to us that the organization is committed to putting its best foot forward."

Days later Griffey and the Mariners reached agreement on a four-year, $24 million contract.

On February 19 the M's opened their first spring training camp under Lou Piniella. It was also the first season in their new spring training facility in Peoria, Arizona. Although the team had to play all thirty of their Cactus League games in 1993 on the road, the team was able to practice in Peoria. As spring training began, Piniella told the *P-I* that the M's were a first-class organization, remarking, "We just have to bring a winning tradition to it."

Just days later, Woody Woodward, GM of the "first-class organization," welcomed Piniella to the Mariner way, announcing that the M's were $2 million over budget and that cost-cutting moves would need to be made by opening day. "We have some cutting to do and we expect to be busy," Woodward said.

Asked for his reaction, Piniella said he hoped budget cuts would not cost him a pitcher, as Johnson's name had been prominent in trade rumors.

The M's got off to a slow start in spring training of 1993, losing each of their first six Cactus League games and Mount Piniella erupted more than once. After one of the early spring training losses, Piniella ordered the food room in the Mariner clubhouse closed. When several players complained about it, Piniella exploded. "This isn't a fucking country club … I'm sick and tired of this shit."

With the M's playing all their exhibition games on the road, there were plenty of bus rides; on one of those bus rides back to Peoria, Piniella, angered by yet another loss, muttered loudly, "I can't believe this. There's no way these guys are this fucking bad." Suddenly, out of the corner of his eye, Piniella spotted some kids playing baseball on a field and ordered the driver to stop the bus. He then addressed his struggling team, yelling "I ought to let you sons of bitches off the bus and see if you can beat those kids … because you sure as hell can't beat anyone else!"

The M's beat Toronto 8-1 on Opening Night of 1993 at the Kingdome. A crowd of 56,120 saw Johnson strike out fourteen Blue Jays. Afterward, Johnson dedicated the game to his father, Bud, who had passed away in the offseason.

"I was really emotional, thinking about my dad," said Johnson. "All I have are good memories. I know he's up there smiling and that he'll be with me every outing."

1993 TOP PERFORMERS

Ken Griffey Jr., .309, 45 HR, 109 RBI

Jay Buhner, .272, 27 HR, 98 RBI

Mike Blowers, 280, 15 HR, 57 RBI

Randy Johnson, 19-8, 3.24 ERA, 255.1 IP

Erik Hanson, 11-12, 3.47 ERA, 215 IP

On April 22, in just his fourth start for Seattle, Bosio pitched the second no-hitter in Mariner history, beating Boston 7-0 before a Kingdome crowd of 13,604. Bosio, pitching on three days' rest, walked the first two batters in the Red Sox half of the first inning, but retired the final twenty-six Boston hitters to come to the plate. The last out came on an incredible barehanded play by shortstop Omar Vizquel.

With the annual amateur draft approaching, the baseball world was anxious to see who the Mariners, selecting first, would pick. Seattle had a choice of seventeen-year-old shortstop Alex Rodriguez or college pitcher Darren Dreifort.

"That's a good-looking kid in Miami," Lou Piniella said of Rodriguez. "He has superstar potential."

Scouting Director Roger Jongewaard said, "Rodriguez is one of those special guys like Griffey, Strawberry, or Dunston. He could be a Cal Ripken or a Barry Larkin, a power-hitting shortstop."

Mariners' representatives met several times with Rodriguez, who indicated he would welcome playing for Seattle. But once noted agent Scott Boras got involved, everything changed. While Boras technically could not act as Rodriguez's agent because Rodriguez had not yet signed a professional contract, Boras acted as an "advisor" and reportedly advised Alex to try to dissuade the Mariners from picking him, presumably so he could be selected by the wealthier Los Angeles Dodgers, the team picking second in that year's draft.

On the day before the draft, Rodriguez, apparently on instructions from Boras, called the M's, speaking in a way Jongewaard described as "weirdly rushed, as if he were reading from a piece of paper." Alex reportedly said to Jongewaard, "Please don't draft me. I want to go to a National League team and Seattle is too far away. I don't want you guys to draft me."

Despite Boras' efforts, the Mariners selected Alex Rodriguez with the first pick of the '93 amateur draft on June 3.

On June 23, Buhner became the first Mariner to hit for the cycle, finishing off the unlikely feat with a fourteenth-inning triple and proceeded to score the winning run in Seattle's 8-7 win over Oakland.

The slow-footed Buhner hit a total of nineteen triples in fifteen seasons in the majors.

Griffey tied a major-league record in July by hitting home runs in eight consecutive games. The record-tying home run came on July 28 off Minnesota's Willie Banks in a 5-1 Mariner loss before 45,607 at the Dome. The streak ended the next night, with Junior going 2-for-4 with a double against the Twins in a 4-3 Seattle win.

Meanwhile, Rodriguez was debating whether to sign with the Mariners as a deadline approached to register for classes at the University of Miami. If Rodriguez had started classes, he would have gone back into the draft the following season. Ultimately, Rodriguez went against the advice of Boras and Rodriguez's half-sister, Susy Dunand, accepting a $1 million signing bonus instead of the $3.2 million bonus Boras and Dunand had advised him to hold out for.

On September 16 Johnson came within five outs of pitching his second no-hitter in a 14-1 drubbing of Kansas City. Instead, he had to settle for his seventeenth win in a game in which he struck out fifteen Royals. Instead of his usual number fifty-one jersey, Johnson wore number thirty-four as a one-game tribute to his mentor, Nolan Ryan, who had made the final start of his Hall of Fame career four days earlier against Seattle.

On September 27 the M's lost 4-2 to Chicago, as the White Sox clinched the A.L. West title. As the Chicago players celebrated, Lou Piniella gathered his team in the visiting clubhouse and told them, "What you're seeing and what you hear, that's why you play the game. Soon, we'll be the ones celebrating."

SHIPWRECKED

The M's closed out the '93 season on October 3 with a 7-2 loss to Minnesota, finishing in fourth place with a record of 82-80. Just for fun, Johnson played left-field in the ninth inning of the season finale, the only appearance at a position other than pitcher in his twenty-two-year career.

Chapter 6

BEWARE OF FALLING CEILING TILES

On November 2, 1993, the Mariners traded pitcher Erik Hanson and second-baseman Bret Boone to Piniella's former team, the Cincinnati Reds, for a pair of promising youngsters, catcher Dan Wilson and relief-pitcher Bobby Ayala. While the deal was motivated by finances, Piniella was high on Wilson, saying, "I know he can catch and throw. We expect him to hit some homers for us, too."

Piniella barely waited for the '93 World Series to be completed before predicting the Mariners would win the realigned four-team American League West in 1994. Woodward concurred, saying, "Baseball has given us a favorable new division alignment — Texas, California and Oakland — teams we can compete with and come out on top."

It seemed to be no idle boast. Shortstop Omar Vizquel had just won his first Gold Glove award and Griffey his fourth, and on December 9 the M's signed Johnson to a four-year, $20 million contract, which included a club option for 1998.

While Piniella was happy with those moves, he hoped the Mariners weren't finished.

"This gives us a nice little ballclub," he said. "But if we want a nice little solid ballclub, we need to add a fourth starter and a hitter, a left-handed hitter with some power. We're two players away from being solid. I figure we can do that for a million and a half dollars."

Unfortunately, Mariners ownership wasn't thinking along the same lines, as Ellis looked a *Seattle Times* reporter in the eye in early December and repeatedly stated, "The budget is $28.5 million."

Woodward found a way to get what Piniella wanted, but at a high cost to the future of the team. On December 10, Woodward traded out-fielder Mike Felder and twenty-one-year-old left-hander Mike Hampton to Houston for left-fielder Eric Anthony, who had hit .249 with nineteen home runs in 1993. Hampton would become a twenty-game winner for the Astros, while Anthony played just one season with Seattle. This deal marked the second time in three years that Woodward had traded a future twenty-game winner for an outfielder who'd last just one year with the Mariners.

Another terrible move was made ten days later when Vizquel was traded to Cleveland for shortstop Felix Fermin, DH Reggie Jefferson, and $400,000 in cash. Woodward, under orders to reduce the payroll to $28.5 million, said the move would free up money to sign a fourth starter.

Piniella seemed happy with the deal. "It's not easy to trade Omar," he told reporters, "but we need to add two more pitchers — and to do that, we had to free up some dollars. We've had to do some things we wouldn't do if this organization had endless bucks. But every club is caught in the same scenario." That wasn't quite true. The Mariners were the only team in baseball trading its Gold Glove shortstop for financial reasons that year.

Indians GM John Hart was ecstatic about the trade, telling the *Seattle P-I*, "We've been trying to move Fermin all winter, but the return wasn't good enough until now. We've listened to several offers, but this was by far the best." The light-hitting Fermin had led American League shortstops in errors in 1993, with twenty-three.

On January 14 the M's spent the money saved by the salary dump of Vizquel by signing the fourth starter Piniella coveted. Free-agent left-hander Greg Hibbard, most recently with the Cubs, signed a three-year, $6.75 million contract. While it seemed like a good idea at the time, as Hibbard had won fifteen games in 1993, he would win just one game for the Mariners, going 1-5 with a 6.69 ERA the next year before suffering a torn rotator cuff. He never threw another pitch in a major-league game.

On January 27, Ken Griffey Sr. resigned as hitting coach despite having signed a two-year contract before the '93 season. Presumably he had served his purpose for the Mariners — helping persuade his son to sign a long-term deal to stay with Seattle.

The M's opened the '94 season in Cleveland on April 4, playing in the first game ever at the Indians' new Jacobs Field. Johnson took a no-hitter into the eighth inning before Sandy Alomar broke it up and the Tribe tied the score and won in extra innings. On April 9, four Mariner errors, including three by third-baseman Edgar Martinez, led to six unearned runs as the M's lost to Toronto 8-6. While the club had had the best record in baseball in spring training that year, after five games the Mariners were 0-5.

The M's arrived home on April 11 to the largest Opening Night crowd in their history, 57,806, and beat Minnesota 9-8 in eleven innings. On May 14, before 33,579 at the Dome, the M's came back from a 7-0 deficit to beat the Angels, 10-7. Catcher Jerry Willard hit a three-run homer in the eighth inning to cap what was then the biggest comeback in team history in a nine-inning game. On May 19 the M's scored two runs in the ninth inning to nip Texas 5-4 on the first-ever Buhner Buzz Cut Night. More than five-hundred fans, including two women, got in free with shaved heads.

"These people are crazy," said Buhner, who took a break from pre-game warm-ups to meet some of his disciples. Buhner Buzz Cut Night returned for the next five seasons, 1995 to 1999, and again in 2001.

1994 TOP PERFORMERS

Ken Griffey Jr., .323, 40 HR, 90 RBI

Jay Buhner, .279, 21 HR, 68 RBI

Tino Martinez, .261, 20 HR, 61 RBI

Edgar Martinez, .285, 13 HR, 51 RBI

Randy Johnson, 13-6, 3.19 ERA

The next night the M's set a team record for runs in a 19-2 drubbing of the Rangers before 22,406 at the Dome. The night after that, the M's hit five home runs and once again clubbed Texas, 13-2. The M's then completed the four-game sweep of the Rangers with an 8-2 pasting and moved into first place in the A.L. West. Griffey hit his twentieth home run of the season in the game, the team's forty-second of the season. In so doing, he became the second-quickest in major-league history to hit twenty homers. On May 27 Las Vegas odds-maker Danny Sheridan gave Junior a 15-1 shot to break Roger Maris' 1961 home run mark of sixty-one homers.

Then, just a week after the M's had briefly reached first place, Griffey told the *Tacoma News Tribune* he wanted to be traded.

"I want out," said Griffey. "I can't see staying. I hate to lose. I love Seattle. I'm building a home there and I love the people. But losing is killing me. It's killing me. It takes heart to win and we don't have enough here. There's not enough heart here to win the division. For some players here it's easier to let losing keep happening than to try and change it."

Woody Woodward's response: "Hell will freeze over before we trade him."

On July 18, Edgar Martinez's two-run double in the eighth inning gave the M's a 7-5 comeback win over Baltimore before 22,694 at the Kingdome. It was to be the last game at the Dome for more than nine months. The next day, at about 4:30 p.m., several panels of tiles fell from the Kingdome ceiling. Fortunately, it happened about thirty minutes before fans were to be allowed into the stadium, so there were no casualties. County and team officials decided to call off the game, the first postponement in the eighteen-year history of the Kingdome.

Later that week, Mariner players met with CEO John Ellis and told him that if they couldn't play at the Kingdome, they preferred to play in Peoria, Arizona, at the team's spring-training stadium, or even at Dodger Stadium, "if it were available." Ellis later told the team they had two options: play the games at Cheney Stadium in Tacoma or play on the road. The M's players voted unanimously to play in Tacoma, but the Major League Baseball Players Association, under pressure from the California Angels, vetoed that plan the next day.

On August 10 Mike Blowers hit a game-winning home run in the tenth inning to beat Texas, 3-2. The next night, Griffey hit his fortieth home run of the season as the M's beat Oakland for their sixth straight victory. It would be Griffey's last homer of the '94 season. The players went on strike the next day and didn't return. The M's finished the shortened season with a 49-63 record, two games out in the weak A.L. West.

As disappointing as the baseball strike was for a Mariners team that seemed on the verge of coming together, the strike actually helped the Mariners. In the short-term, it put an end to a seemingly endless twenty-two-day road trip. The trip was not only the longest in team history, but also one of the longest in baseball history. If the season had resumed, the M's might have had to play the balance of that season on the road.

The longer-term effect was that the experience of being on the road together for such an extended period of time helped the players on that '94 team grow closer, developing a bond that would serve them well during the pressure-packed '95 season. As Jay Buhner put it, "We lived together, hung together, pulled together. It was like us against the world, man, and we all wanted to show we could rely on one another."

Chapter 7

"NINETEEN LONG YEARS OF FRUSTRATION IS OVER!"

On September 14, 1994, with the players' strike more than a month old and no settlement in sight, the remainder of the season, including the World Series, was canceled by interim baseball Commissioner Bud Selig. It was the first time in ninety years that there would be no World Series.

While there had been no settlement and no certainty at the time that there would even be a '95 season, on September 16, 1994, an upbeat Griffey told the *Seattle Times*, "I hope we can keep this team together for a change. The way we finished (winning nine of the last ten games in 1994) makes you eager to come back, makes stopping even uglier, tougher to deal with. But at least this time we really have something to look forward to."

Despite Griffey's optimism, most people familiar with the situation realized that even if the strike were settled, Seattle's ownership wasn't likely to keep the team intact for 1995. Several players were free agents, most notably Buhner, who had his best year to that time in the strike-shortened '94 season, batting .279 with twenty-one home runs and sixty-nine RBI. Extended over a full season, those numbers put him on a pace for thirty-three homers and 108 RBI — numbers that would have ranked the thirty-year-old Buhner among the top sluggers in baseball.

Seattle Times beat writer Bob Finnigan, who'd covered the team since 1982, didn't offer much hope that the team would stay together. "No matter what the outcome of the current labor war," he wrote, "something will have to give or someone will have to go in the Mariners' usual small-market scenario."

To this point, the Mariners had been a self-proclaimed "small-market" team, but this tag was due more to the franchise's position as perennial losers on the playing field than the actual size of the Seattle market. In truth, Seattle was the nation's twelfth-largest television market in 1995 with a median household income of $40,350, higher than all but seven markets in the country.

There had been no settlement of the strike by late October, but the Mariners still had crucial decisions to make. In early November, Buhner, who'd filed for free agency, talked to a reporter about his desire to stay.

"I purposely did not file for free agency until the very last day to give the Mariners as much chance as I could. I've never made any secret that I want to stay," Buhner said. "I realize Seattle cannot pay as much as some teams and I'm willing to work with that - within reason. If the Mariners want me to sign, let's get an offer on the table and let's get something worked out."

On December 14 it appeared the M's had lost Buhner to the Baltimore Orioles, who had offered him a four-year, $16 million contract. The *Seattle Times* headline that day read "Buhner on His Way to Baltimore — Departure Leaves M's with Big Hole Behind Griffey." Team President Chuck Armstrong told the newspaper, "We never even really got a chance to bid. We've been waiting to see how the situation of baseball itself would evolve from the current contract talks, to see how it might affect our own financial situation so we might work out a contract with Jay."

Buhner's departure looked like a done deal when the right-fielder told the *Seattle Times*, "While I wanted to stay here, and I understand and feel for the Mariners' economic situation, I have to say it is nice to be wanted, to go to an organization that has treated me first class. I never heard a word about a contract from the Mariners."

Steve Kelley of the *Times* was appalled that a team that was seeking a new stadium would make little effort to keep one of its most important players. He wrote:

"Buhner is gone and Ken Griffey Jr. won't be far behind — another sad day for baseball in Seattle. By letting Buhner go to Baltimore, the Mariners practically showed Ken Griffey Jr. the door. Where is the gesture of good faith? Where is the commitment to excellence? They are about to lose Buhner and eventually Griffey and probably Johnson and we're expected to cough up the cash to build them a new ballpark."

"How about winning first? How about making your product more attractive? Instead of preaching to us the importance of Major League Baseball to the fabric of a city, how about making your baseball team competitive? Is one September pennant race in twenty years too much to ask? What's the sense of building a StarDome, if the Mariners keep losing their stars?"

"NINETEEN LONG YEARS OF FRUSTRATION IS OVER!"

Fortunately, although Buhner had passed an Orioles' physical, before his contract with Baltimore was finalized, the M's swooped in at the eleventh hour to sign him to a three-year, $15.5 million deal.

Piniella called it "a good come-from-behind, ninth-inning win for the M's." Griffey admitted to the *Seattle P-I* that he would have asked for a trade if Buhner had left. "I couldn't go through another rebuilding stage," he said. "There comes a time when you have to put your money in a basket and go for it. Basically that is what this organization is doing this year."

Junior might have thought the team was going for it, but on the day of Buhner's signing, Jim Street reported in the *Seattle P-I* that Edgar Martinez was being shopped by the Mariners "to several teams, including the New York Mets."

After President Bill Clinton's efforts to force a settlement failed, and with the start of spring training just a week away, the baseball owners decided to put pressure on the striking players by bringing in replacements. Each team in baseball, with the exception of the Orioles, signed these non-union players. While Lou Piniella readily admitted that replacement baseball wasn't going to be close to what baseball fans were used to watching, he insisted that it was his job to get his team prepared to play the '95 season, whether with regular players wearing the Seattle uniforms or no-name replacement players who had been dubbed the "InterM's."

"We want it to be major-league players," Piniella said, "but, if not, our obligation is to do the best we can."

On March 11, more than a week into the '94 Cactus League season, John Ellis, who had become one of the hardliners pushing the baseball owners' agenda, told reporters that how the replacement teams and their games were covered in the media would determine the success or failure of the owners' strategy.

"I still believe people will come (to games) unless they are discouraged from coming," said Ellis, who insisted that the media should be more supportive of the replacement-player scheme and "focus on the game" rather than on the inferior players playing it. Ellis said he expected that if the owners' plan was successful, players would cross the picket line.

"I think players will cross," he said. "It's only a matter of when. With replacement games on, there is a place for guys to cross to."

Finally, just days before the '95 season was to begin with replacements, the regular players and owners came to an agreement ending the 232-day strike, the longest in baseball history. With the regular players coming back, it was agreed that a shortened schedule of 144 games would start on April 25.

With the strike settled, the Mariners faced their next challenge, putting together a team that could compete on the field. A shortened spring training of three weeks began in early April amid questions about whether Edgar Martinez or Johnson would be traded and whether the team would offer a contract to first-baseman Tino Martinez.

"We're putting our heads together trying to figure out what we're going to do," Chuck Armstrong said. "The payroll will be lower, but so will revenues. We have a lot of evaluating to do the next few days. Our objective is to win the A.L. West."

The M's took a huge risk with Tino Martinez, who had hit a career-high twenty home runs in the shortened '94 season. Rather than offering him arbitration, where he might have made $1.5 million, the club offered Martinez a take-it-or-leave-it deal for $1 million. If he declined the offer, he'd immediately have become a free agent. While Martinez said he didn't think he'd have a problem finding a job, he accepted the offer because he liked the direction the Mariners were headed.

As the Mariners' regular players showed up in Peoria on April 6, the team reached agreement with veteran second-baseman Joey Cora, who had played the previous four seasons with the White Sox. While this signing wasn't considered a major one at the time, Cora would prove to be a significant addition to the '95 team.

On April 7, the headline in the *P-I* read "Mariners to make a deal — Edgar or Johnson the likely target." The article relayed that Woodward needed to cut costs to meet Mariner ownership's payroll budget.

"I anticipate making at least one trade that will be budget influenced," Woodward told the newspaper. The story said that Edgar Martinez, who was due to make $3.3 million in 1995, was the likeliest player to be traded, but also said if the team couldn't find a taker for Martinez, they'd likely be forced to trade Johnson. Rumors were rampant that Johnson would be dealt to the Yankees, with the pitcher asking reporters every day that spring, "Where am I going this time? How would I look in pinstripes?"

Fortunately, Piniella and Woodward went to Mariners ownership and persuaded them to withdraw the order to cut payroll by trading players. Woodward credited Piniella, telling a reporter later, "I was there, but give Lou the credit for his sales pitch. He was very persuasive."

On April 27 the Mariners opened the '95 season by defeating the Detroit Tigers 3-0 before a crowd of 34,656 at the Kingdome. Given the long strike and reports of demonstrations by angry fans in ballparks in other cities, the M's weren't sure what to expect from fans at the first game at the Dome in more than nine months, but a total of 100,999 flocked to the ballpark to see the M's take three of four games from the Tigers in the season's opening series. The club then headed out on the road, where it swept a three-game series in Texas. The M's 6-1 record equaled the best start in franchise history.

Despite the impressive record, it quickly became apparent that the M's would need better starting pitching behind Johnson and Bosio. On May 15 Woodward acquired thirty-three-year-old right-hander Tim Belcher from Cincinnati for Roger Salkeld, a twenty-three-year-old right-hander who had been Seattle's first pick (third overall) in the 1989 draft. Belcher had turned down a minor-league deal from Seattle just two weeks before, opting for a similar deal with the Reds. Belcher had won fifteen games for Cincinnati in 1992, Lou Piniella's last year there, and he didn't bust the team's budget either; he was on a one-year contract with a base salary of $200,000. The addition of Belcher proved to be a good one, as he capably filled one of the M's problem rotation spots.

Just five days later Woodward made another trade for a starting pitcher, but this one wasn't as effective. In acquiring right-hander Salomon Torres from the San Francisco Giants, Woodward gave up left-hander Shawn Estes, Seattle's first-round pick in 1991, and infielder Wilson Delgado. It was a hefty price to pay for a pitcher such as Torres, who had fallen out of favor in San Francisco after going 2-8 with a 5.44 ERA in 1994. The twenty-three-year-old Estes became an All-Star just two years later when he went 19-5 with a 3.18 ERA for the Giants, and had a long big-league career that spanned parts of thirteen seasons. However, Torres was a failure for the '95 Mariners, going 3-8 with a 6.00 ERA.

On May 26 disaster struck at the Kingdome. Griffey fractured his wrist crashing into the center-field wall while catching a ball hit by Baltimore's Kevin Bass. The M's won 8-3, but would lose Junior, who had surgery to insert a plate in the wrist, for three months. At the time of the injury, Seattle was in third place with a 15-12 record, two and a half games behind the division-leading Angels. Most experts didn't think the M's could stay in the hunt with Griffey out of action.

However, bench players Rich Amaral and Alex Diaz performed admirably in Junior's absence, especially in the field. Three days after Junior went down, the Yankees came to town and the M's swept them three straight. It was an emotional series, highlighted by a twelfth-inning walk-off home run by Amaral in the May 29 game and a bench-clearing brawl on May 31 fueled by a beef between Johnson and New York's Jim Leyritz, who'd been hit by a Johnson pitch.

While Leyritz promised retaliation and waited for Johnson outside the Mariners' clubhouse after the game, the Kingdome staff eventually asked Leyritz to leave. In response to Leyritz's threats, Johnson said, "If he wants satisfaction, maybe we can do it like the 1600s, with swords or pistols at ten paces. I can see it now: 'High Noon in Times Square.' Actually, if he wants me, he knows where to find me. I'm only sixty feet, six inches away. Part of my game is intimidation, and you can't intimidate the intimidator. I'm the intimidator; Leyritz is the intimidatee."

In June the Mariners briefly experimented with a four-man rotation, becoming one of the first teams in twenty years to do so. The reason was a lack of five solid starters. Bob Wells and Tim Davis, who'd started the season in the rotation, had failed and were replaced by Belcher and Torres, but the Mariners were giving away a game every fifth day by starting left-hander Dave Fleming. The twenty-five-year-old Fleming had been one of the top pitchers in the league as a rookie in 1992, when he won seventeen games, but his career had gone downhill since.

Neither Piniella nor pitching coach Bobby Cuellar had any solutions for getting Fleming straightened out. In mid-June, after Fleming couldn't make it out of the second inning in New York, Piniella had seen enough.

"I love Dave Fleming," Piniella said, "but we can't keep going like this with him, throwing away games."

Fleming was moved to the bullpen without improvement and eventually was shipped off to Kansas City. Fleming's stats for 1995 included a 1-5 record and a 7.50 ERA, with Seattle losing twelve of the sixteen games in which he pitched. The four-man experiment lasted about three weeks, with the starters going 7-7.

As the July 31 trade deadline approached, the Mariners, just four games out in the A.L. West at the beginning of July, had fallen eleven games behind the red-hot California Angels, who went 20-7 that month. In a typical year, that sort of a deficit might have the M's trading some of their established players for prospects, but in 1995 MLB had added a Wild Card spot and the 43-44 Mariners were just one game behind the Yankees in the Wild Card race.

With the team that close to a playoff spot and needing a successful season to win approval for a new stadium, Mariners ownership agreed to provide Woodward with additional funds for midseason reinforcements.

"NINETEEN LONG YEARS OF FRUSTRATION IS OVER!"

It was a critical move, one that Seattle's ownership typically had not been willing to do, either before 1995 or since. Ownership's decision was made easier in 1995 because the team was getting $2.4 million back on insurance policies taken out on injured players Griffey and Hibbard.

The approval to take on payroll allowed Woodward to shop around for a premium starting pitcher. While Woodward considered deals for David Cone, David Wells, and Jim Abbott, he made a trade on July 31 with the San Diego Padres for right-hander Andy Benes. The price appeared steep at the time; outfielder Marc Newfield and left-handed pitcher Ron Villone had both been first-round picks of the Mariners. But Newfield and Villone never amounted to much, and the acquisition of Benes solidified the Seattle rotation for the remainder of the season. While his overall ERA of 5.86 wasn't pretty, it was skewed by two disastrous outings. More important, the Mariners won ten of his twelve starts, with Benes going 7-2 in his two months with the team, a 21-win pace.

The move to add payroll didn't go unnoticed in the Mariner clubhouse. "This is the first time we've ever had a transaction of this magnitude this time of year," Buhner said. "It's awesome. It's definitely one of the ingredients to help us make a run at it." Blowers said the trade for Benes would help the September 19 stadium vote. "Being from the area, I'd love to see a new stadium for Seattle," he said. "I'd like to play in it, but after I retire I'd like to take my kids to watch baseball in the Northwest."

The Seattle media noticed, too, with Steve Kelley writing in the *Times*, "Let's celebrate the commitment. For the first time in Seattle, a late-season trade was made that didn't turn out the lights on another losing season. And to think it only took nineteen years."

In addition to the trade for Benes, the M's made two low-cost acquisitions that summer for players who became a big part of the team's success during the '95 stretch run. Left-handed reliever Norm Charlton, who'd been discarded by the Mariners after tearing an elbow ligament in 1993, missed the entire '94 season, but was signed by the Philadelphia Phillies for 1995. After posting a 7.36 ERA in twenty-five appearances, Charlton was released by Philadelphia on July 10. Four days later he came to Seattle for a tryout. Lou Piniella liked what he saw of his former closer and the southpaw was added to the team.

Not long after Charlton returned, Bobby Ayala, who'd pitched well in the first half of 1995, faltered and Charlton took over as Seattle's closer. Remarkably, the same pitcher who'd posted a 7.36 ERA in the National League, morphed into an unhittable reliever for the M's. He saved fourteen games in fifteen opportunities with Seattle, posting a 1.51 ERA and allowing just twenty-three hits in 47 2/3 innings while striking out fifty-eight batters. Because Charlton had been released by the Phillies, the M's were responsible for just the pro-rated portion of the major-league minimum salary — Charlton would cost the club roughly $50,000 in 1995.

The other player acquired on the cheap was left-fielder Vince Coleman, who was obtained from Kansas City on August 15 for a player to be named later (pitcher Jim Converse). The thirty-three-year-old Coleman had been having a decent season for the Royals (.287 with twenty-six stolen bases), who had decided to go with a youth movement. The sixth-most prolific base stealer in baseball history, Coleman gave the M's the leadoff hitter they'd lacked all season. In forty games with Seattle, Coleman hit .290 with sixteen stolen bases, a sixty-four-steal pace, and delivered several clutch hits. The Mariners were responsible for just $55,000 of Coleman's $250,000 salary.

Riding a six-game win streak, Seattle found itself leading the Wild Card race on August 11. Despite the additions of Benes, Coleman, and Charlton and the mid-August return to action of Griffey, the team followed that streak with one of its worst slumps of the season, losing eight of twelve to fall four games behind Texas in the Wild Card race and eleven and a half games behind the Angels in the A.L. West. With the Yankees coming to Seattle for a crucial four-game series, the usually reserved Edgar Martinez called a players' only meeting about an hour before the start of the first game of the series.

The M's trailed 7-6 entering the ninth inning, but Coleman led off with a walk and easily stole second and third. He scored when Cora hit a single off the glove of New York shortstop Tony Fernandez. Then, with Cora running, Griffey hit the first pitch from Yankee closer John Wetteland into the second deck in right field to give Seattle a 9-7 win.

That win seemed to be a turning point for the '95 club. They took two of the next three games from New York, and then went 5-5 on a tough, four-city road trip, which included stops in Boston, Cleveland and New York, all playoff teams that season. When the M's returned home on September 8, their record stood at 62-61 and they were one game back in the Wild Card chase and just six games behind the struggling Angels, who had lost eleven of their previous twelve games.

1995 TOP PERFORMERS

Edgar Martinez, .356, 29 HR, 113 RBI

Jay Buhner, .262, 40 HR, 121 RBI

Tino Martinez, .293, 31 HR, 111 RBI

Mike Blowers, .257, 23 HR, 96 RBI

Randy Johnson, 18-2, 2.48 ERA, 214.1 IP

With twenty-one games left in the '95 season the schedule looked favorable. Fourteen of those games would be played at the Kingdome. Remarkably, the M's won twelve of those games while the Angels continued their free fall, suffering through a nine-game losing streak for the second time in a month. With the Angels coming to Seattle on September 26 for two of the most important games in Mariners history, the M's led the division by two games. Each team had six games left to play.

When the Mariners destroyed the Angels 10-2 to move three games up with five to play, California appeared dead, having lost twenty-two of their last twenty-eight games. Yet the Angels recovered to win their last five games of the season while Seattle lost three of their last five. After 144 games, both teams were tied with identical records of 78-66.

A one-game playoff to decide the A.L. West was set for the afternoon of Monday, October 2. It was just the third one-game playoff in American League history. Fortunately for the Mariners, Seattle won a coin toss on September 18, correctly calling tails, so the game was played at the Kingdome instead of in Anaheim. Even better, the M's had Johnson ready to pitch on three days' rest. Johnson was at his best, throwing a complete game in the M's 9-1 victory. A crowd of 52,356 saw the Mariners win their first division title and clinch the first playoff berth in franchise history.

The Mariners' comeback from thirteen games behind the Angels was the third-greatest in major-league history, surpassed only by the 1978 New York Yankees, who overcame a fourteen-game Boston lead, and the 1951 New York Giants, who trailed Brooklyn by 13½ games on August 11. Since divisional play began in 1969, the '95 Mariners are the only team to win their division after being seven or more games behind at the beginning of September.

There was no time to relax, though, as the M's had to start their first-ever playoff series the very next night — in the hostile environment of Yankee Stadium. It would be the Mariners' third game in three days — in three different time zones. Worse, with Johnson needed to get the Mariners into the playoffs, Seattle's ace would be available to start just one game in the best-of-five series.

The first game featured a pitching mismatch, with eighteen-game winner David Cone starting for New York against Bosio, who had allowed a .313 average to opposing batters that season. Bosio lasted 5 2/3 innings, allowing four runs and departed trailing 4-2. Griffey, playing in his first post-season game, tied the score in the bottom of the sixth with a two-run home run off Cone, his second homer of the game, but Ayala, on in relief, blew the game in the eighth, allowing hits to four of the five batters he faced, including two doubles and a home run. Seattle fell 9-6.

Game 2 was a hard-fought battle, won by New York on a home run by Jim Leyritz in the bottom of the fifteenth inning. Griffey hit another home run, his third of the series, in the twelfth inning to put Seattle ahead, but the Yankees tied the score in the bottom of the inning on a double by Ruben Sierra. After five hours and thirteen minutes, the M's found themselves down two games to none and facing elimination.

A crowd of 58,905 filled the Kingdome on Friday, October 6 to see the first-ever postseason baseball game in Seattle. Johnson struck out ten and allowed just two runs as the M's prevailed 7-4. The next day saw New York tee off on Bosio, who allowed five runs before he was removed two batters into the third inning. Down 5-0, Seattle got four runs back in the bottom of the third, three of them on a home run by Edgar Martinez.

Jeff Nelson came on in the third and pitched four gutty innings of relief, throwing seventy-nine pitches, nineteen more than he threw in any other game during his fifteen-year career. Seattle tied the score with a run in the fifth and went ahead 6-5 when Griffey hit his fourth home run of the series in the sixth. New York tied the game in the eighth on a wild pitch by Charlton, but Edgar Martinez brought 57,180 fans to their feet with a grand-slam home run over the center-field wall in the bottom of the eighth to put Seattle up 10-6. The game ended with the M's victorious 11-8.

With the series tied, the game on Sunday October 8 was a winner-take-all contest between the Mariners and the Yankees. It was a game for the ages. With the Yankees leading 4-2 going into the bottom of the eighth, Seattle scored two runs off New York's ace Cone, whose 147th pitch of the night was ball four to pinch-hitter Doug Strange to force in the tying run.

"NINETEEN LONG YEARS OF FRUSTRATION IS OVER!"

But the Yankees threatened in the ninth, getting their first two runners of the inning on base. In came Johnson to thunderous applause from 57,411 at the Dome. It was just the second relief appearance of his Mariners career.

Johnson retired the next three batters and kept New York from scoring. He returned for the tenth and struck out the side in order, but the Yankees grabbed the lead in the top of the eleventh inning on a single by Randy Velarde.

Just as quickly as Seattle fell behind, the Mariners came back in the bottom of the eleventh to win the game and the series, shocking the Yankees. It took just eight pitches to three batters. Cora started the inning with a bunt single, Griffey singled Cora to third and Edgar Martinez plated both with a double down the left field line. The call of Mariners announcer Dave Niehaus went like this:

> "Right now, the Mariners are looking for the tie. They would take a fly ball; they would love a base hit into the gap, and they could win it with Junior's speed. The stretch and the 0-1 pitch on the way to Edgar Martinez; swung on and lined down the left-field line for a base hit! Here comes Joey! Here is Junior to third base; they're gonna wave him in! The throw to the plate will be ... LATE! The Mariners are going to play for the American League Championship! I don't believe it! It just continues! My, oh my! Edgar Martinez with a double ripped down the left-field line and they are going crazy at the Kingdome!"

The Mariners were going to play for the American League pennant, but once again there wasn't much time for reflection. Game 1 of the ALCS was due to start at the Kingdome less than forty-eight hours later.

Hours after the series with the Yankees was over, Piniella was undecided about who would start the first game of the ALCS against the Cleveland Indians. He told reporters, "We might pitch Bob Wells, then (Tim) Belcher in Game 2. Bosio's available, too."

While starting Wells, a journeyman reliever, was an option, it was far from a good option. Wells hadn't started a game since May, had only started four games all year, and had averaged a tick over three innings in those starts — with an ERA of 9.45.

Ultimately, the Mariners, through some clever maneuvering, managed to get rookie Bob Wolcott onto their twenty-five-man roster for the championship series. While Wolcott had only made six major-league starts, he'd won three of them, including late-season victories over two playoff teams, the Red Sox and Yankees.

The decision to start a raw rookie like Wolcott in the most important game in franchise history nearly backfired. The twenty-two-year-old walked the first three hitters in the first inning of Game 1, throwing twelve balls in his first thirteen pitches. The bases were loaded with nobody out and Albert Belle, Eddie Murray, and Jim Thome due up. Piniella came to the mound to try to settle Wolcott down, telling him to just relax and throw strikes, adding "If we lose this game 11-0, we'll all have a good offseason."

Wolcott settled down, retiring the next three batters without allowing a run, Belle on a strikeout, Murray on a pop-up and Thome on a hard grounder to second. Wolcott made it through seven full innings, allowing just two runs in Seattle's surprising 3-2 win.

Cleveland evened up the series the next night with a 5-2 win, as thirty-seven-year-old Orel Hershiser limited the powerful Mariners offense to four hits and one run in eight innings. Belcher started for Seattle and kept the Tribe off the board for the first four innings, but allowed two runs in the fifth and two more in the sixth.

The series moved to Cleveland, with Randy Johnson starting Game 3 for Seattle. The game went into the eighth with the M's clinging to a 2-1 lead and Johnson allowing just three hits in the first seven innings. He retired the first batter of the eighth, but the second batter, Alvaro Espinoza, hit a fly ball to right field that was dropped by Buhner, allowing the tying run to reach second, where it scored on a single by Kenny Lofton. The game went to extra innings, but Buhner redeemed himself with a three-run homer to win the game in the eleventh. Charlton, who'd come on to replace Johnson in the ninth, pitched three hitless innings for the victory.

The Indians took the next two games, 7-0 and 3-2, as Seattle managed just eleven hits, to go ahead in the series, three games to two. Nevertheless, the Mariners and their fans felt they had Cleveland right where they wanted them — back in the Kingdome for the final two games, with Johnson ready to pitch Game 6.

It wasn't to be. Seattle's hitters couldn't get to forty-year-old Dennis Martinez, who held them scoreless for seven innings in Game 6. With the M's trailing 1-0 heading into the eighth, every Mariner fan in attendance felt that the M's would find a way to continue their incredible "Refuse to Lose" run. But Cleveland scored two runs on a passed ball by Dan Wilson to go up 3-0 and added a fourth run on a Carlos Baerga home run. The Mariners went down meekly in the final two innings, managing just one base runner, a walk to Tino Martinez — in his final at-bat as a Mariner — and the M's miracle season ended in disappointment without a trip to the World Series.

As the Indians' players celebrated on the field, Mariner fans stood and cheered for nearly fifteen minutes after the final pitch. Finally, many of the M's players returned to the field for a curtain call. The crowd of 58,489 cheered wildly while the players waved to the fans and tossed souvenir balls and caps into the stands.

With the '95 season over, there was plenty of work to do to keep the Mariners in Seattle, but one obstacle seemed to have been overcome; baseball fans in Seattle had proven that they would support a winning team. While the M's had averaged just 20,013 fans for their first sixty-seven home games of the '95 season, the team's final twelve home games drew 648,539, an average of 54,045 fans per game.

Chapter 8

STADIUM ISSUES

The Mariners' first home stadium, the Kingdome, officially known as the King County Multipurpose Domed Stadium, was the subject of significant controversy during its twenty-four year history. This controversy began years before the stadium was erected when ballot referendums to fund the stadium were rejected by King County voters in 1960 and 1966. Public funding finally was approved when the Kingdome was included as part of a major capital-improvement plan approved by King County voters in 1968.

Construction on the stadium was delayed for several years because of the loss of the Seattle Pilots, but groundbreaking for the Kingdome finally took place on November 2, 1972. A group of twenty-five Asian protesters threw mudballs at dignitaries attending the ceremony, upset about the stadium's potential impact on the neighboring International District.

The Kingdome opened on March 27, 1976. The Mariners played their first game there a little more than a year later, on April 6, 1977.

The Mariners and King County, which operated the Kingdome, had a contentious relationship over the years due to many disputes between the two entities over issues large and small. One of the first occurred in 1978, when Mariners Executive Director Kip Horsburgh threatened to block the '84 NCAA Basketball Finals from being held at the Kingdome because of a possible "practice game" the M's "might" need to play at the stadium. Eventually the Mariners relented and the Kingdome was able to host the finals.

The relationship between the county and the Mariners worsened after George Argyros bought the club in 1981, with Argyros on many occasions blaming the M's poor attendance on the Kingdome. A major dispute occurred in 1984 when somehow the Mariners and the Seahawks were both scheduled to play at the Dome on the same date. Argyros used this conflict to threaten to move the team, filing a lawsuit against King County and the Seahawks six weeks before the disputed date. The suit, filed in Kittitas County Superior Court in Ellensburg, sought to cancel the remaining twelve years of the Mariners' Kingdome lease. The Seahawks eventually backed down and moved the date of their season opener.

On April 8, 1985, two thousand Mariner fans gathered at Westlake Mall for a rally sponsored by local civic groups and businesses to generate support for the team, which had stated in the offseason that attendance for the '85 season would need to increase to 1.2 million (from 870,000 in 1984) in order to remain in Seattle.

"Baseball is important," Seattle Mayor Charles Royer told the crowd. "That's why there are a number of mayors in cities without teams that would like to steal ours." Denver, Tampa, and Vancouver, British Columbia, were prominent cities actively seeking a baseball team at the time.

In June of 1985, Argyros demanded that King County renegotiate the M's stadium lease, threatening that the club might file bankruptcy to terminate its lease and seek to move the team if the county didn't offer significant lease concessions.

"We'd like to make Major League Baseball successful in the Northwest and I think we can do it," Argyros told the Seattle Times, "but we're at the point where we need help."

Later that year King County and the Mariners agreed to a renegotiated Kingdome lease to run through the '96 season. The lease contained an escape clause allowing the M's to leave Seattle if attendance remained below 1.4 million and season ticket sales did not reach a minimum of ten thousand.

Yet, in a shocking turn of events, Argyros made a backroom deal less than two weeks before the 1987 season opener to purchase the San Diego Padres. Since he couldn't own two teams at the same time, the Mariners were put into a trust. Two months later the Padres deal fell through, and Argyros resumed control of the Mariners. Now hated in Seattle, Argyros was booed relentlessly on Opening Night and needed a police escort to leave the Dome. As far as Seattle baseball fans and local government officials were concerned, Argyros couldn't sell the Mariners soon enough. But Argyros rebuffed all local efforts to buy the team and two years later sold the club to Indiana native Jeff Smulyan, who would in turn sell the team to The Baseball Club of Seattle in 1992.

By the end of 1993, with three years remaining on the team's lease at the Kingdome, King County officials began talks with the M's about improvements to the Dome that they hoped would entice the team's owners to extend their lease. The owners were not persuaded and determined that only a new stadium would provide the revenues they believed were needed to make baseball viable in Seattle.

An early advocate of building an open-air baseball stadium with a retractable roof was John Torrance, who used his own money to push a project called StarDome and was the first to produce an elaborate drawing of what such a stadium might look like. Torrance's plan was for the stadium to be located on the site of the Kingdome's north parking lot, allowing the stadium to be well integrated into Pioneer Square. The Mariners preferred a site south of the Kingdome, an area with fewer bars and restaurants so that fans would be forced to spend more money on food and drink inside the new stadium.

In early 1994, King County Executive Gary Locke ordered a study done on the feasibility of building a new retractable roof stadium as part of a public/private partnership. The Mariners were encouraged by Locke's efforts, with Chuck Armstrong telling a reporter, "We certainly do not want to be a burden on the taxpayers."

Later that year two events occurred that had divergent impacts on the possibility of the Mariners getting a new stadium. The first was the collapse of several ceiling tiles at the Kingdome on July 19, 1994. The M's were forced to play the rest of their "home" games on the road during the '94 season.

The second event was the baseball players' strike that began on August 12 and didn't end until April 1995. This was the longest strike in baseball history and inflicted serious damage to the national pastime. Angry baseball fans stayed away in droves. Twenty-seven of the thirty teams suffered a decline in their average attendance in 1994-95, with nine teams each losing more than eight thousand fans per game.

While the falling ceiling tiles helped the Mariners' argument that the Kingdome needed to be replaced, the strike turned off so many fans that it seemed highly unlikely voters would approve a tax for a new baseball stadium that year.

Still, Mariners ownership insisted it would put the team up for sale if there wasn't a plan for a new stadium in place by the end of the year. While the terms of the team's Kingdome lease stipulated that the team had to be offered first to a local buyer if it were put up for sale, few believed another local buyer would emerge.

That made 1995 a do-or-die season; if the M's didn't get their stadium, the team likely would move out of Seattle. After several starts and stops, including opposition from both activist Frank Ruano, who for years had been a key opponent of the Kingdome, and a group called Citizens for More Important Things, the stage was set for a September referendum that would have King County voters decide whether to approve a sales tax to fund a new baseball stadium.

The referendum seemed destined to fail and was trailing heavily in pre-election polls all summer, but the timing of the vote coincided with the most exciting baseball played by the Mariners in their nineteen-year history. On September 18, the day before the vote, the Mariners beat Texas to move within two games of the first-place California Angels, who had been 12½ games ahead of Seattle just a month before.

Despite the excitement caused by the team's unprecedented run and a comeback win on election night, the referendum was narrowly defeated and the Mariners quickly announced that the team would be put up for sale if there wasn't a stadium plan in place by October 30. The Mariners continued their incredible run on the playing field, winning their division in a one-game playoff over California and beating the New York Yankees in a thrilling five-game playoff series.

The M's incredible run, coupled with the closeness of the referendum, galvanized support for a new stadium in the state capital of Olympia. An emergency session of the Washington State Legislature was called and a plan for a $320 million stadium, to be paid for with new taxes on restaurant and car-rental receipts, was hastily approved. The move angered groups who'd opposed the referendum and tens of thousands of people who'd voted against a public subsidy for the Mariners. Nevertheless, the team's improbable playoff run had created enough political support to keep the M's in Seattle. Even though the referendum failed, the Mariners got their stadium, complete with a retractable roof, and they were staying in Seattle. Mariner fans rejoiced.

Little did fans know that they'd have to go through yet another significant threat to baseball in Seattle. More than a year after the legislature approved funding for the stadium, the deal nearly fell apart. The Public Facilities District (PFD), created to oversee construction of the stadium, realized that the retractable roof the Mariners demanded was going to cost $45 million more than originally estimated. Before agreeing to pay the increased costs for the roof, the PFD wanted the Mariners to sign a lease to play in the stadium.

The possibility that an impasse over the lease would delay the stadium's opening past the target date of April 1999 so outraged the Mariners that within two days they announced that the team was up for sale. Mariner

CEO John Ellis said at a news conference that the decision was final and that the team would no longer engage in discussions with the PFD.

"We've done all we can do," Ellis said "We're now on a different course." Ellis detailed how even slight delays in construction would push the stadium's opening back by a full year and claimed the team's owners could not withstand another year of losses playing at the Kingdome. That Ellis managed to utter such words with a straight face was a bit surprising, given that the Mariners had set a team attendance record in 1996, with more than 2.7 million fans coming through the turnstiles.

For a couple of weeks in December 1996 it looked as if baseball's run in Seattle might come to an end. The Mariners refused to budge. But then Senator Gorton, who had brokered the original deal for Nintendo to purchase the team, stepped in and persuaded the Mariners to reconsider. The deal was on again, and groundbreaking for the new stadium took place in March 1997. The opening was delayed, but only until midseason of 1999, with the new stadium, named Safeco Field, opening on July 15.

Despite having a deal, cost issues lingered. The construction of the stadium went way over budget and became the most expensive stadium ever built to date in North America at a cost of $517 million. The Mariners had agreed to cover all cost overruns, a promise Ellis reaffirmed in July 1998 when the cost overruns were estimated at $81 million. In May 1999, two months before the stadium opened, the team faced a $100 million bill for the cost overruns and tried to back-pedal on its promise, claiming that a legal loophole obligated King County to pay the costs to complete the stadium project.

In a letter to the PFD, Ellis implied that if the Mariners had to pay the cost overruns, they might be unable to afford to keep Ken Griffey Jr. and Alex Rodriguez. According to PFD board member Sue Taoka, the Mariners did more than imply. Taoka told the *Seattle Times* in July 1999 that she had met with Ellis and Mariner board member Howard Lincoln earlier that year and the pair was unable to persuade the PFD to let the Mariners off the hook for the overruns. She recalled that one of the two men said to her on the way out the door, "Ask your kids what they'll think when we couldn't afford Griffey or Rodriguez."

An angry public soon made itself heard and even Senator Gorton, the Mariners' staunchest supporter, believed the team should pay the cost overruns and move on. The Mariners, he said, "were swimming upstream against a strong current."

SHIPWRECKED

It took nearly two years, but eventually the team agreed to pay. The attempt to avoid paying for the overruns didn't sit well with the public, especially when it was revealed that most of the overruns were caused by a large number of change orders requested by— you guessed it — the Seattle Mariners.

Chapter 9

THE POST-1995 FALLOUT

The '95 season was barely complete when word came down from Mariners ownership that the team needed to trade first-baseman Tino Martinez for financial reasons. Despite taking in millions of dollars in extra revenue from the capacity crowds in September and from six home playoff games, the team's ownership was insistent that the player payroll for the '96 season would be increased by a mere five percent from the club's payroll in 1995.

While the Mariners ownership had lost millions of dollars in the years leading up to 1995, the team had pulled off a major coup, winning a new publicly financed palace despite strong opposition to public funds being used to benefit a private enterprise.

Despite taking in more revenue than anticipated in 1995 and a significant increase in season ticket sales for the 1996 season — at higher prices — the team's ownership decided once they had their stadium they would not authorize enough of a payroll increase to keep the M's first playoff team intact.

Few teams have ever had three first-ballot Hall of Famers in the prime of their careers playing for them at the same time. The Mariners had the most popular player in the game in Ken Griffey Jr., the most feared pitcher in the game in Randy Johnson, and perhaps the greatest shortstop in the history of baseball in Alex Rodriguez. Add to that a borderline Hall of Famer in DH Edgar Martinez, who won two batting titles (and hit .322 or better six seasons in a row) and Jay Buhner, who had three forty-home-run seasons and you begin to understand why this was a team that should have competed for a World Series title several years in a row.

After winning the A.L. West for the first time in 1995 and getting approval for a new outdoor ballpark, the Seattle Mariners should have been on the verge of a dynasty. No other team in baseball could match their level of talent on a daily basis — if they just would have surrounded this group of young stars with decent supporting talent.

Ownership's decision not to finance their operation properly in the years leading up to the opening of Safeco Field repeatedly would play a key role in the team's personnel decisions, and ultimately, the team's place in the American League standings, during this critical period when the team's three superstars — Griffey, Johnson and Rodriguez — would make their decisions on whether to stay with the Mariners.

The path chosen by the Mariners owners would be the single most important reason why the team never reached the World Series and would lead directly to the departure of those three future Hall of Famers.

Was the Mariners ownership ungrateful that they were being handed a new publicly funded stadium that would provide a massive increase in revenue and a major bump in the value of the franchise? With that new stadium by then a virtual certainty, it would seem incumbent that ownership keep the club together in the intervening years.

But the M's ownership group didn't take that view and they had a critical ally in *Seattle Times* beat-writer Bob Finnigan, who had covered the team since 1982 and had developed strong ties to Chuck Armstrong and other Mariner executives. Whenever the club wanted to propagate a specific agenda, such as cutting payroll or trading a popular player, it seemed as if Finnigan would agree to present the team's point of view as if it were his own, selling the team's decisions to Mariner fans as reasonable decisions made by a competent management team. This continued on a regular basis until Finnigan retired late in the 2006 season.

On October 18, 1995, the day after the Mariners were eliminated from the ALCS by the Cleveland Indians, alongside the story of the M's 4-0 defeat and the end of the team's miraculous run, the *Seattle Times* published an article headlined "No Pressure, Just a Challenge".

In it, Finnigan planted the seed that the Mariners might not be able to afford to keep some of the key players from the '95 team. There was even a quote from an unnamed Mariner official about the team's desire to cut payroll despite that same official acknowledging the team's revenues were likely to increase in 1996 because of the success of the '95 season. The candid quotes from that official seemed at odds with Manager Lou Piniella's hopeful words in the article. "I don't see any reason why we can't assemble a club competitive enough to take this further next year. We have a nucleus, solid and experienced," Piniella said. "*We just have to add to it.*"

Finnigan wrote two more articles, one on October 28 (M's Next Miracle: Fitting '96 Payroll) and another on November 12 (Lovefest Can't Fill Need for Contract) in which he reported that the M's were not likely to keep Tino Martinez, third-baseman Mike Blowers, and key setup man Jeff Nelson.

Then, on November 23, Finnigan confirmed suspicions that the team would not be increasing the player payroll significantly from what had been spent in 1995. Chuck Armstrong was quoted as saying, "Our payroll for next season will be at the 1995 figure or a little higher. There is a perception out there that we are cutting payroll and that is not the case."

While Armstrong didn't like that perception, essentially it was correct. Even if the M's payroll technically didn't decrease for 1996, because the team's revenue was surely going to increase in 1996 with higher attendance and higher ticket prices, even if the M's spent a few more dollars than they had in 1995, they would certainly spend a smaller percentage of revenue on player payroll than they had in 1995.

In any event, the important message was that the team's budget for 1996 was not going to be large enough to keep Tino Martinez, revealing for the first time that the M's were in trade talks with the Yankees regarding Martinez. When Tino heard about those talks, he expressed disappointment that the Mariners had not called him or his agent to talk about a contract, saying "Before I left the Mariners, I'd like to think they'd call and see what it might take to sign me."

In a December 1, 1995 article headlined "For Mariners, Focus Turns to Edgar, Tino — Piniella Wants Team Intact," Finnigan reported that the Mariners not only were in discussions to trade Tino Martinez to the Yankees, but they were talking to the New York Mets about Edgar Martinez, who'd hit .356 in 1995 and won his second batting title. An unnamed Mariners official confirmed the talks regarding Edgar, but told Finnigan, "Our talks with the Mets have not been as strong as (with the Yankees) on Tino."

Lou Piniella told Finnigan that he didn't want to see anyone leave the team, but his pleas were apparently ignored as the M's were preparing to trade Tino Martinez and seriously considered trading Edgar Martinez a mere six weeks after Edgar's double had put Seattle in the 1995 ALCS.

"I hope we don't do anything else, trade Tino or anyone," Piniella said. "We don't actually have to pay payroll until April 1, and a lot can happen between now and then to change circumstances."

With the team tipping its hand by saying in public that it could not afford to keep Martinez, and with few teams in need of a first-baseman other than New York, whose veteran first-baseman, Don Mattingly, was retiring after a twelve-year career, Seattle sabotaged much of its negotiating leverage and was forced to accept a deal favorable to the Yankees. It had taken Martinez, the team's No. 1 pick in the 1988 amateur draft, several years to deliver on his potential, but he'd just had his breakout season in 1995, hitting .293 with 31 home runs and 111 RBI.

With the future of the franchise no longer in jeopardy and a deal in place for a new stadium, it hardly seems believable that the M's continued to claim financial hardship and traded away one of their best young players. When the trade was announced on December 7, 1995, on Martinez's twenty-eighth birthday, Mariner fans had more cause to complain. The deal sent Martinez to the Yankees, the team the M's had just beaten in the playoffs. Strengthening one of its chief American League competitors would prove to be a foolish and costly move.

Vocal Mariner fans wrote in to the local newspapers and complained loudly on the radio airwaves that trading Martinez was an outrage, especially in light of the team's new stadium deal, leading *Seattle Times* columnist Blaine Newnham to come to the M's defense on December 19.

In a column titled "Will New Fans Just Fly Away? — True Believers Realize Team Is Doing Right Thing," Newnham called the five-year, $20 million contract that Tino signed with the Yankees "absurd," writing "Martinez has a nice smile and a nice stroke, but he might never again have the year he had for the Mariners. And even if he does, the team would have to generate nearly a half a million extra ticket sales to pay the salary the Yankees are giving him."

I'm not quite sure how Newnham arrived at such a ridiculous and irresponsible conclusion. According to a report in Newnham's own newspaper, the Mariners' average ticket price in 1996 was $12.34. Averaging out the cost of Martinez's five-year contract and assuming the M's would have had to pay him a $4 million salary in 1996 (instead of the $2.3 million the Yankees paid him that year by backloading the contract with higher salaries in the later years) you'd still have to factor in the cost of the first-baseman signed to replace Martinez — Paul Sorrento, whom the Mariners paid $1.025 million in 1996.

Subtracting Sorrento's salary from that $4 million meant that *at most* the M's might have had to pay Martinez $2.975 million more than they paid Sorrento. Dividing that amount by the M's average cost of $12.34 per ticket comes to a total of 241,085 extra tickets needing to be sold to pay for Martinez's contract — less than half the amount Newnham claimed. That estimate also assumed that the Mariners wouldn't derive any additional concession and parking revenue from those additional ticket buyers and also failed to take into account the Mariners' revenues from other sources, such as their broadcast contracts. Seattle's cut of a new national TV deal with NBC and ESPN was due to jump from $3.4 million in 1995 to $7.4 million in 1996.

Martinez not only matched his breakout '95 season in the pressurized atmosphere of New York, but he was a remarkably consistent performer the next six seasons, averaging 28 HRs and 115 RBI and became a hero on several World Championship teams. At the end of the day, the contract Newnham called absurd was a bargain for the Yankees, much as it would have been had the Mariners signed Tino to a similar contract.

It certainly wasn't out of line for M's fans to be outraged about a trade that handed over one of the team's best players to one of Seattle's chief A.L. rivals, but with sportswriters like Finnigan and Newnham quick to defend short-sighted, financially motivated moves like the trade of Tino Martinez, the M's would make many more such moves in the ensuing years, leading to a sad and discouraging decline in the franchise's fortunes.

In actuality, it wouldn't have been that difficult for the M's to keep Martinez. He earned just $1 million in 1995, so he was certainly deserving of a significant pay raise. The money was there; the team's season-ticket numbers were growing even while ticket prices were increasing by a significant margin. The M's average ticket price rose 23.5% from 1995 ($9.99) to 1996 ($12.34), broadcast revenues were increasing, and a new stadium with new revenue streams was in sight. Competent management would have realized that Martinez was an asset the team needed to keep.

If trading Martinez, who'd hit .322 with thirteen home runs and thirty-two RBI against the Yankees in his Mariners career, wasn't insulting enough to Seattle fans, the deal also sent lockdown relief pitcher Jeff Nelson to New York. The M's had apparently decided that they not only couldn't afford Martinez, but they couldn't afford to retain their best setup man either. Nelson, paid a mere $860,000 by the Yankees in '96, had appeared in sixty-two games for Seattle in 1995, going 7-3 with a 2.17 ERA, striking out ninety-six batters in 78 2/3 innings while allowing just 58 hits.

One day after the trade, Finnigan wrote about the Nelson element of the deal. "Another key factor for Seattle was, as usual, financial. Nelson, good as he was, was in line to make more than $1 million as a setup man. In the Mariner Nation, those numbers don't add up, now or ever."

It's unclear what Finnigan was talking about. Within two years the Mariners would be paying three different setup men, none of them as good as Nelson, well in excess of $1 million a season, with one of them, Mike Timlin, paid more than $3 million in 1998.

Martinez's new contract with New York elicited a defensive response from Woody Woodward.

"We figured Tino was going to get upwards of $3 million in arbitration, and there was just no way we could afford that," he said. "I can assure you there's no way we could have afforded that (Yankees contract). I trust people will understand that circumstances, our payroll situation, dictated that we make this trade ... I don't like breaking up a successful club any more than anyone else. We hated to trade Tino, but we've succeeded in unloading a lot of payroll."

So, while most of the other major-league teams measured success by how well they developed their players and by how they finished in the standings, the Seattle Mariners of the mid-1990s apparently judged themselves as a success for their ability to dump star players who were making too much money.

By those standards, the Mariners had a very successful offseason, ridding themselves of seven of the fourteen best players from the team that had just won the American League West.

In addition to trading Martinez and Nelson to New York, where both played major roles in the Yankees' winning four of the next five World Series, Seattle also traded its starting third-baseman, Mike Blowers (23 HRs, 96 RBI in 1995) and its second-best setup man Bill Risley (2-1, 3.13 ERA, 65 strikeouts in 60 1/3 innings), and allowed starting pitchers Andy Benes and Tim Belcher and leadoff man Vince Coleman to leave as free agents. Valuable resources had been expended to acquire Benes, Belcher, and Coleman in the middle of the '95 season; four prospects, including three former No. 1 draft picks, were traded to acquire those players, yet each of the players was allowed to leave as free agents without much effort to retain them.

To say that the M's didn't get much return for the seven key players who departed after the '95 season would be an understatement.

Sterling Hitchcock and Russ Davis, the two players they received from the Yankees in the Martinez/Nelson deal (in which Seattle also threw in reliever Jim Mecir, who went on to have a solid eleven-year career as a setup man), didn't do much for the M's. Hitchcock, a left-handed starter, posted a 5.35 ERA in his only season in Seattle, while Davis was a defensive liability at third base and actually had more errors (71) in his four seasons in Seattle than home runs (66).

Risley, traded to Toronto eleven days after Martinez and Nelson were shipped off to New York, brought back two of the worst pitchers in team history, Edwin Hurtado and Paul Menhart. Hurtado pitched in twenty-nine games for the M's in 1996-97, going 3-7 with an ERA of 8.10. It didn't take as long for the M's to figure out what they had in Menhart, who went 2-2 with a 7.29 ERA in eleven games for the '96 Mariners before he was dumped on the San Diego Padres for a pitcher of little note.

Seattle's motivation in trading Blowers was all about shedding salary; neither of the two players the M's acquired from the Dodgers in the November 25 trade that sent Blowers to LA — infielders Miguel Cairo and Willis Otanez — were still with Seattle a few weeks later when spring training began.

The most notable addition to the Mariners for 1996 wasn't acquired in trade or free agency. Twenty-year-old Alex Rodriguez, who'd played in sixty-five games with Seattle in 1994-95, took over from Luis Sojo as the team's starting shortstop and added a big bat to the Mariners lineup. First-baseman Paul Sorrento and relief-pitcher Mike Jackson were signed to one-year free-agent contracts for a combined $2.2 million to replace Martinez and Nelson.

So it was with both hands tied behind their backs that the Mariners began their defense of their American League West title in 1996.

Opening Day saw 57,467 fans fill the Kingdome for a thrilling 3-2 win in twelve innings over the Chicago White Sox. It was the sixth-largest crowd in the history of the Dome and the ninth straight crowd of more than fifty-five thousand. Rodriguez, the new starting shortstop, had the game-winning hit.

On April 15 the M's took on the Angels at the Kingdome. A four-game winning streak looked to be at an end when California surged to a 9-1 lead by the fourth inning. But the magic of 1995 returned for a night as the M's rallied for an 11-10 victory and the biggest comeback in franchise history. The victory improved the club's record to 9-4 and moved the team into first place.

The M's win streak reached eight games before it was snapped on April 19 when Toronto's Pat Hentgen, who went on to win the A.L. Cy Young Award that year, outdueled Bob Wolcott. On April 26, Randy Johnson, who'd won the Cy Young Award in 1995 when he went 18-2 with a 2.48 ERA, left his start at Milwaukee's County Stadium after 3 1/3 innings with a stiff back. Johnson was able to take his regular turn five days later against Texas, but lasted just two innings and had to leave with what was later diagnosed as a nerve irritation in his back.

Johnson returned on May 12 and went five innings in an 8-5 Mariners victory over Kansas City. "It was a big step in the right direction," Johnson said of his ninety-eight-pitch, seven-strikeout performance. While Johnson put on a brave face, he pitched through a lot of pain that night. Two days later, after being placed on the disabled list, Johnson said "I'm not helping either the team or myself by continuing to try to pitch. So I miss two weeks now, a couple or three starts, and get well. There's plenty of season left."

While there was indeed plenty of season left, the start against Kansas City would be Johnson's last of the '96 season.

The Mariners rotation, which was already struggling because of the failure to re-sign Benes and Belcher, could ill afford to lose its ace. Seattle started no fewer than fifteen different pitchers during the '96 season, but only two of them, Johnson and Jamie Moyer, who made eleven second-half starts for the M's after he was acquired from Boston at the July 31 trade deadline, posted ERAs under 4.00. Meanwhile, Benes, who signed a two-year, $8.1 million deal with the Cardinals, went 18-10 that year with a 3.83 ERA for St. Louis, and Belcher, who signed a one-year deal for $1.4 million with Kansas City in early February, finished the '96 season with a 15-11 record and a 3.92 ERA.

On May 1 the M's lost 5-4 to Texas, which moved into first place, where it remained for the balance of the '96 season, reaching the postseason for the first time in its twenty-five year history.

While the Mariners had a tremendous offense in 1996, setting a major league record with 245 home runs, a record broken a year later by a Seattle team that hit 264 home runs, the M's starting pitching in 1996 was abysmal.

In early July the Mariners took three out of four from the Rangers in Texas to pull within four games of the division lead, fueling speculation about whether the Mariners would try to improve their starting pitching before the July 31 trading deadline.

1996 TOP PERFORMERS

Ken Griffey Jr., .303, 49 HR, 140 RBI

Alex Rodriguez, .358, 36 RBI, 123 RBI

Jay Buhner, .271, 44 HR, 138 RBI

Edgar Martinez, .327, 26 HR, 103 RBI

Sterling Hitchcock, 13-9, 5.35 ERA, 196.2 IP

THE POST-1995 FALLOUT

The M's took care of an important piece of business in late July, agreeing to a four-year, $10.55 million contract extension with Rodriguez on his twenty-first birthday. In his first season as a starting player, Rodriguez established himself as a star. He'd finish the '96 season as the American League batting champion, hitting .358 with 36 home runs and 123 RBI. Rodriguez's new deal paid him $900,000 in 1997, $2 million in 1998, $3 million in 1999, and $4.2 million in 2000.

At the time of the signing, Rodriguez said, "My intention was not to get the largest amount or the biggest contract." He then turned to Chuck Armstrong and said, "Chuck, that'll come in four years." No truer words have ever been spoken in the history of the Seattle Mariners.

On July 30 the M's record stood at 57-47, ten games over .500 and just two and a half games behind Texas in the A.L. West. As they'd done the year before, the Mariners made a move at the trade deadline to improve their starting rotation, trading outfielder Darren Bragg to the Red Sox for the left-handed Moyer, who went 6-1 with a 3.31 ERA the rest of the season.

While the Mariners got lucky with the thirty-three-year old Moyer, who established himself as a starter and remained with Seattle for another ten seasons, eventually becoming the franchise leader in victories, Seattle could have had another ace if it hadn't been so averse to spending money. The M's were in trade talks at the deadline for Philadelphia's Curt Schilling, but backed away after learning that his contract guaranteed him $3.5 million for the '97 season if he started twenty-six games in 1996. Instead of acquiring Schilling, the M's traded for a lesser Phillies starter, southpaw Terry Mulholland, who left as a free agent at season's end.

With the M's having two routes to the postseason, through the A.L. West or the Wild Card, the club made two more trades to improve its offense in August, adding veteran left-fielder Mark Whiten in a trade with Atlanta on August 14 and bringing in third-baseman Dave Hollins from Minnesota on August 29. While both players contributed to the cause the rest of the '96 season, neither was brought back for 1997 and the deal for Hollins was particularly costly, as the M's dealt away a minor-league prospect who would come back to haunt Seattle for years to come.

While Hollins hit .351 and knocked in twenty-five runs in twenty-eight games with Seattle in 1996, the player to be named later headed to the Twins literally was a player to be named later; twenty-year-old first-baseman David Arias changed his name to David Ortiz the following season. A few years later he became a folk hero in Boston, averaging thirty-six home runs a year for nine seasons and would be a key player on two World Series winning teams. Ortiz entered 2012 needing just twenty-two home runs to reach four-hundred for his career, while Hollins played one month for Seattle.

In early September, the Rangers ran off a five-game win streak to extend their division lead to a season-high nine games. Prospects seemed dim for the Mariners, who had just nineteen games remaining on their '96 schedule. But the Mariners suddenly got hot and the Rangers began to lose. The limping Rangers arrived in Seattle for a four-game series on September 16 having lost their previous four games by a combined score of 35-16. The M's had won four straight to pull within six games of the Rangers when they met in the first game of a four-game series at the Kingdome in mid-September.

It seemed like 1995 all over again as everything that could go right for Seattle went right. The M's swept the four-game series by scores of 6-0, 5-2, 5-2, and 7-6 to pull within two games. Seattle got within one game of Texas when it routed the Oakland A's in consecutive games on September 20 and 21, 12-2 and 9-2, to extend its winning streak to a franchise-record ten games.

However, that was as close as the M's got in 1996. The ten-game win streak ended the next day as the M's lost a 13-11 slugfest to Oakland in their final home game of the season. With seven games left in Anaheim and Oakland, the M's still had a shot, but slumped at the wrong time, losing two of three to the Angels and three of four to the A's, and finished the season in second place at 85-76. Meanwhile, Texas got back on the winning track to take six of its last eight games and win the West at 90-72. The Mariners finished second in the Wild Card race, two and a half games behind Baltimore.

While the '96 season came to a disappointing end there was great hope for the future. The Mariners were coming off the first consecutive winning seasons in franchise history, a new ballpark was on the horizon, and fan support was at an all-time high. More than 2.7 million fans came indoors to the Kingdome to see the Mariners in 1996, with the average attendance of 33,628 more than eleven thousand fans per game more than the team had drawn on average in 1995.

With an exciting, winning team finally in place, the '97 season couldn't come soon enough for baseball fans in Seattle.

Chapter 10

DEVELOPING THROUGH THE DRAFT

O ne of the keys to building a winning major-league team is selecting and developing young players through the annual amateur draft. Unfortunately the Seattle Mariners have been one of the worst teams in baseball at doing so.

In its first fifteen years, the team was undercapitalized and had virtually no chance to win. In the 1980s there was a time when the M's, through the good work of Scouting Director Hal Keller, drafted and promoted several promising players to the majors. In fact, from 1984 to 1986, position players Alvin Davis, Danny Tartabull, Harold Reynolds, Jim Presley, Ivan Calderon, and Spike Owen, and pitchers Mark Langston and Bill Swift all graduated to the majors.

This was a core of good young players that would have been envied by any team in baseball. A good organization would have been able to build a winning team around this foundation of inexpensive players by filling its other spots with free-agent signings and a shrewd trade acquisition or two. But the Mariners wouldn't spend the money to sign free agents, they didn't have the smarts to make good trades, and their baseball people constantly faced interference from owner George Argyros and team President Chuck Armstrong.

The M's of the 1980s failed to capitalize on that influx of young talent, eventually trading away most of their good players for players that were either old, or bad, or both. The M's got another chance in the 1990s, thanks to finishing with the worst record in the American League at two opportune times, enabling them to select Ken Griffey Jr. and Alex Rodriguez with the first overall picks in the 1987 and 1993 amateur drafts. The early 1990s saw the Mariners graduate several more players from their farm system, including Tino Martinez, the club's first-round pick in 1988, and two players signed as international free agents, Edgar Martinez and Omar Vizquel.

The Mariners of the 1990s were underfunded, too, despite the purchase of the team by Nintendo. Every year there seemed to be a budget crunch, with the team forced to trade talented stars such as Vizquel (1993) and Tino Martinez (1995) to meet ownership's arbitrarily set budgets. Other young players were traded away before they had a chance to develop, including Bret Boone (1992), David Ortiz (1996), Jason Varitek (1997), Jose Cruz Jr. (1997) and a trio of pitchers who'd each go on to win nineteen or more games in a season with their new teams, Mike Hampton (1993), Shawn Estes (1995), and Derek Lowe (1997). In fact, in a twenty-six-month period from 1995 to 1997, GM Woody Woodward traded away no fewer than seven players who had been first-round picks by Seattle.

Trading young talent for stopgap players acquired for half a season and let go for financial reasons was one thing, but the Mariners of the early 2000s had a different problem; due to a series of mistakes and miscalculations, they no longer were drafting and developing good talent. Year after year, they'd fill one hole or another with free agents or trades, but ultimately, when the core of the Seattle team got old at the same time there were no young players ready to step in, leading to the Mariners' inevitable decline.

Remarkably, from the time that Rodriguez became the team's regular shortstop in 1996, for the next fifteen years the Mariners didn't have even one position player they'd taken in the amateur draft become a starting player in Seattle for a full season. While second-baseman Dustin Ackley seemed poised to end that dismal streak in 2012, this was a level of failure unprecedented in baseball history. While the first few years of this draught can rightly be blamed on Woodward, who traded away young players like Varitek and Cruz, there was plenty of blame to be placed on the shoulders of the two GMs who followed him in Seattle — Pat Gillick and Bill Bavasi.

Gillick, the architect of Seattle's 116-win team of 2001, typically preferred to acquire veteran players with postseason experience rather than building through the draft. But other forces may have been at work. After the 2000 season, the Mariners spent a good chunk of money, $13.1 million, to win the rights to Ichiro Suzuki. That deal has worked out quite well for the franchise, but it coincided with a long period of fallow drafts, which may not have been a coincidence. Given the conservative spending nature of the team's ownership, it seems that the Mariners may have deliberately shortchanged their amateur scouting operation during this period of time.

There's certainly enough circumstantial evidence from the M's next few drafts to make a case that the team cut back its budget for amateur signings to help fund the initial outlay for Ichiro. In 2003 and 2004, the Mariners unnecessarily lost their first-round draft picks. In 2003 they gave up their first pick, the nineteenth overall selection, to Arizona for signing backup first-baseman Greg Colbrunn, who played just one season in Seattle. In 2004 they lost their first pick to Kansas City for signing Raul Ibanez. If the M's had waited three weeks to sign Ibanez, they would have kept their first-round pick; the Royals already had revealed they were not going to offer arbitration to Ibanez, meaning the M's would not have had to compensate the Royals in any way to sign Ibanez.

Further, in 2002, the M's used their first-round pick to draft a high-school player, John Mayberry Jr., who had decided to attend Stanford University. Given that scenario, it would have taken an extraordinary signing bonus to sway Mayberry and his parents, but the Mariners held the line at a modest signing bonus and for the first time in franchise history, the team failed to sign its first-round pick.

To summarize, the Mariners didn't sign a first-round pick in any of the first four seasons after acquiring Ichiro (the M's had also lost their first-round pick in 2001 to the Yankees when they brought back relief-pitcher Jeff Nelson). By doing so, the M's avoided paying millions of dollars in first-round bonus money to amateur players in each of those seasons.

While the signing of Nelson was defensible, needlessly forfeiting two first-round picks and spending another first-round selection on a player who was unlikely to join the organization, was not. Whether this was a deliberate move on the M's part or sheer negligence, it was the biggest factor in the dearth of position players ready to contribute to Seattle's major-league roster in the mid to late 2000s.

With the pick the M's wasted on Mayberry, Seattle could have chosen first-baseman Jocy Votto, who instead developed into one of the top sluggers in the game with the Cincinnati Reds. With the pick they lost for signing Colbrunn, they could have picked outfielder Carlos Quentin, who averaged twenty-seven home runs a season for the White Sox from 2008 to 2011. Finally, with the pick the M's surrendered to Kansas City for signing Ibanez, Seattle could have drafted Hunter Pence, a perennial twenty-five-home-run hitter and one of the best outfielders in the National League (or, if they'd preferred pitching, they could have selected one of two big league aces — Yovanni Gallardo or Gio Gonzalez).

There were other inexplicable misses as well. When the M's took Willie Bloomquist in the third round of the 1999 draft, they passed on a third-baseman from Maple Woods Community College in Missouri. While Bloomquist reached the majors and spent six seasons in Seattle as a light-hitting reserve infielder, that third-baseman, Albert Pujols, out-homered Bloomquist 445 to 17 through the end of the '11 season.

In 2001, the M's used the thirty-sixth pick overall, compensation for losing Alex Rodriguez, to select Michael Garciaparra. While his older brother was an All-Star shortstop, the younger Garciaparra was barely even a baseball player, having spent most of his time in high school focusing on soccer. He never reached the majors. But the player selected two picks after Garciaparra, third-baseman David Wright, became a five-time All-Star for the New York Mets.

In the same draft, Seattle passed up first-baseman Ryan Howard seven times. Among the players the M's preferred to Howard, who would average forty-four home runs a season from 2006 to 2011, were middling talents like Rene Rivera and Mike Wilson. One player Seattle selected ahead of Howard, catcher Lazaro Abreu, not only didn't reach the majors, he played in just four games in his entire minor-league career.

During Bill Bavasi's tenure in Seattle, the M's swung and missed three times early in the first round. When you're picking as high as Seattle did in 2005 (third overall) and 2006 (fifth overall), an organization cannot afford to get the pick horribly wrong. But the M's did, selecting catcher Jeff Clement in 2005 while passing up shortstop Troy Tulowitzki and third-basemen Ryan Braun and Ryan Zimmerman. The M's were reportedly all set to pick Tulowitzki until the night before the '05 draft, when Bavasi was said to have overruled his scouts because the M's needed a catcher. Tulowitzki, Braun, and Zimmerman became perennial All-Star candidates, while Clement was traded after playing just seventy-five games for the M's. In 2006, Seattle eschewed the popular local choice, passing on University of Washington standout Tim Lincecum to pick right-handed pitcher Brandon Morrow, who was traded after the '09 season. Lincecum won Cy Young Awards in each of his first two full seasons with the Giants and was an All-Star in each of his first four full seasons. And when the Mariners picked Canadian hurler Phillippe Aumont with the eleventh overall pick in 2007, they passed on promising catchers J.P. Arencibia and Devin Mesoraco.

To be fair, during the fifteen-year period where the M's failed to pull a regular position player from the draft, they did develop a handful of pitchers, but just three became solid contributors for Seattle — starters Joel Pineiro and Gil Meche, and reliever J.J. Putz.

Compared to the rest of the major-league teams, the Mariners record of drafting and developing position players during this fifteen-year period was abysmal. Between 1996 and 2011, twenty-four of the other twenty-nine teams drafted and developed at least ten position players who became regular players for at least one season, while every team except Seattle had at least five draftees become regular position players. Topping the list was the Minnesota Twins, who had twenty-five different draftees become regular players for them between 1996 and 2011. The Twins culled eighty-nine seasons out of those position players, who were named to the All-Star team fifteen times.

While Seattle's track record of drafting position players was exceptionally weak during that time, there's reason for hope. The Milwaukee Brewers were high on that list, having drafted seventeen position players who became regulars, including five who have been named to at least one All-Star team (Prince Fielder, Rickie Weeks, J.J. Hardy, Corey Hart, and Ryan Braun). The man responsible for drafting those All-Stars was none other than Jack Zduriencik, who was hired as Seattle's general manager after the '08 season. At this writing, while Zduriencik had been on the job in Seattle for only three years, the M's had already seen returns from his first Seattle draft class; infielders Dustin Ackley and Kyle Seager, both selected in the 2009 draft, made it to the majors in 2011.

Chapter 11

MORTGAGING THE FARM

Despite setting a franchise record in attendance in 1996, when more than 2.7 million people showed up at the Kingdome and with season tickets sales at an all-time high (17,200), Mariners ownership inexplicably cut the team's player payroll for 1997 by $2.5 million. This was done after the M's had enjoyed the fourth-highest attendance in the American League in 1996. The Mariners, playing in a terrible indoor stadium, had drawn nearly a half-million more fans than the New York Yankees, who won the World Series that season.

While the Mariners had whined for much of their twenty-year existence of a lack of support in Seattle, now that the team had found an unprecedented level of fan support, the club's wealthy owners were figuratively extending a middle finger to the fans filling up their stadium. The decision to cut payroll for 1997 would be one that would haunt the franchise for years to come.

The M's made a move that offseason to shore up one area of the team, their starting rotation, acquiring left-hander Jeff Fassero from the Montreal Expos just four days after the World Series ended. Fassero had won twenty-eight games for Montreal in two years as a full-time starter, but the Expos were cutting costs and felt they had to move him. Other teams coveted Fassero, but Seattle had an edge in the dealings — Montreal's general manager was former Mariner pitcher Jim Beattie, who had been Seattle's farm director until October 1995. Questioned after the trade as to why he didn't get more for Fassero, a defensive Beattie sounded much like his former boss Woodward after so many cost cutting Mariner trades.

"I did not think that I could do any better than this," Beattie said. "It's no secret that I have to move salary to get players who I think can help us win."

Fassero and the Mariners agreed to a three-year contract that paid him nearly $3.5 million in 1997. Two weeks later the club re-signed Moyer to a two-year deal with a club option for a third year. Concerned about an abundance of left-handers in the rotation, Seattle traded the left-handed

Sterling Hitchcock to San Diego for right-hander Scott Sanders in early December. While Hitchcock wasn't great in his only season in Seattle, he turned out to better than the home-run prone Sanders, who allowed sixteen home runs in 65 1/3 innings and posted a 6.47 ERA before the M's traded him to Detroit three months into the '97 season.

While the M's had done reasonably well in solidifying their rotation for 1997, there were no such illusions about the team's bullpen. The cut in payroll led to a foolish decision not to retain right-hander Mike Jackson, who had made seventy-two appearances in 1996. Jackson wanted to re-sign with Seattle, but he asked for a raise from his '96 salary of $1.2 million to $2 million, and the M's offered $1.5 million.

"Mike did not fit into our financial picture," Mariners Assistant GM Lee Pelekoudas told a reporter, "We discussed a contract with him and didn't have a fit."

Jackson signed a two-year deal with the Cleveland Indians for $4.2 million. He started out as a setup man before taking over as the Tribe's closer midway through the '97 season. Jackson recorded fifteen saves and followed up by saving forty games in 1998, posting ERAs of 3.24 and 1.55.

Another experienced reliever, twenty-eight-year-old Shigetoshi Hasegawa, who'd pitched six years in Japan, wanted to sign with Seattle in December 1996 because of his friendship with Jim Colborn, the M's Pacific Rim scouting director. But bad timing led to him signing with the Angels instead. Because Mariners ownership had put the team up for sale that month, Woodward was forbidden from signing new players at the time. Hasegawa eventually joined the M's years later, but not in time to save the team's bullpen in 1997.

If the Mariners had somehow managed to sign either Jackson or Hasegawa, they might have gotten through the '97 season without having to panic to add bullpen help in midseason. Given that Jackson asked for just a few hundred thousand dollars more than the team offered, there should have been an effort made at compromising or offering a two-year deal like the one the pitcher eventually received from Cleveland. Seattle could have backloaded that two-year deal, with a higher salary in the second year, but apparently wasn't flexible enough to consider that option. Charlton, one of two veteran relievers the M's retained for the '97 season, wasn't happy about the loss of Jackson. "We had a good bullpen last year, but they took from it when they didn't bring back Jax," Charlton said. "Some teams with good bullpens added to them - Cleveland, Baltimore ...why couldn't we?"

Charlton had had a decent year in 1996, but the other veteran pitcher brought back, the right-handed Ayala, had struggled. Ayala, whose ERA rose from 2.86 in 1994 to 4.44 in 1995, posted a 5.88 ERA in 1996 and missed two months of the season with a broken hand after punching a hotel window in a rage. In a separate incident, Ayala was facing drunken-driving charges from an auto accident that year during spring training.

Ayala's presence on the team was a puzzle to most Mariner fans who couldn't understand why he was allowed to blow game after game in the late innings. While there appeared to be no truth to the widely circulated rumor that Ayala was dating a member of Lou Piniella's family, many fans clung to this misplaced belief because at least it offered a reasonable explanation why Seattle stuck with Ayala so long while allowing better relief pitchers to slip away. Ayala earned $900,000 in 1997 and was inexplicably signed to a two-year, $3.3 million deal for 1998-99.

When Ayala went 1-10 with a 7.29 ERA in 1998 and was again the target of booing fans at the Kingdome, the M's finally shipped him off to a foreign country — Canada — where he'd pitch one season for the Montreal Expos. While M's fans were glad to see Ayala go, Seattle was still responsible for two-thirds of his $1.8 million salary in 1999.

Left-field was another problem area. The M's didn't make an offer to free-agent Mark Whiten, who hit .300 with twelve homers in forty games for Seattle late in the '96 season. Greg Vaughn, a free agent from the San Diego Padres, was said to be interested that winter in signing with Seattle, but the M's claimed they couldn't afford him. In early December, Bob Finnigan wrote in the *Times*, "Vaughn reportedly wants at least a three-year deal worth $5 million to $6 million a year. Seattle's offer to a left-fielder will be closer to five or six ... dollars. Not millions."

Assistant GM Lee Pelekoudas told Finnigan, "All our money is going into pitching." Vaughn averaged thirty-eight home runs a year the next three seasons.

With management claiming it couldn't afford to sign a veteran left-fielder, Piniella traveled to Puerto Rico in early December for a look at Jose Cruz Jr. the team's first-round pick from 1995. After watching him play one game, Piniella declared that Cruz, who had just 160 games of minor-league experience, was ready for the major leagues. While Cruz did well in spring training, he started the season at Triple-A Tacoma. Seattle opened the '97 season with a left-field platoon of Lee Tinsley and Rich Amaral.

SHIPWRECKED

On April 1, 57,586 fans jammed into the Kingdome for Opening Night against the World Champion Yankees. The M's didn't disappoint, as Ken Griffey Jr.'s two home runs led them to a 4-2 win.

Randy Johnson, who had recovered from the back surgery that had shortened his '96 season, faced his first test of the '97 season on April 5 and did well. Johnson allowed just five hits, didn't walk anyone, struck out eight, and left after six innings with a 3-2 lead. But it took right-hander Bob Wells, in a setup role for which he wasn't qualified, all of three batters to blow the lead for Johnson in the seventh inning. Seattle's offense added two runs in the seventh and a run in the eighth to head into the ninth leading 6-4. But in the first of many bullpen meltdowns during the '97 season, Charlton gave up a double to former Mariner Bill Haselman, walked another former Mariner, Darren Bragg, and then allowed a three-run home run to Nomar Garciaparra. The M's fell 8-6.

On May 1, Griffey, who had set a major-league record with thirteen home runs in April, was named American League player of the month. Griffey also hit .340 in April with thirty RBI. New York's Tino Martinez was runner-up. The M's had sellout crowds on May 17 (57,304) and 18 (57,435) when they gave away Alex Rodriguez T-shirts and two games to Baltimore. The second game was lost in another bullpen meltdown. Ayala gave up single runs in the sixth and seventh and Charlton coughed up the deciding two runs in the ninth to seal the Orioles' 8-7 victory. Ayala and Charlton were booed by the capacity crowd at the Kingdome.

The 1-4 homestand over, the M's headed out on the road where they had posted a 14-7 record to that point in the season, significantly better than their 10-14 record at the Kingdome.

On the first night of the trip, Piniella talked to his players for ten minutes before batting practice.

"Lou was intense, the most intense I've seen him in three years," Alex Rodriguez said. "I think it helped all of us. He expressed his confidence in us despite the recent losses, reminded us we are a good ballclub and, like any club, even good ones go through tough stretches. But the really good ones keep the slumps short."

Fueled by a 4-for-4 night by second-baseman Joey Cora, who doubled and homered, the M's won 13-4. Cora, in the midst of a fifteen-game hitting streak, during which he hit .475, described Piniella's rant as "awesome," telling the *Seattle Times*, "It affirmed some things to us about our team, pointed out some things we had to change."

Cora's hit streak reached a team-record twenty-four games before it was snapped on May 31 against Detroit.

The M's lost eight of eleven games during this stretch, including three games blown by Seattle's abysmal bullpen. By late May, the staff ERA had inflated to 5.93, worst in the majors.

Assistant GM Lee Pelekoudas made it clear that help was not on the way for the struggling bullpen, telling the *Seattle Times*, "We have tried to upgrade what we have," he said. "We can't. We have talked to other clubs. No one wants to give up pitching. Anyway, these guys should be doing the job themselves."

Asked by a reporter about the team's strategy in putting together the '97 bullpen, which had posted a collective ERA of 6.72 for the year — and 10.16 over the previous dozen games, Woodward said, "We made a decision. We had a consensus. It hasn't worked to this point. But I don't consider it a mistake."

Asked about possible changes, Woodward insisted, "There's no place else to go. Every time we talk to another club about a young pitcher who might help us, they talk about an older pitcher who makes a ton of money. There's no fit."

Woodward's comments seemed to indicate that if the Mariners had been willing to take on salary at the time, they could have avoided surrendering some of the club's best prospects at that year's trading deadline. But Woodward apparently had his orders that the '97 payroll could not be increased to improve the bullpen. Piniella was naturally displeased with the state of his bullpen.

"It isn't easy to be this bad," he said. "Really, it isn't. You don't get mad. You get busy."

1997 TOP PERFORMERS

Ken Griffey Jr., .304, 56 HR, 147 RBI

Edgar Martinez, .330, 28 HR, 108 RBI

Randy Johnson, 20-4, 2.28 ERA, 213 IP

Jeff Fassero, 16-9, 3.61 ERA, 234.1 IP

Jamie Moyer, 17-5, 3.86 ERA, 188.2 IP

SHIPWRECKED

One move the club made was to call up Jose Cruz Jr. from Tacoma on May 31. Cruz had hit .268 with six home runs in fifty games in the minors, but he represented an improvement. Seattle had gone the first two months of the '97 season with little to no production from left field.

No longer the team's closer, Charlton continued to struggle. On June 10 he entered the M's game in Toronto in the seventh inning, with Seattle clinging to a 3-1 lead. By the time he was finished putting the game in the "L" column, he'd faced nine batters, given up five extra base hits, walked one batter, hit another, and retired just two batters. His ERA for the season stood at 8.19. But while Piniella was concerned, he insisted that the team's only choice was to hope that Charlton could figure things out.

"He'll have to," Piniella said after the game. "He's one of the people we count on out there."

Piniella's continued faith in Charlton was unfounded that year, as the southpaw didn't improve much the rest of the way, finishing the season with a career-high 7.27 ERA.

Despite the bullpen's struggles, Seattle still led what was a weak A.L. West that season by four and a half games on July 11, when Steve Kelley wrote in the *Seattle Times*:

> It will take a rash of injuries and a complete pitching collapse for the Mariners to lose the West. They have the best nine-man order in the game. They have the deadliest pitcher in baseball. Randy Johnson practically guarantees them two wins in every playoff series. They have dependable Nos. 2 and 3 starters in Jeff Fassero and Jamie Moyer. But winning the West shouldn't be enough for this team. Not with Ken Griffey Jr., Alex Rodriguez, Joey Cora, Edgar Martinez, Jay Buhner, not with Johnson on an inexorable push toward another Cy Young Award.

> This is a franchise with greater promises to keep, which means it has to bust some moves. The bullpen remains a dangerous Twilight Zone. Without a bullpen that, at least, can approximate Baltimore's, the Mariners won't linger long into October. This franchise owes you - one starter and one reliever. If it doesn't make any significant deals it runs the risk of breaking a trust with the fans. Trades can be made. Quality arms are out there.

That same day, Finnigan wrote in the *Times* about several pitchers, starters, and relievers rumored to be available. When the name of Kansas City starter Kevin Appier, in the middle of a three-year contract that paid him $5 million per year, was brought up, Finnigan quoted an unnamed Mariner official as asking, "Where would we get the money?"

If the Mariners needed to find money in 1997, all they needed to do was check the Kingdome coffers, which were overflowing from the team's increased attendance that season. The M's would draw a team-record 3.2 million fans to the Dome in 1997. The fans were doing their part, filling the Kingdome on a nightly basis, averaging over thirty-nine thousand per game, but management still seemed unwilling to do its part.

On July 17, after watching his Mariners suffer another late-inning loss to reduce their division lead to a mere half game over the Angels, Piniella had seen enough.

"We've tried a lot of different combinations here," Piniella said. "And if you want to know the truth, we need to go out and get some help, okay? I do the best I can with what we have. But if we get some pitching help, we'll be a much better ballclub."

On July 30, the day before the trade deadline, the M's bullpen imploded in Boston, turning what had been a 7-2 eighth-inning lead into an 8-7, ten-inning loss. The culprits were the usual suspects, with Ayala giving up two runs in the eighth and Charlton allowing three in the ninth. Hurtado coughed up the winning run in the tenth.

If there was any doubt left in Seattle — or in the front offices of teams with relief pitchers to trade — that the M's would now be willing to trade Cruz and other highly rated prospects, they were erased with the latest bullpen disaster. Two weeks before the trade deadline, Woodward had gone on KJR Radio saying Cruz was an "untouchable" and would not be traded. But on the day of the trade deadline, the *Times* revealed that "two Mariner sources" had said that the team had become desperate enough to find an effective closer that they were now willing to trade Cruz.

And so it was that in the top of the fifth inning of Seattle's game on July 31 in Milwaukee, that Cruz, who had hit twelve home runs and driven in thirty-four runs in forty-nine games since his call-up from Triple-A, was summoned back to the dugout from the on-deck circle and told that he'd been traded to Toronto for relief-pitchers Mike Timlin and Paul Spoljaric. A few hours after the announcement, details of another trade emerged, this one with Boston. Catcher Jason Varitek, Seattle's first-round pick in the 1994 draft and pitcher Derek Lowe were both headed to the Red Sox for reliever Heathcliff Slocumb.

With the trades of Varitek and Cruz, Woodward had now traded seven Mariners' first-round picks in a twenty-six-month period, leaving Griffey, Rodriguez and two pitchers drafted in the first round of the 1996 and 1997 drafts, Gil Meche and Ryan Anderson, as the only Seattle first-rounders left in the organization.

"It came down very close to the twelfth hour," Woodward said. "It's true; I did not want to make that deal. But as we got closer to the deadline, we realized that to get the help we need to win this year, we were going to have to put a good young player like Cruz in the deal, but it needed to be done. We've got a shot this year and we've got to go for it."

Bob Finnigan revealed in the *Times* that the inclusion of Spoljaric was a "dealmaker" from Seattle's standpoint. Toronto had offered veteran left-hander Dan Plesac instead of Spoljaric and also offered outfielder Joe Carter, who could have replaced Cruz in the Mariners' outfield, but according to Finnigan, "the M's could not take on one-third of Carter's $6.5 million salary" (which would have amounted to less than $2.2 million).

The deal Seattle passed on would have served the team much better, but would have required approval to add Carter's salary from ownership. The thirty-five-year-old Plesac had twelve years of experience, held left-handed hitters to a .200 average in 1997 and his $800,000 salary wouldn't have been intrusive. Carter had hit the biggest home run in Blue Jays history, a walk-off job to end the 1993 World Series. He was still a very good player, belting twenty-one home runs and driving in 102 runs that season and would have fit nicely in the M's lineup. More important, if Seattle had acquired two veteran relievers in Timlin and Plesac, they may not have felt a need to make the trade for Slocumb, a deal many consider the worst in franchise history.

Still, Seattle insisted on Spoljaric, who did little to help the M's bullpen in 1997, walking fifteen batters in 22 2/3 innings and posting a 4.76 ERA. He was worse the following season, his last with the Mariners, pitching to a 6.48 ERA in 83 1/3 innings, walking fifty-five.

In Slocumb, the Mariners picked up a pitcher that Red Sox fans had booed mercilessly that season. There had even been talk in Boston of releasing Slocumb, who had an ERA of 8.04 on June 3, but Boston GM Dan Duquette held on to the struggling right-hander in the hopes that if Slocumb could have a few good outings, he might be able to get something of value from a team desperate for relief pitching. He found just such a team in the Seattle Mariners.

MORTGAGING THE FARM

The Red Sox received two players who turned out to be the heart and soul of the Boston team that would win the World Series in 2004, breaking the dreaded Curse of the Bambino (the 1920 trade that sent Babe Ruth to the Yankees) that some believed had kept the Sox from winning a World Series for more than eighty years. Catcher Jason Varitek hit as many as twenty-five home runs in a year for Boston in his fourteen seasons and became a solid defender behind the plate, but he also brought leadership to the Red Sox clubhouse, eventually being named the team's captain. Right-hander Derek Lowe pitched seven seasons in Boston and won the deciding game of all three Red Sox postseason series in 2004. He spent two seasons as Boston's closer, saving forty-two games in 2000 and then became a successful starter, winning twenty-one games in 2002, his first year in the Red Sox rotation. He entered the '12 season with 166 career wins. Just two of them came with Seattle.

Worst of all, Mariner sources confirmed reports out of Boston that the original trade discussions to acquire Slocumb had been for Varitek *or* Lowe, but when Woody Woodward called Duquette back to accept the deal, somehow he wound up agreeing to part with both players.

Unfortunately for the Mariners, Slocumb was a pitcher who was always pitching in and out of trouble, allowing nearly two baserunners an inning. While he managed to convert thirteen save opportunities in the second half of 1997, he did so with a high-wire act that drove fans and Piniella crazy. And while Seattle wasn't obligated to hold onto Slocumb past the '97 season, because they'd given up so much to get him, they decided to keep him in 1998 (and pay him a $3 million salary). He recorded just three saves that year (at $1 million per save) and didn't get his ERA below 10.00 until late May.

If the Mariners had managed to retain Jackson or Nelson, or both, the trades at the 1997 deadline that sent future stars packing wouldn't have become necessary. Surprisingly, Blaine Newnham of the *Times*, who'd been one of the Mariners' most vehement defenders when they claimed they couldn't afford Tino Martinez, was the only member of the mainstream media who dared criticize the Mariner processes in 1997. He wrote:

> When will this organization start thinking like a big-market, pennant-contending team, spending money up front instead of waiting until oil is leaking on the ground? They waited this year to see if Norm Charlton and Bobby Ayala could somehow bail them out when there was ample evidence to suggest they wouldn't. They could have — should have —

spent the $2 million to keep Mike Jackson and saved themselves the $2.25 million they'll have to pay Mike Timlin next year. They didn't act like a team averaging 38,000 fans a game and tracking on a World Series berth. They acted like the old Mariners."

The midseason trades helped stabilize the shaky bullpen somewhat, and the Mariners clinched the A.L. West title on September 23 with a 4-3 win over the Angels. Two days later team President Chuck Armstrong told the *Seattle Times* that the Mariners would turn a profit for the first time under the current ownership. Despite being just the twelfth team in major-league history to draw more than three million fans, Armstrong said, "We still consider ourselves a small-market team, because of our population base and geographic isolation."

The Mariners met the Baltimore Orioles in the first round of the '97 playoffs, but the magic from 1995 was not evident: Baltimore won the first two games of the series at the Kingdome by identical 9-3 scores despite crowds of more than fifty-nine thousand for both games. The teams headed to Baltimore with the Orioles needing one win to capture the series. Seattle took the third game 4-2 behind eight shutout innings from Jeff Fassero. However, Mike Mussina outpitched Randy Johnson for the second time in the series on October 5, and Baltimore won the game and the series 3-1. The Mariners' vaunted offense, which set a major-league home-run record that season that still stands, scored just eleven runs in the four playoff games. Seattle's supposedly revamped bullpen allowed sixteen hits and eleven runs in 9 1/3 innings.

The M's had won their division at a high cost to the team's future, yet hadn't been able to advance out of the first round of the playoffs.

Chapter 12

THE BEST AND WORST TRADES IN MARINERS HISTORY

This analysis of the best and worst trades in Mariners history focuses almost exclusively on deals that have occurred in the past twenty years. While there were good and bad trades made in the team's first decade, the non-competitive state of the franchise during that period of time was such that no single transaction, good or bad, could possibly have had the same impact on the team as those transactions that have been made since Nintendo purchased the team in 1992.

It might be a surprise to find that the February 2008 trade that sent five players to Baltimore to obtain Erik Bedard isn't on this list. There are two main reasons why. While Bedard had an injury-riddled tenure in Seattle, if the M's hadn't traded for him in the first place, it's highly unlikely they'd have had the relationship necessary to sign him to an incentive-based deal prior to the '11 season, when he was one of the top pitchers in the league in the first half, with his performance enabling the M's to acquire two outfield prospects from Boston at the trade deadline. Additionally, none of the three pitching prospects sent to Baltimore panned out.

TEN WORST TRADES

1. Jason Varitek and Derek Lowe to the Boston Red Sox for Heathcliff Slocumb (July 31, 1997).

This trade ranks as the worst trade in M's history for several reasons. Slocumb went 2-9 with a 4.97 ERA in a season and a third in Seattle, while Varitek and Lowe both have had long, productive major-league careers with other teams.

Slocumb had a terrible season with the Red Sox in '97 before the trade and the Red Sox should have been happy just to dump Slocumb's salary. But Boston GM Dan Duquette took advantage of a desperate Woody Woodward and was able to acquire two prospects who were close to being major-league ready and would help the Red Sox win their first championship in eighty-six years. This one hurt even more when it was later revealed that the original deal for Slocumb was Varitek *or* Lowe.

2. Tino Martinez, Jeff Nelson, and Jim Mecir to the New York Yankees for Sterling Hitchcock and Russ Davis (December 7, 1995).

Trading a young, power-hitting first-baseman is never a good idea, but it's far worse when you trade that first-baseman to the team you just beat in the playoffs, throw in your best setup man, and help that team win the World Series four of the next five seasons.

The M's claimed they couldn't afford to pay Martinez $3 million and Nelson $1 million for 1996, but with a new stadium on the way and season ticket sales on the rise, the decision to trade these two players was indefensible.

The players received by Seattle in the deal didn't take the sting out of losing Martinez and Nelson either; Hitchcock lasted one year in Seattle, while Davis was a poor fielding third-baseman who hit the occasional long ball.

3. David Ortiz to the Minnesota Twins for Dave Hollins (August 29, 1996).

While Hollins solidified third base for the M's over the last month of the '96 season, that team didn't make the playoffs and Seattle didn't make an effort to re-sign him at the end of the year.

The twenty-year-old prospect sent to the Twins, David Arias, had hit .322 and drove in ninety-three runs in Single-A ball that year. He later changed his name to David Ortiz, was named to seven All-Star teams, and entered the '12 season with 378 career home runs in the majors. If the Mariners hadn't traded away third-baseman Mike Blowers after the '95 season for financial reasons, it's likely this trade never would have happened.

4. Rafael Soriano to the Atlanta Braves for Horacio Ramirez (December 7, 2006)

This trade ranks among the worst in franchise history because it was done with sheer stupidity — it made absolutely no sense on the day it was made. Soriano was one of the best setup men in baseball, had closing potential, and was under club control for three more years. Ramirez was almost certain to be made a free agent by the Braves the following week, not offered arbitration for fear he'd make too much money.

Soriano continued his dominance with the Braves, while Ramirez had a 7.16 ERA in his lone season in Seattle. Mariner President Chuck Armstrong angered Mariner fans further when he revealed after the '07 season that he'd ordered GM Bill Bavasi to trade Soriano because of some mysterious off-the-field issues.

5. Asdrubal Cabrera to the Cleveland Indians for Eduardo Perez (June 30, 2006)

Like Ortiz, Cabrera was just twenty and an unfinished product when Seattle traded him in 2006. He was already in Triple-A, but seemingly blocked by the young double-play combo of Yuniesky Betancourt and Jose Lopez. While Eduardo Perez was a good hitter against left-handers, giving up anything of value for a DH who'd play once a week was ridiculous. Giving up a player such as Cabrera, who hit twenty-five home runs and was an All-Star for Cleveland in 2011, was ridiculous times ten.

Bavasi later admitted that he didn't disclose the deal to Bob Engel, Seattle's head of international scouting, until after it was made, presumably to avoid being talked out of making the deal.

6. Shin-Soo-Choo and Shawn Nottingham to the Cleveland Indians for Ben Broussard (July 26, 2006)

Choo never got much of a chance in Seattle, batting just thirty-three times for the M's in 2005 and 2006 before being shipped off to Cleveland. This trade might not have made this list if Broussard had managed to hit as well with the M's as he had for the Tribe. His left-handed power swing seemed perfectly suited for Safeco Field, but he hit .238 and drove in just seventeen runs for the M's in 2006.

Choo exacted swift revenge on the M's with a game-winning home run against Seattle in his first game with Cleveland. While the Mariners have desperately sought outfielders with pop the past few years, Choo hit .300 or better with good power three times for the Tribe.

7. Jose Paniagua, Denny Stark and Brian Fuentes to the Colorado Rockies for Jeff Cirillo

This one seemed like a good idea at the time. Cirillo was a career .300 hitter who was thought to be perfectly suited for Safeco Field. The M's had had a run of success with Washington-connected players in John Olerud and Aaron Sele and logically thought they could replicate that with third-baseman Cirillo, who made his home in Redmond after marrying into a Seattle-area family.

While Fuentes evolved into a solid closer years later, the failure of this trade was all about Cirillo. The M's essentially paid him nearly $14 million not to play for the Mariners the final two years of his contract.

8. Bill Swift, Mike Jackson, and Dave Burba to the San Francisco Giants for Kevin Mitchell, Mike Remlinger and $500,000 (December 11, 1991)

The Mariners were desperate for a power hitter and the temperamental Mitchell was just three years removed from an MVP season in which he'd hit forty-seven home runs. But he hit just nine homers in one injury-shortened season in Seattle and the loss of the three arms decimated Seattle's pitching staff.

Swift, a reliever with the M's, became a twenty-one-game winner as a starter, Burba was a reliable starter in the majors for the next nine seasons and Jackson continued his run as one of the best relievers in baseball for several more years.

9. Jeff Clement, Ronny Cedeno, Nathan Adcock, Brett Lorin, and Aaron Pribanic to the Pittsburgh Pirates for Jack Wilson and Ian Snell (July 29, 2009)

While none of the five players sent to the Pirates in the deal have warranted much regret, it was the performances and the salaries of the two players Seattle acquired that made this deal a stinker.

Jack Zduriencik likely wouldn't have made this trade, which added over $9 million to the M's 2010 payroll, if he'd known at the time that ownership would cut his player payroll by more than $10 million for 2010, leaving the team without a legitimate DH or left-fielder. The M's paid Wilson $10 million to hit .249 in 123 games in 2010 and 2011 and paid Snell $4.25 million to go 0-6 with a 6.41 ERA in 2010.

10. Carlos Guillen to the Detroit Tigers for Ramon Santiago and Juan Gonzalez (January 8, 2004)

The M's were so anxious to get rid of the twenty-eight-year-old Guillen for off-field reasons that they gave him away for a light-hitting utility infielder and a minor-leaguer who lasted just one season in the organization. Guillen was one of the Tigers' best players for most of the next eight years, making three All-Star teams.

DISHONORABLE MENTION

Omar Vizquel to Cleveland for Felix Fermin and Reggie Jefferson (December 20, 1993)

Mike Hampton and Mike Felder to Houston for Eric Anthony (December 10, 1993)

Jose Cruz Jr. to Toronto for Mike Timlin and Paul Spoljaric (July 31, 1997)

Matt Thornton to the White Sox for Joe Borchard (March 20, 2006)

Chris Snelling and Emiliano Fruto to Washington for Jose Vidro and cash (December 18, 2006)

Danny Tartabull and Rick Luecken to Kansas City for Scott Bankhead, Mike Kingery, and Steve Shields (December 10, 1986)

TEN BEST TRADES

1. Mark Langston and Mike Campbell to the Montreal Expos for Gene Harris, Brian Holman and Randy Johnson (May 25, 1989)

The Mariners got lucky here because the player they considered to be the key to this deal was Gene Harris, who would win just two games for Seattle. Yet Randy Johnson became the most dominant pitcher in baseball, winning five Cy Young Awards — though just one with Seattle. Johnson is likely to make the Hall of Fame in his first year of eligibility in 2015.

2. Ken Phelps to the New York Yankees for Jay Buhner, Rich Balabon, and Troy Evers (July 21, 1988)

The Mariners GM who made this trade, Dick Balderson, was fired six days later and replaced by Woody Woodward. While Phelps didn't pan out in New York, Buhner quickly became a fan favorite in Seattle, averaging forty-one home runs a year from 1995 to 1997 when the M's won the A.L. West twice.

3. Darren Bragg to the Boston Red Sox for Jamie Moyer (July 30, 1996)

While the twenty-six-year-old Bragg was a gritty fourth outfielder type, the thirty-three-year-old Moyer had bounced around the majors since breaking in with the Cubs in 1986; few expected him to develop into one of the top left-handers in the game. And nobody expected Moyer to pitch into his late forties, coming within thirty-three wins of joining the

300-Win Club. Moyer is the M's all-time leader in wins with 145. Felix Hernandez trailed him by sixty entering the '12 season.

4. Three-way trade with the Indians and Mets where Seattle dealt J.J. Putz, Jeremy Reed, Sean Green and Luis Valbuena and received seven players in return — Franklin Gutierrez, Jason Vargas, Mike Carp, Endy Chavez, Ezequiel Carrera, Aaron Heilman, and Maikel Cleto (December 10, 2008)

In Jack Zduriencik's first deal as Mariners GM, he traded a broken-down closer and a bunch of spare parts for a package that would net the M's a Gold Glove center-fielder, a No. 3 starter and a middle-of-the-order hitter. As if that weren't enough, Cleto was traded two years later for a starting shortstop, Brendan Ryan.

5. Randy Johnson to the Houston Astros for Freddy Garcia, Carlos Guillen, and John Halama (July 31, 1998)

We still wish the Mariners had held onto The Big Unit and gone to a few World Series, but since Seattle decided it had to trade him, the deal worked out as well as could be expected. The Mariners received a top-notch starting pitcher, an above-average shortstop, and a serviceable back-end starter. This trade turned out significantly better than either of the previous Johnson deals that came close to fruition — a July 1993 trade of Johnson to Toronto for pitchers Steve Karsay and Mike Timlin and a June 1998 trade of Johnson to the Dodgers for pitchers Hideo Nomo and Ismael Valdes and an outfielder.

6. Ken Griffey Jr. to the Cincinnati Reds for Mike Cameron, Brett Tomko, Antonio Perez and Jake Meyer (February 10, 2000)

Cameron wasn't the same impact player as Griffey, but neither was Griffey after he left Seattle, because of significant injuries in his thirties. While Cameron became a fan favorite in his own right in Seattle, the best part of being forced to trade Griffey was not having to pay him $17 million a year for the next eight seasons.

7. Roger Blanco to the Atlanta Braves for Mark Whiten (August 14, 1996)

While Whiten hit .300 with a dozen home runs in forty games with Seattle, which helped the M's contend until the last week of the '96 season, Blanco never made it out of A ball. This trade might have landed higher on the list if the Mariners had bothered to try to keep Whiten for another season.

8. Joey Cora to the Cleveland Indians for David Bell (August 31, 1998)

While Cora flamed out in Cleveland and never played again after 1998, Bell was an adequate starter at second and third base for the M's the next three seasons, averaging nineteen homers per season with above average defense.

9. Chris Widger, Matt Wagner, and Trey Moore for Jeff Fassero and Alex Pacheco (October 29, 1996)

Fassero solidified the M's rotation in 1997-98, winning twenty-nine games and averaging 233 innings a year before a big drop-off in '99. While Widger did okay in Montreal, the M's were dealing from surplus, with Dan Wilson in his prime at the time. The twenty-four-year-old Wagner hurt his shoulder and never pitched in the majors again.

10. tie — Marc Newfield and Ron Villone to the San Diego Padres for Andy Benes (July 31, 1995) and Jim Converse to the Kansas City Royals (August 15, 1995) for Vince Coleman.

Both of these deals were significant as they served to solidify the M's rotation and lineup for the 1995 stretch run. While Andy Benes had an inflated ERA due to a couple of bad outings, he won seven of his twelve starts for Seattle, a twenty-one-win pace. Coleman hit .290 and stole sixteen bases in forty games, a sixty-four-steal pace, and gave the Mariners the legitimate leadoff hitter they'd lacked for years. Without either trade, the M's wouldn't have made the '95 playoffs and would be playing in some other city now.

Chapter 13

TEARING DOWN

On November 13, Ken Griffey Jr. was named the Most Valuable Player of the American League for the '97 season having hit .304 and led the league with fifty-six home runs and 147 RBI. It was the first time in the club's twenty-one-year history that a Mariner player had won the MVP Award, but M's fans had little time to celebrate because on the day of the announcement Chuck Armstrong revealed that the team would not offer Randy Johnson a contract extension and announced that Johnson was on the trading block.

Armstrong claimed that Johnson's agent was seeking "Maddux Money" for the 6-foot-10 pitcher who'd finished second in Cy Young Award voting in '97.

"Talking further along those money lines was a waste of time good only as PR eyewash," Armstrong said, adding that he also had concerns about Johnson's ability to remain healthy. Despite undergoing back surgery in 1996, Johnson hadn't missed any starts because of the injury in '97, when he made 29 starts and went 20-4 with a 2.28 ERA.

Johnson was said to be seeking a two-year deal for $22 million to $24 million, in the annual salary range of Atlanta ace Greg Maddux, who had recently signed a five-year, $57.5 million contract extension with the Braves. An unnamed Mariner official told the *Seattle Times*, "To pay Randy, we'd have to be have committed twenty to twenty-five percent of our team payroll annually to him. We couldn't do that."

The next day the *Seattle Times* ran an editorial with the headline, "No Magic to Be Found in Slam on M's Fans," writing

On the same day that Ken Griffey Jr. collected his well-deserved American League Most Valuable Player award, the geniuses in Mariner management spit in the party punch bowl. They told pitcher Randy Johnson, the club's other world-class player, to take a hike. The Johnson fiasco is another in a series of events that suggest a haughty attitude toward the ticket-buying public...

In the days ahead, you'll hear endless analyses as to why the Mariners couldn't afford the reported $22 million necessary to keep Johnson for two years. You'll hear he's a 34-year-old-guy with a 54-year-old arm, bad back, and lousy attitude. The spinmeisters will be out in force. But fans remember how Johnson came back from surgery and pitched like a dream. For nine years, he helped fill the seats and sell the beer.

Recently, the team revealed a budget-busting pricing system for seats in the new ballpark. Some will be among the most expensive in the country. What's the plan here, fellas, first-class team or just first-class ticket prices? Can't somebody get through to these owners that Johnson is a big, 6-foot-10 reason the Mariners are still in Seattle and a new ballpark is rising in the dirt south of the Kingdome?"

The M's talked with several teams that winter about Johnson, but did not get an offer they liked. On November 17, under the headline, "Mariners Reject Johnson for Rivera Swap — Yankee Closer Not Considered Enough," Bob Finnigan reported that the Yankees had offered closer Mariano Rivera for Johnson. The twenty-seven-year-old Rivera had just finished his first season as New York's closer, posting a 1.88 ERA and recording 43 saves.

An inflexible Woody Woodward said of the Yankee offer, "We need a starting pitcher back in any deal for Randy. If we don't get one, if we don't get what we are looking for, then we are fully prepared to go into the season with Randy on our team."

An unnamed Mariner official said that the team had concerns about Rivera's arm. Those concerns were every bit as unfounded as the M's supposed concerns about Johnson's back, given that Rivera racked up thirty or more saves in thirteen of the next fourteen seasons. The twelve-time All-Star was still going strong in 2011, setting a major-league record for career saves.

On November 21, Steve Kelley talked to Johnson, who said, "I think the question the Mariners have to ask is: Are they closer to a World Series with me or without me? I feel like I've given my best years to date to the Mariners. I helped them save baseball in Seattle. I was one of twenty-five guys that kept baseball alive in Seattle. They're getting rid of the pitcher who has every pitching record there, and then they're turning around and raising ticket prices. But it's a business, so I guess it's selfish of me to think I could stay in Seattle. I was comfortable there the last nine years. This is where my children were born and where my wife's family is from. But it's time to move on, I guess."

With trade offers for Johnson not to the Mariners' liking, GM Woody Woodward said that the team would keep him, but told the *Seattle Times* that if the Mariners didn't trade Johnson and had to pay his $6 million salary for 1998, the club wouldn't be able to sign a closer. Reminded of the team's bullpen failures in 1997, Woodward said, "I'm looking forward to the new stadium and new revenues. Then maybe we can do a little more in the offseason."

On February 18, the M's reached a working agreement with the Orix Blue Wave of the Japanese Pacific League. "As a distinct possibility, Seattle could have an inside track on acquiring Ichiro Suzuki," Bob Finnigan wrote in the *Times*.

At the time, Suzuki was a four-time batting champion in Japan, with a career average of .359, but he was a virtual unknown in the states. Asked about the possibility of signing Suzuki, who had come to Seattle that winter and worked out at the Kingdome, Mariners Scouting Director Roger Jongewaard said such a deal could only be made with the cooperation of the Orix club.

"It would be wonderful to work something out should Orix ever wish to allow him to play in the U.S.," Jongewaard said. "But until then, for us to try and get him from them without total agreement would be like Orix coming and taking Junior from us. We wouldn't like it." While Suzuki would not be joining the Mariners for the '98 season, his was a name for Mariner fans to tuck away for the future

On March 31, 57,822 fans filled the Kingdome for Opening Day and saw the M's jump out to a 9-3 lead over the Cleveland Indians after five innings. Coming off a season in which Seattle had hit a major-league record 264 home runs, the team's hitters didn't disappoint as Griffey, Edgar Martinez, Jay Buhner, and Russ Davis all hit home runs. But the M's bullpen quickly showed that they were no better than the '97 bunch, allowing four runs in the eighth inning, resulting in a 10-9 defeat. A trio of relievers, Ayala, Timlin, and Tony Fossas shared the blame, with the forty-year-old Fossas taking the loss in his first appearance in a Mariner uniform. Former Mariner Mike Jackson retired Martinez for the final out to record the first of his forty saves that season.

"Not to say anything bad about another club, but Seattle has the same bullpen as last year," Jackson said after the game. "Unless those guys step up and do the job, they'll be in the same situation as last year."

The M's lost the next night, too, 9-7, as Heathcliff Slocumb allowed two runs in the ninth. A two-home run, five-RBI game by new first-baseman David Segui was wasted as the M's fell to 0-2 on the season. Seattle won the next two games, both against Boston, as its offense erupted for twenty-three runs, belting seven home runs.

The M's lost the last two games of the homestand against the Yankees, 13-7 and 4-3. The first of the two games was settled early as new addition Jim Bullinger gave up six runs in the first inning, but the second was lost in the eighth inning when Ayala gave up two runs to break a 2-2 tie.

Despite scoring sixty-one runs and hitting nineteen home runs on the opening homestand, the M's headed out on the road with a dismal 3-5 record. The bullpen that led the league in blown saves in 1997 deserved a good share of the blame — Seattle relievers allowed 20 walks and 25 hits in 27 2/3 innings in the first eight games of the new season.

The road didn't treat the Mariners any better though; the first game of a ten-game trip resulted in one of the most devastating losses in franchise history. Johnson struck out fifteen Red Sox hitters and allowed just two hits before departing after the eighth inning. While a 7-2 lead was safe with most bullpens, Seattle's was not most bullpens. Four relievers pitched in the ninth for the M's and not one recorded an out as Boston scored seven runs to emerge victorious 9-7. The final blow was a long grand slam by Mo Vaughn off Paul Spoljaric.

Naturally, Piniella was upset after the game. "It's not a slump, not nine games into the season," he said. "It's got to be a confidence thing … It's got to be. There's talent out there; there's talent that's had success. Those guys just have to do better … the bullpen needs a kick in the butt."

The M's were only nine games into the '98 season, but to fans who'd lived through the team's bullpen struggles the year before, the new season already seemed to be slipping away.

"We've talked about trying to trade," said Lee Pelekoudas. "But our feeling is that we have the arms and ability in the bullpen. It's a matter of getting them to pitch to their abilities. Admittedly, they have not done that yet, but there is no reason they cannot do the job we need."

On April 12, Slocumb gave up two runs in the ninth to finish off another collapse by Seattle's moribund bullpen, which allowed five runs in the 8-7 loss to Boston. It was the fifth consecutive loss for the M's and pitching coach Nardi Contreras paid the price; he was fired and replaced by Stan Williams.

Johnson helped the M's snap a seven-game losing streak in mid-April. After the Indians' Kenny Lofton jawed at him about a slider that was a little bit inside, causing both benches to clear, Johnson threw the next pitch, a fastball, under Lofton's chin. The benches cleared again and Johnson was ejected, but his teammates appreciated what he had done.

"Randy fired us up," said Joey Cora. "He made a statement with that pitch. It was up to us to follow that up with a great game, and we did."

That win was the first of a six-game win streak. The M's swept a four-game series from the Twins. The series in Minnesota included a game in which Seattle built a lead even Slocumb couldn't blow — on April 17, leading by 11-2, Piniella put Slocumb in to try to get him some work in a non-pressure situation, ostensibly to try to get him straightened him out — only to watch as Slocumb allowed four runs in an inning of work, increasing his ERA to an unsightly 27.00.

The winning streak ended on April 21 with a 5-3 defeat to Kansas City, a loss that had the bullpen's fingerprints all over it. Fossas entered a tie game to start the eighth inning and couldn't get anyone out, allowing hits to three consecutive hitters.

Four days later, the situation was identical, with Seattle tied with Minnesota entering the eighth. A Kingdome crowd of 51,880 looked on in horror as Timlin allowed four hits and got only two batters out. He left with the bases loaded, trailing 4-2, and a few minutes later the fans headed for the exits when Slocumb gave up a grand slam to Ron Coomer. Five days after that, Ayala tried to protect a one-run lead at Yankee Stadium, but instead gave up a game-tying home run to Tim Raines. As if that wasn't enough, Ayala stuck around for the tenth and hit the leadoff batter, who came around to score the winning run on a Tino Martinez single.

One of the few highlights of the '98 season happened on May 3 when Dan Wilson hit an inside-the-park grand slam in the first inning of a 10-6 win over Detroit at the Kingdome. Wilson sent a ball to deep left center field that left-fielder Luis Gonzalez got a glove on but couldn't catch. The ball bounced past center-fielder Brian Hunter and Wilson knew he had at least a triple.

"I really picked up on the excitement and energy of the crowd," he said after the game. "It took me a couple of innings to catch my breath."

1998 TOP PERFORMERS

Ken Griffey Jr., .284, 56 HR, 146 RBI

Alex Rodriguez, .310, 42 HR, 124 RBI

Edgar Martinez,.322, 29 HR, 102 RBI

David Segui, .305, 19 HR, 84 RBI

Jamie Moyer, 15-9, 3.53 ERA, 234.1 IP

On May 12 the Mariners beat Detroit 4-2 to move over .500 for the first time with a record of 19-18. Unfortunately for a Seattle club coming off three straight winning seasons, it was the *only* day of the '98 season that the team would be above .500. The Mariners lost nine of their next eleven games to fall ten and a half games behind division-leading Texas by May 23. While trade talks had been quiet, with the team falling out of contention so early in the season, it seemed just a matter of time before the Mariners would trade Johnson.

There was one problem with that scenario, though. Johnson wasn't having the best of seasons, perhaps distracted by the possibility of a trade. After departing from his May 19 start in Texas after just three innings (allowing six runs and striking out just two batters), his ERA for the season stood at 6.83, the highest in any of his ten seasons with Seattle after May 1.

"My problem is not mechanical," Johnson said. "It's between my ears."

Piniella acknowledged the obvious when he said, "If it comes to a trade, Randy isn't making Woody's job any easier pitching like this."

Piniella and Williams, the new pitching coach, met with Johnson for an hour the day after the pitcher's early exit in Texas, with the manager reportedly telling Johnson that the easiest way for him to be traded was to pitch well. Johnson pitched better in his next two starts, both against the expansion Devil Rays, allowing just two earned runs in seventeen innings.

Trade talks began to heat up with the Dodgers, one of the teams interested in trading for Johnson the previous offseason. The proposed deal with LA was said to be for two starting pitchers, Hideo Nomo and Ismael Valdes, and an outfielder, either Wilton Guerrero or Todd Hollandsworth. But the trade was reportedly killed at the last minute by the M's absentee Japanese owner, Hiroshi Yamauchi. Yamauchi was typically content to stay out of the running of the team, but intervened when Japanese players, such as Nomo, were involved. When Nomo first came to the U.S. to pitch in 1995, Yamauchi wanted the Mariners to sign him; because they weren't interested then, he didn't want the team to acquire Nomo now.

The failed trade of Johnson seemed to affect the entire ballclub; the M's lost twelve of their next fifteen games. On June 18, after Ayala and Spoljaric teamed up to give up seven runs in the eighth and ninth innings to turn a 5-3 lead into an 11-5 loss, a frustrated Edgar Martinez said "We haven't been hitting, or fielding or making plays or pitches. We stink."

Griffey corrected Martinez. "We don't stink," Junior said. "We suck."

Pelekoudas, who was traveling with the team on the M's worst road trip (2-8) since 1992, told the *Seattle Times*, "What we need is to stop playing this crap baseball. We know what we need. We need to start playing better baseball. We need for this team to start playing as well as it should."

Pelekoudas, Woodward, and Piniella could complain all they wanted, but they were responsible for this mess. The team they'd put together in 1998 was flawed — in much the same way the '97 team was flawed — in the bullpen and in left field, with the uncertainty over the Johnson situation not helping matters any. The '98 team would be fortunate to escape last place, finishing with a 76-85 record, two and a half games ahead of last place Oakland.

As the July 31 trade deadline approached, focus turned to the New York Yankees, who arrived in town for a weekend series. Woodward hoped to play the Yankees and the Cleveland Indians off against each other, but neither team made serious offers for Johnson, offering players who weren't as significant as the ones they'd offered Seattle over the winter. This forced Woodward to call back teams he'd already cut off talks with — San Francisco, Houston and Baltimore. As the 9 p.m. trade deadline approached, no announcement had come, and it seemed Seattle might keep Johnson.

Finally, in the middle of the game against New York the Mariners announced that Johnson had been traded to Houston for two minor-leaguers and a player to be named later. The two players announced at the time, pitcher Freddy Garcia and infielder Carlos Guillen, were virtual unknowns. Chuck Armstrong remarked that he wouldn't know Garcia or Guillen "if they walked into the room."

After the game, recognizing that Mariner fans would be disappointed that the team hadn't received any recognizable names in the Johnson deal, Woodward claimed "It's hard to believe, but there was very little interest in Randy Johnson." Griffey, who admitted that he had been ordered not to say anything about the trade, presumably by Mariners management, said that if Johnson was only worth three unknown minor-leaguers, "they would get a bag of balls if they traded me."

SHIPWRECKED

The next day several Mariner players met with Piniella in his office. The players were angry that Johnson had been traded for players that wouldn't provide immediate help to the '98 team. Even at 48-60 and ten games out of first, this group of players still believed it could make a run at the division title — if only it had gotten some reinforcements for the second half.

But Seattle wasn't going to make a run in 1998, or in 1999 for that matter. It wasn't revealed at the time, but Mariners management had made a conscious decision to sacrifice those two seasons in order to rebuild for the time when the new stadium was up and running. As Piniella told *Seattle Post Intelligencer* sports columnist Art Thiel years later for Thiel's book, *Out of Left Field,* "We were tearing the team down to get ready for the new park. We took our lumps, but it was the right thing to do. If we got beat, so be it. It turned out to be a nice strategy."

It's hard to believe that the ultra-competitive Piniella went along with a plan that would ensure the M's inability to contend, especially with the futures of Griffey and Rodriguez in doubt. While the team wouldn't own up to this plan, even to its own players or most team employees, it had to be obvious to Griffey and Rodriguez that the M's weren't making the moves necessary to address the problems with the team and get it back to contention.

The dismal '98 season ended on September 27, with a 12-6 loss to Texas before 37,986 at the Dome. Spoljaric, getting a late-season audition as a starter, lasted just 3 2/3 innings in what would be his final appearance with Seattle. Fittingly, Fossas, who started the season in the M's bullpen and was released on June 10 with an 8.74 ERA, picked up the victory for the Rangers in his tenth straight scoreless outing. While Seattle finished the year only nine games under .500, it played much worse that year against good competition, going 19-45 (a .297 winning percentage) against teams with winning records.

In early November, Finnigan reported that the M's had about $10 million to spend on new players for the '99 season. Considering that the team needed two starting pitchers, a closer, an outfielder, and a leadoff hitter, the front office had a lot of work to do.

There were discussions of trading for Minnesota ace Brad Radke, who'd won thirty-two games the previous two seasons, but he was deemed too expensive, even though his contract for 1999 called for him to be paid just $2.25 million. Instead, on November 9, Seattle traded Spoljaric to Philadelphia for right-hander Mark Leiter. While Leiter, who'd be paid $3 million in 1999, had saved twenty-three games for the Phillies the year before, he'd also blown twelve save opportunities, most in the majors in 1998.

Still, Piniella liked Leiter. "He's a better pitcher than he's shown the past few years," Piniella said. "He gives us insurance in the bullpen and some protection in the rotation. With the market as it is for starters, there's no telling what we'd wind up against in bidding for them."

When Seattle signed free-agent reliever Jose Mesa to a two-year deal for $7 million, Leiter was shifted to one of the club's open rotation spots. Mesa had lost his closing job in Cleveland to Jackson and Mesa's 5.17 ERA in a setup role for the Tribe in 1998 meant the M's didn't have much competition for his services.

Mesa and Leiter would make a lot of money for pitchers who were considered mediocre at best. Worse, Leiter pitched in just two games in 1999 before tearing his rotator cuff, an injury that required surgery and ended his season and his Mariners career. Since Leiter faced just six hitters that year, Seattle paid him $500,000 for each batter he faced. While Mesa saved thirty-three games for Seattle in 1999, it took him half a season to get his ERA below 7.00 and he allowed nearly two base-runners an inning.

Salaries exploded that winter all over baseball — right-hander Kevin Brown, who signed a seven-year deal with the Dodgers for $105 million — was the poster child for such craziness, but Mariner management seemed unwilling to make any adjustments in its approach to the offseason. Several players the M's thought they could sign, among them starting-pitcher Todd Stottlemyre and third-baseman Robin Ventura, agreed to terms with other clubs for much more money than Seattle had been willing to pay.

On the eve of the annual winter meetings, a concerned Jay Buhner spoke out about his concerns for the '99 season.

"What are we doing?" he asked. "What are Woody Woodward and our front office doing? Anyone with any common sense can see that our team needs a lot more than it's doing to be competitive. We owe it to a lot of people who supported us in the fight for the new stadium. We had cracks in the foundation of our team last year. Woody and his people, even our owners, don't seem to have done much about them so far."

Seattle seemed intent on sticking with a $53 million payroll that had not been increased from 1998 despite a free-agent market that saw players receive higher salaries than ever. On November 10, Woodward was asked by the *Seattle Times* if he would ask ownership for an increased budget in light of the unexpected shift in the free-agent market.

A flustered Woodward appeared insulted. "Go back and ask for more money?" Woodward exclaimed. "Don't even ask me that! I won't comment on our payroll situation in that sense. What is going on around us is crazy, but I have a $53 million payroll. We should be able to win with $53 million."

Buhner revealed that he and several other players had met with management late in the '98 season.

"We were looked in the eye and promised there would be changes," Buhner said. "As players, as the guys who have to get this done on the field, what are we supposed to think? We need help and we're not being given it. Right now, we're upset and we're thinking if we have to dig down deeper and work harder, then Woody Woodward and his people have to do that, too. Our window of opportunity only lasts so long."

While Buhner was critical of Woodward, he recognized that the team's ownership deserved its share of the blame.

"In fairness to Woody on payroll, we should be higher, a lot higher, maybe $10 million higher," he said. "I know $53 million is a lot, but these days it isn't enough. I understand how ownership worries about salaries going crazy. But if we have enough to put a contending team into the new park in the second half of the season, they'll make big money in return."

With spring training a couple of weeks away, Armstrong said he was confident. "We have a darn good chance to win the A.L. West," he said. "We have a better ballclub than last year and I don't think the competition has improved as much as we have."

Armstrong addressed Buhner's recent complaints about the team's payroll, asking "What is $65 million going to bring you that you can't get at $54 million or $55 million? What other moves might we have made?" While Armstrong surely didn't mean for his rhetorical question to be answered, an appropriate response at the time might have been that another $10 million would have allowed the team to keep Johnson instead of having to trade the Hall of Fame talent.

On February 10, Piniella spoke at the M's annual spring training luncheon and, despite the lack of impact additions, predicted that his team would win the A.L. West in 1999.

"I'm sure people are going to pick us third in our division," he said. "I'll tell you this: We're not going to finish third. We're going to finish on top."

Piniella would be wrong again, as the '99 team would finish third. He'd been wrong before. At the spring training luncheon in 1998 he'd declared that year's team his best team ever.

The Mariners had three guests at spring training in 1999, all members of the Orix Blue Wave — pitchers Nobuyuki Hoshino and Nobuyuki Ebisu, and Ichiro Suzuki. The three players trained with the M's for the first two weeks that year and even made appearances in the M's first four exhibition games. Unfortunately, Suzuki got food poisoning and had to leave his first game after two at-bats and wasn't able to play in the next three. It was a good opportunity for the M's to get to know Suzuki, but it was still considered a longshot that Orix would ever allow him to transfer to a team in the U.S.

On Opening Night, the M's lost 8-2 to the White Sox, when Jeff Fassero allowed six runs in six innings. The M's lost their second game of the '99 season too, 11-3, with Jamie Moyer giving up eight runs in six innings. The next night, Freddy Garcia, acquired in the Johnson trade, made his major-league debut and picked up his first big league win with 5 2/3 innings of two-run ball.

On April 9, rookie pitcher Mac Suzuki was arrested for drunk driving and hit-and-run after crashing his yellow Hummer into a parked car in Seattle. Williams, the pitching coach, was surprised, saying, "I didn't even know he imbibed. You can't find a finer young man." While Suzuki, the first Japanese player to play for Seattle, might have been a fine young man, he wasn't much of a pitcher. After sixteen forgettable appearances in 1999, which featured a 9.43 ERA and thirty-four walks in forty-two innings, he was traded in mid-June to the Mets.

On April 29 the Mariners beat Detroit 22-6 to set a franchise record for runs that still stands. Griffey hit two home runs, a grand slam and a solo shot, and had six RBI while Davis doubled twice and had five RBI. In mid-May, Seattle won six consecutive games to reach .500 (21-21) and pulled within two games of the division-leading Rangers. It was the closest the Mariners would get to first place for the rest of the '99 season. A four-game win streak in mid-June improved the M's record to 35-31, the high water mark for the '99 team.

1999 TOP PERFORMERS

Ken Griffey Jr., .285, 48 HR, 134 RBI

Alex Rodriguez, .285, 42 HR, 111 RBI

Edgar Martinez, .337, 24 HR, 86 RBI

Freddy Garcia, 17-8, 4.07 ERA, 201 IP

Jamie Moyer, 14-8, 3.87 ERA, 228 IP

SHIPWRECKED

On June 27 the M's beat Texas, 5-2 in the 1,758[th] and final baseball game of the Kingdome's history. Fittingly, Griffey hit the last home run in the stadium's history, a three-run blast off Aaron Sele in the first inning. Junior also added a spectacular catch to his personal Kingdome highlight reel, robbing Juan Gonzalez of a three-run home run.

"We've closed our Kingdome chapter, and we like to think it read well," Buhner said. "Hopefully, the next chapters will make a book no one will want to put down."

Safeco Field opened on July 15 to a packed house of 44,607. Dave Niehaus threw out the ceremonial first pitch, while Moyer threw the first actual pitch. While Moyer held San Diego to a single run in the first eight innings, striking out nine and throwing a season-high 129 pitches, the M's were held scoreless until the eighth when they scored twice on back-to-back-to-back doubles by Wilson, Segui, and David Bell to take a 2-1 lead. But Mesa, who entered the game sporting a 6.94 ERA, ruined the night, walking four batters in the ninth and surrendering two runs without allowing a hit to give the Padres a 3-2 win. Mesa lives on in history as the first player booed by the home crowd at Safeco Field.

After the game, Piniella said, "Walks have killed us out of the bullpen. It always hurts, but tonight, the big night for our fans, for our organization, it hurts more." Asked what he said to Mesa when he went to the mound in the ninth, Piniella replied, "I told him 'You have to throw strikes. If you can't throw strikes, I can't let you pitch.' "

The M's losing streak was extended to seven the next night, when Seattle couldn't manage to score off ex-Mariner Sterling Hitchcock in the first seven innings and lost 9-1, falling eight games back. On July 20, in just the sixth game played at Safeco, Johnson, now with the expansion Arizona Diamondbacks, pitched a complete game shutout, striking out ten as his new team won 6-0. Mariner fans cheered Johnson before and during the game.

Asked about the reception Johnson had received, Alex Rodriguez said "Anything less would have been uncivilized. He was standing on the mound he built."

On July 23, after a 5-4 loss to Minnesota, the M's fell ten games out of the division lead, but were still six and a half games out in the Wild Card race, prompting Woodward to proclaim, "We have to start playing a hell of a lot better than we are, but I think our club can be in the race."

Five days later, with the Mariners having lost sixteen of their last twenty-four games, Seattle traded first-baseman Segui (hitting .293 with nine home runs) to Toronto for relief-pitchers Tom Davey and Steve Sinclair. The trade came just two days after the club had traded their left-fielder, Butch Huskey (batting .290 with fifteen home runs) to Boston for another relief pitcher, Rob Ramsay.

Reached for comment after the trades of two of the M's starting-position players, Edgar Martinez said, "These deals give you the sense we are looking for next year. But there is still a lot of baseball left this year. If we don't make other moves, it looks like they [the front office] are preparing for next year, not this one. I hope in the time before the deadline [three days away at the time] something more happens." But the M's were done dealing; at the time, Seattle was twelve games behind Texas in the A.L. West and seven and a half games behind Boston for the Wild Card.

The M's managed a six-game win streak in early August to reach .500, but there would be no playoffs in 1999. Seattle faded down the stretch, finishing the season with a 79-83 record, sixteen games behind Texas in the A.L. West and fifteen games behind the Wild Card-winning Red Sox.

This cartoon originally appeared in the September 1998 issue of *The Grand Salami*.

Chapter 14

OFF-THE-FIELD ICONS

T hree icons, each connected with Mariner baseball for much of the team's history — Dave Niehaus, Rick the Peanut Man, and the Tuba Guy — passed away between 2008 and 2011. All three were characters in their own right and each made the experience of being a Mariner fan more special.

DAVE NIEHAUS

While players, managers, and front-office people have come and gone during the Mariners' thirty-five-year history, announcer Dave Niehaus was the one constant for the first thirty-four. For every one of those years, nobody represented the Mariners with more class and excellence.

Niehaus, who died at seventy-five of a heart attack after the '10 season, called 5,284 Mariner games, missing just 101 games over three and a half decades. And because he traveled with the team and called the team's road and home games, it's pretty safe to say that nobody has seen more Mariner games in person than Niehaus.

Somehow he managed to make bad baseball entertaining for the people of the Pacific Northwest — and save for a nine-year run from 1995 to 2003, the Mariners have played plenty of bad baseball.

When Randy Johnson struck out the final Angels' batter in the ninth inning of the one-game playoff in 1995 to put the M's in the postseason for the first time, you could feel the relief in Dave's voice as he exclaimed, "NINETEEN LONG YEARS OF FRUSTRATION IS OVER!"

He was well known for his great stories, which he used to entertain fans during blowout games, but also for his many signature calls, which included "My Oh My!" (an incredible play or game), "Fly Away!" (a home run), and "Get out the Rye Bread and Mustard Grandma, it is Grand Salami Time!" (a Mariners' grand-slam home run).

While he was a Mariner employee, Niehaus was no homer. If a player was dogging it in the outfield or not running out ground balls, he pointed it out on the air. "I've got to report what I see," he told *The Grand Salami* in 1997. He disliked announcers who used the term "we" or "our" when referring to the team they were covering. And he wasn't too fond of the attitudes of some modern-day ballplayers. In an interview with AP sportswriter Jim Cour in 1986, Niehaus told the tale of one Mariner slugger who refused to do radio interviews, saying he didn't want any blue jeans — the gift M's players received at that time for an appearance. Niehaus said he told the player, whom he wouldn't name, that he would never talk to him again "even if he hit five home runs in a single game." That player can now be revealed as Gorman Thomas, who had led the team in home runs the previous season.

Niehaus' insistence on reporting the truth didn't sit well at times with his Mariner bosses. Team President Dan O'Brien was slow to offer Niehaus a contract for the '80 season, unsure if he wanted to keep the then forty-five-year-old on as the voice of the Mariners. Niehaus' commitment to Seattle never wavered though. Approached by other teams for broadcasting jobs, he always said, "I want to be here when it happens." And he was, calling every single postseason game in franchise history.

Niehaus received many honors for excellence in broadcasting. In 2008, he was inducted into the broadcaster's wing of the Baseball Hall of Fame in Cooperstown, New York. Fittingly, he was the first person to be honored by the Mariners with a statue, which was installed on the main concourse of Safeco Field in September 2011.

When the Mariners finally win the World Series, whether this century or next, we're certain Dave Niehaus will have a front-row seat and will be smiling down on Seattle.

RICK KAMINSKI aka "THE PEANUT MAN"

If you attended even a handful of Mariner games, you knew Rick Kaminski, who made an art out of throwing peanuts to fans at sporting events in Seattle. Rick worked the first events at the Kingdome, among them Sounders and Seahawks games in 1976, and then the Mariners, when the franchise began play in 1977.

Kaminski smiled a lot and had a quick wit and a clever sense of humor, but he was at his best throwing peanuts to fans at Mariners games. Despite a top speed of 72 mph — once timed by the radar gun of a Mariner scout — he was spot-on accurate with his tosses, even when he threw the peanuts behind his back across entire sections of seats. He also knew baseball and could carry a conversation about what the Mariners needed to do to improve — and for most of the thirty-five years Rick threw peanuts at M's games, the team was in serious need of improvement.

Over the years, some of Rick's famed peanut tosses found their way onto the ESPN highlight reel and he won many honors, including an MVP Award (Master of Vending Prowess) in 1991. Rick died from a brain aneurysm in July 2011. He'll be remembered for being an original and a steady presence at Mariner games at the Kingdome, Safeco Field, and spring training in Arizona.

ED MCMICHAEL aka "THE TUBA GUY"

Ed McMichael, known to everyone in Seattle simply as "The Tuba Guy," was a fixture outside sports events in town since the early 1980s. A classically trained musician, he could play just about any song imaginable on request at a moment's notice. Because he was a gentle soul, it was especially tragic when he died from injuries suffered from a beating at the hands of street thugs late in 2008.

Ed had a unique brand of humor and he loved to entertain. Even though he wasn't inside the ballpark watching the games, he always knew what was going on with the Mariners.

In 2007, the year before he died, he asked me "Why did Mike Hargrove really leave the Mariners?" And he'd often ask "When are the Mariners going to the World Series?" I was able to answer the first question, but not the second.

Chapter 15

PAT GILLICK TAKES OVER

As the '99 season ended, change was coming to the Seattle Mariners front office. Long-time General Manager Woody Woodward resigned on September 17.

While there were whispers that Woodward was forced out by the team's ownership, with incoming Chairman Howard Lincoln not a big fan of his, Woodward claimed that the decision was his own. He said he didn't want to have to be the one to trade Ken Griffey Jr., who had one year remaining on his contract.

The fifty-nine-year-old Lincoln, who took over for John Ellis late in the '99 season, had represented the interests of Hiroshi Yamauchi on the Mariners board of directors for many years and was stepping down as chairman of Nintendo to take over the team.

"The Mariners need every dime we can get our hands on," he told a *Seattle Times* reporter. "We need to maximize our revenues at Safeco Field, and we need to control costs."

The Mariners hired Pat Gillick on October 25 to be the team's new general manager. Gillick, sixty-two, had been successful with the Toronto Blue Jays and Baltimore Orioles, and had built the Blue Jays organization that won the World Series in 1992 and 1993. Recognizing the importance of keeping the team's two remaining superstars, Gillick said on the day of his hiring, "We must be persuasive and creative. We must do enough to show Griffey and Rodriguez that we are putting a contender together."

One person familiar with Gillick was John Olerud, Sr., whose son, John, one of the top first-baseman in baseball, had been signed by Gillick in Toronto.

"Pat is an extremely creative person," the senior Olerud told the *Times*. "As a Mariner season-ticket holder, I am delighted and excited about what this means for the ballclub."

With the younger Olerud eligible for free agency, there was immediate speculation that the M's could have the inside track on signing him. Olerud had hit .298 with 19 home runs and 96 RBI for the Mets in 1999.

Within days of taking the job, Gillick set up separate meetings with Griffey and Rodriguez and their agents. On November, 1 Gillick, Lincoln, and Armstrong went to Griffey's home in Orlando, Florida to talk with Junior and his agent, Brian Goldberg. It wasn't a long meeting. Griffey quickly informed the Mariners' brass that he wanted to be traded to a team closer to Orlando. The Mariner executives inquired if there was anything they could do to change his mind, including the ultimate question: Would Junior agree to stay in Seattle if the M's won the World Series in 2000? After he said that not even a title would change his mind, the team realized there was nothing it could do but try to honor his trade request.

The M's also met with Alex Rodriguez and his agent, Scott Boras, but it was more of a getting-to-know-you meeting. Boras had insisted before the meeting that Rodriguez would not agree to any contract before testing the free-agent market after the 2000 season.

A month later Griffey was still a Mariner because no team had been willing to meet Seattle's asking price, and the possibility that Junior might play a final season with the Mariners loomed. The Cincinnati Reds were considered the frontrunner and the Reds reportedly offered ten to fifteen combinations of players, but the sticking point seemed to be shortstop Pokey Reese, who Cincinnati refused to include in the deal. Reds GM Jim Bowden at one point pulled out of the negotiations, leaving Gillick incredulous that the Reds would allow one player (Reese) to prevent a potential trade.

"We're talking a player of the decade, an all-century player, a future Hall of Famer, and they're going to let this one player hold up a deal?" he told a reporter.

While there was no movement on the Griffey trade front, Gillick was busy trying to lure free agents to Seattle. On December 3, Gillick told the media he had made offers to eight different free agents. Among those players considering whether to come to Seattle were Olerud, starting-pitcher Chuck Finley, and relievers Arthur Rhodes and Graeme Lloyd.

Additionally, the Mariners were trying to woo a Japanese relief pitcher, Kazuhiro Sasaki, to come to Seattle. Sasaki, thirty-one, had pitched for ten seasons for the Yokohama Bay Stars and was Japan's all-time saves leader. Competition for Sasaki was fierce with the Yankees, Mets, and Diamondbacks all bringing the pitcher in for visits. Sasaki's agent, Tony Attanasio, said he expected the Mariners to be serious contenders to sign Sasaki, adding that his client might help deliver outfielder Ichiro Suzuki to the team in the future.

"If you get one, you might get two," Attanasio told a reporter. "They happen to be pretty good friends."

At the winter meetings in early December the Mariners had a trade worked out to deal Griffey to the New York Mets, one of four teams on the list of teams Junior would agree to join. Two different versions of the story exist. Griffey's agent, Brian Goldberg, insisted that Armstrong had called and told him he needed an answer in fifteen minutes or the deal was off. Armstrong claimed he told Goldberg to call within the next fifteen minutes (because he and Lincoln were going out to dinner) or to call the next morning. If Armstrong had only been willing to take this important call during dinner, Griffey might have been traded to the Mets.

The situation angered Junior so much he told the Mariners that he would accept a trade to one team, and one team only: the Cincinnati Reds. However, the M's and Reds were still at a stalemate, and the general managers seemed to have tired of dealing with one another. At one point, Goldberg offered a compromise, saying that Junior would be amenable to signing a two-year extension to stay in Seattle. Lincoln refused to discuss such an arrangement.

On December 6 the Mariners made the biggest free-agent signing in franchise history to date, adding first-baseman John Olerud with a three-year, $20 million contract. Then, shockingly, from December 18 to 21, the Mariners signed four more free agents: Kazuhiro Sasaki (three years, $9.5 million), Arthur Rhodes (four years, $13 million), Mark McLemore (one year, $2.25 million), and Stan Javier (one year, $1.8 million).

The burst of spending surprised Piniella. "Look at our club and it's gotten a heck of a lot more solid in a hurry, adding these free agents," he said. "We're starting to fill in some of our deficiencies. If we can add a starting pitcher with some experience, we'll be in much better shape."

Piniella's reaction was understandable. He'd grown accustomed to losing a key player or two each year and not signing free agents of note. With the signing of these veterans, all of a sudden the Mariners had a top-notch bullpen and a solid bench, areas that had been neglected by Woodward the previous few seasons.

The M's even got the starting pitcher they needed to bolster their rotation. The M's signed Poulsbo, Washington native Aaron Sele, an eighteen-game winner in 1999. Sele had initially agreed to a four-year, $29 million deal with the Orioles, but Baltimore had withdrawn its offer because of concerns about Sele's shoulder. Gillick swooped in and signed Sele to a two-year contract for $15 million. The short deal was a good idea, as Sele, after winning thirty-two games in his two seasons with Seattle, had shoulder issues the following year.

Gillick's first months in Seattle were quite a contrast to the eleven-year tenure of Woodward. Gillick's predecessor was known in baseball circles as "the golfing GM" because he didn't seem to work very hard and often was difficult for agents and other general managers to reach. With Gillick in charge, the Mariners made aggressive moves to bring in top-flight players. Additionally, while Woodward typically relied on scouting reports when making trades or signing free agents, Gillick would always make sure that he or one of his trusted aides had seen the players numerous times in person. The change from one of the worst GMs in the game to one of the best was a welcome one for Mariner fans, many of whom were displeased by ticket price increases for the 2000 season.

In addition to the work ethic of Gillick and his solid reputation around baseball, another factor was a significant increase in the Mariners payroll, from $53 million in 1999 to roughly $70 million for 2000.

The prospect of playing their first full season at Safeco Field was a reason ownership had agreed to increase payroll; the increase was larger than expected as part of an effort to persuade Rodriguez to sign long-term. With Griffey wanting out, the M's hoped they could keep Rodriguez beyond 2000. Columnist Jon Heyman wrote in *New York Newsday* that at Gillick's first meeting with Rodriguez, the new GM had asked Rodriguez how he'd like to see the team improved. Rodriguez reportedly offered an exhaustive list of positions he felt needed to be upgraded: veteran starting pitcher, first base, bullpen help, and leadoff hitter. With the exception of the leadoff hitter, Gillick had managed to cross all the items off of A-Rod's shopping list in one offseason.

On February 10 the long-rumored trade of Griffey to Cincinnati was finally consummated. It was Gillick's first deal as Mariners GM. He received a package of four players for the star center-fielder. Coming to Seattle were outfielder Mike Cameron, pitchers Brett Tomko and Jake Meyer, and infielder Antonio Perez, with Cameron and Tomko the key pieces in the deal. Cameron, twenty-seven, had hit .256 with twenty-one homers, sixty-six RBI and thirty-eight stolen bases in '99.

On March 8 the Mariners held a press briefing during spring training to announce that Rodriguez, who had been the subject of rumors, would not be traded.

"The best way to win in 2000 is for Alex to remain, and the best way for us to keep Alex long term is for the team to win in 2000," Lincoln said, discussing what he perceived to be the differences between Rodriguez's situation and Griffey's. "Kenny made it clear he did not want to stay in our organization. Alex is a great young man who has said he wants to stay and wants to win, and not only says these things but demonstrates them on a daily basis. How do you trade a guy who does this?"

GM Pat Gillick sounded a bit more skeptical. "It's a roll of the dice," he said. "We basically have to take his word. He likes to win, and we have a better chance to re-sign him if we win."

On April 4, 45,552 packed Safeco Field for a disappointing Opening Day as the M's were shut out 2-0 by Boston's Pedro Martinez, who continued his dominance over Seattle, allowing just two hits in seven innings for his fifth win in five career starts against the Mariners.

Two nights later, Cameron and David Bell smacked home runs in the bottom of the eighth to snap a 2-2 tie and give Seattle a 4-2 win. Sele had a successful homecoming, allowing just two runs in six innings, and Sasaki struck out all three batters he faced in the ninth to record his first save as a Mariner.

The next night, Cameron leaped over the center field fence at Safeco to take a home run away from the Yankees' Derek Jeter in the eighth inning of Seattle's 7-5 win over New York. The crowd of 40,827, amazed by what it had seen, continued cheering and screaming for several minutes, and when Cameron struck out in the bottom half of the inning, he was given a standing ovation.

"I don't think I've ever seen anyone get an ovation for striking out," Piniella said. It was just Cameron's fourth game with Seattle and he had already won over the fans at Safeco.

On May 19 the Mariners added a new face in outfielder Rickey Henderson, who had been released by the New York Mets. The forty-one-year-old Henderson, the all-time stolen base leader, could still play, having hit .315 with a .423 on-base percentage and thirty-seven steals the previous year with the Mets. The future Hall of Famer provided the M's with the leadoff hitter that year's Seattle team sorely needed and at a cost the team could easily afford. Since Henderson had been released by the Mets, Seattle was on the hook for only the pro-rated portion of the major-league minimum salary and the $260,000 buyout of his option for 2001, which Henderson had insisted on as a condition of signing with Seattle. While Henderson hit just .238 in 2000, he had a very respectable .362 on-base average and stole thirty-one bases.

A 5-3 win over the Angels on June 27 gave the M's a season-high seven-game win streak and a 44-30 record, but the Oakland A's were hanging tough in the A.L. West, just a half-game behind the M's. It was essentially a two-team race that season; the Rangers and Angels trailed Oakland and Seattle by a large margin for much of the year. The M's took two of three from the Dodgers to head into the All-Star break in first place, three games ahead of Oakland. Seattle had won eleven of its last twelve series, a franchise first.

A big reason for Seattle's success in 2000 was first-year pitching coach Bryan Price. Piniella had burned through four pitching coaches in his first seven seasons in Seattle and the team's pitching had suffered for it. But Price quickly won Piniella's trust and was allowed to handle the pitching staff without interference from the manager.

As the trade deadline approached, the M's were in need of a left-handed hitter to improve their lineup. The names of Moises Alou, Johnny Damon, Jeromy Burnitz, Rondell White, and Bobby Higginson were bandied about, with a rumored trade for Detroit's Juan Gonzalez failing because Seattle wouldn't give up young pitchers such as Ryan Anderson, Joel Pineiro, or Gil Meche. Finally, on July 31, the M's acquired outfielder Al Martin from San Diego. While the M's didn't give up much to get Martin — reserve outfielder John Mabry and minor-league reliever Tom Davey — they didn't get much from Martin, who hit just .231 with a dismal .283 on-base percentage the rest of the season. The M's also were saddled with Martin's guaranteed $5 million contract for 2001.

In early August the M's went to New York and Chicago, taking three of four from both the Yankees and White Sox to extend their A.L. West lead to six games. A 7-1 win over Cleveland on August 11 advanced the lead to a season-high seven games. With a 69-47 record, Seattle was on pace for a ninety-seven win season, which would be a new franchise record.

2000 TOP PERFORMERS

Alex Rodriguez, .316, 41 HR, 132 RBI

Edgar Martinez, .324, 37 HR, 145 RBI

Jay Buhner, .253, 26 HR, 82 RBI

Aaron Sele, 17-10, 4.51 ERA, 211.2 IP

Kazuhiro Sasaki, 2-5, 3.16 ERA, 37 saves

However, just as Seattle's chances to seize a playoff berth seemed at hand, the M's hit a nasty slump in August, losing eight games in a row, all to Cleveland and Detroit. Terrible pitching was the main cause of the slump, as Seattle allowed nine runs or more in the last seven games of the losing streak, becoming the first team since the 1901 New York Giants to do that. A leaky defense didn't help either, as the M's made sixteen errors during the eight-game slide, seven of them by third-baseman Carlos Guillen.

After snapping the losing streak with an 8-4 win in Detroit on August 22, the M's lost their next three games — and five of their next six — but still found themselves in first place, but by a slim margin of just one and a half games.

Seattle caught a scheduling break in mid-September and took advantage, reeling off an eight-game win streak against three of the weakest teams in the league — Kansas City, Baltimore, and Tampa Bay. With a three-game lead and ten games left in the season, the M's had a great opportunity to seize control of the division when Oakland arrived at Safeco for a critical four-game series.

Capacity crowds filled Safeco Field for each of the games, but the A's won the first three games of the series to move into a first-place tie. Seattle salvaged the final game and, with a week left in the season the M's were a game up on Oakland in the A.L. West race and two games ahead of the Cleveland Indians for the Wild Card. Over the next six days, the M's won three and lost two while the A's won five of six to take over the division lead. Cleveland won five of seven in the same stretch to stay within a game of Seattle for the Wild Card lead.

The Mariners went into the final day of the 2000 season needing a win against the Angels to clinch a playoff berth. With Oakland winning in Texas, the A's clinched the A.L. West. Cleveland won its game too, forcing Seattle to win or face a one-game playoff at Safeco Field against the Indians the next day. Aaron Sele allowed two runs in the first, but Seattle picked up single runs in the fourth and the fifth. The M's took the lead in the seventh on a Bell home run, and the bullpen did the rest and the M's clinched the Wild Card.

It had taken the Mariners a full 162 games to clinch a playoff spot, but they had done it, leading to a raucous celebration in the visiting clubhouse in Anaheim.

"We've been tense for half a year," said Edgar Martinez, "This celebration is taking all that pressure out and having fun."

Alex Rodriguez called it an emotional win. "I wanted it very badly. I haven't even watched the playoffs the past two years because it hurt too much. This had a seventh-game atmosphere."

The playoffs began two days later against the White Sox at Comiskey Park where the M's jumped out to an early 3-0 lead. But an erratic Freddy Garcia lasted just 3 1/3 innings, departing in the fourth with the bases loaded, one out and Seattle trailing 4-3. In perhaps the turning point of the series, reliever Brett Tomko came up big, with 2 2/3 scoreless innings, to keep the game close. The M's tied the game 4-4 in the seventh on a single by Cameron, but both teams had solid bullpens and the game remained tied after nine. Seattle's offense exploded for three runs in the top of the tenth, on back-to-back home runs by Martinez and Olerud. Sasaki came on for the save and the M's had a 1-0 series lead.

Seattle also won Game 2 with a home run by Jay Buhner supporting 5 2/3 solid innings from starter Paul Abbott for a 5-2 win. Game 3, the first postseason game at Safeco Field, was a hard-fought affair played before a crowd of 48,010. The starting pitchers, Sele and Chicago's James Baldwin, allowed just one run each and the game was tied 1-1 entering the bottom of the ninth. Olerud led off that inning with a single. Pinch-runner Henderson moved to second on a sacrifice bunt by Stan Javier, moved to third on an error, and scored on a perfectly placed squeeze bunt by Guillen. Seattle had swept the series and was headed to New York for the second American League Championship Series in team history.

While the Yankees were a formidable opponent, they had backed into the playoffs that season, losing their last seven games of the regular season and fifteen of their last eighteen before beating Oakland in five games in the Division Series.

Seattle won Game 1 at Yankee Stadium 2-0, as Garcia struck out eight and allowed just three hits in 6 2/3 innings. Game 2 was critical in the series: If the Mariners could somehow win it, they'd be heading back to Seattle up two games to none. And for a while it looked like they would, as John Halama and Jose Paniagua shut out the Yankees for the first seven innings and the M's led 1-0. Seattle pitching held New York scoreless for the first sixteen innings of the series, but that streak ended horridly in the bottom of the eighth when the Yankees exploded for seven runs off Arthur Rhodes and Jose Mesa to take the game 7-1.

New York won Games 3 and 4 in Seattle as Andy Pettitte and Roger Clemens combined to limit the M's to two runs, with Clemens pitching a one-hit shutout and striking out fifteen. Down three games to one, Seattle won the fifth game 6-2 behind home runs by Edgar Martinez and John Olerud to send the series back to New York.

The atmosphere at Yankee Stadium on October 17 was festive with Yankee fans sure that their team could win one of the next two games and reach the World Series for the third straight year. But the Mariners had other ideas, jumping out to a 2-0 lead in the first inning on doubles by Rodriguez and Martinez. When Guillen, who'd hit just seven homers all season, slugged a two-run homer in the fourth off Orlando Hernandez, it looked like the series might be headed for a winner-take-all seventh game.

But Halama, who'd pitched very well in Game 2, imploded in the fourth inning, allowing five consecutive batters to reach base as New York closed to 4-3. Tomko kept the game at 4-3 with 2 2/3 innings of hitless relief, but departed after the sixth. After Paniagua struggled to start the seventh, Rhodes came in to face lefty David Justice with two runners on and one out. Falling behind, Rhodes got the ball up in the zone and Justice hit it deep into the seats in right field for a 6-4 Yankee lead.

While the home run was a crusher for the M's, Rhodes allowed three more runs in the inning and Seattle trailed 9-4. Those extra runs were crucial, because Seattle scored three runs in the eighth, two off the usually unhittable Mariano Rivera, and might have won the game had Rhodes been able to stop the bleeding. Instead, Seattle lost 9-7 and would head home for the winter while the Yankees headed to the World Series. A bright spot in the game for Seattle was the performance of Alex Rodriguez, who went 4-for-4 with a home run and two doubles in what would be his final game as a Mariner.

The M's headed into an uncertain offseason not knowing what their 2001 club would look like and whether they'd have a chance to return to the postseason.

Wry Bread   *by Tim Harrison**

LIFE WITHOUT JUNIOR

The Mariners counted on Ken Griffey Jr. for a lot more than 50 home runs a year. Now that he's been traded, different players will have to assume Junior's other responsibilities:

GOOD LUCK IN CINCY, JUNIOR -- DON'T WORRY ABOUT US, WE'VE GOT EVERYTHING COVERED.

*with a tip o' the pen to Erik L. for inspiration

This cartoon originally appeared in the April 2000 issue of *The Grand Salami*.

Chapter 16

WHO NEEDS SUPERSTARS?

In the mid to late 1990s the Seattle Mariners had three of the biggest stars in the game, Ken Griffey Jr., Alex Rodriguez, and Randy Johnson. Griffey was the most popular player in baseball and a perennial fifty-home-run hitter. Rodriguez was the best shortstop in the game and Johnson was the most dominant pitcher, the kind of ace who could lift a team on his shoulders and take it to a World Series.

Entering the '97 season, each of the three players was in the prime of his career. Rodriguez was 21, Griffey, 27 and Johnson, 33. While some might have argued that Johnson was not in his prime at age 33, he hadn't established himself as an ace until 1993, when he was already 29.

It would be difficult for any team in baseball not named the New York Yankees to fit all three of these superstars into its player payroll, but the Mariners somehow managed to lose all three of these unique players through a combination of mismanagement, misguided arrogance, and too much executive ego.

While Griffey and Johnson both joined the Mariners in 1989, Rodriguez's first full season in the majors wasn't until 1996, when he burst on the scene with an MVP-caliber season, hitting .358 with 36 home runs and 123 RBI.

As it turned out, 1997 was the only year in which the team had the services of all three stars for a full season. The Mariners had a contract option on Johnson for 1998, but the team's management apparently had decided by the middle of the '97 season that it wasn't going to sign the pitcher to a contract extension. That might help explain why the team was so anxious to go for broke in 1997, making two midseason trades for three mediocre relief pitchers, trading away three potential stars — Jason Varitek, Jose Cruz Jr., and Derek Lowe — in the process.

Those midseason trades became necessary because Mariners ownership routinely refused to raise its budgets high enough to keep the team intact. Attendance at the Kingdome had climbed from eighteen thousand fans a game in 1990 to thirty-nine thousand a game by 1997, but the team was repeatedly forced to trade or lose key players for financial reasons. One year it was shortstop Omar Vizquel; another year it was first-baseman Tino Martinez and pitchers Jeff Nelson, Bill Risley, and Tim Belcher; and in yet another year it was relief-pitcher Mike Jackson, third-baseman Dave Hollins and left-fielder Mark Whiten.

While the Mariners lost all that talent in the 1990s, they still had the three superstars. But the M's were foolish if they thought the stars wouldn't take notice of what was going on around them. Each year the team fell short, in large part because it had lost valuable players. The stars had to question the motives of Mariners ownership and whether it was more interested in winning a World Series or making money. Why would any of these players want to stay in Seattle when there were other teams desirous of their services that wanted to win and would be willing to build championship-caliber teams around them?

The Mariners' approach to setting budgets in the 1990s and constant dumping of players wouldn't be the only reason the three stars left, but it certainly didn't help the team in its efforts to keep their stars.

When the Mariners announced late in 1997 that they would not offer Johnson a contract extension, Chuck Armstrong claimed that the decision was based on the pitcher wanting "Maddux money" and having a bad back, but those concerns were a smokescreen. Johnson said in the media he wanted to stay in Seattle and was happy to take a two-year contract. While it's likely he wanted "Maddux money," he deserved it; Greg Maddux, a Hall of Famer in his own right, should have been happy to earn "Randy Johnson money." Johnson was a huge part of the M's success on the field and at the box office, and his heroics were a major factor in the club getting its publicly financed stadium.

A two-year contract, even for a thirty-four-year-old pitcher, should not have been too big of a risk for the M's. Armstrong's supposed concerns about Johnson's back were disingenuous; the pitcher had just completed a season in which he was arguably better than in his Cy Young season of 1995. Johnson went 20-4 with a 2.28 ERA in 1997, the season *after* he had back surgery. He made twenty-nine starts that season and his back wasn't an issue. In the first four and a half seasons after leaving Seattle, Johnson won ninety games and four Cy Young Awards.

More likely the real reason the Mariners didn't offer Johnson a contract extension was that Armstrong despised the pitcher and couldn't wait to be rid of him. The two had engaged in a petty feud that had lingered since 1993 when Johnson believed Armstrong had been insensitive after the death of the pitcher's father. While Johnson could be a pain in the ass, and he often was, most star players are difficult to deal with. A sports team is going to have to deal with managing and massaging the egos and whims of their star players. Armstrong should not have let his ego get in the way of the Mariners keeping an irreplaceable talent such as Johnson.

After trading Johnson to the Houston Astros in mid-1998, the Mariners turned their attention to keeping Griffey and Rodriguez. Seattle had a plan to try to keep the two remaining superstars, but it didn't have much chance of success and probably served to hasten the departures of both players.

In an ironic twist, the contracts of both players would expire at the same time - after the 2000 season. One reason this occurred was because of the time Rodriguez had spent in the majors in 1994 and 1995, years when he wasn't a starting player, he had accumulated enough service time to become a free agent after just five regular seasons, not the usual six.

Further, the M's were aware in late 1998 that Griffey would gain so-called "ten and five" rights at the end of that season. Players in the majors for at least ten seasons, with the last five with the same team, automatically receive protection from being traded without their approval. Having dealt with the moody Griffey for many years, Mariner executives surely realized that when the time came that the M's wanted or needed to trade Junior their return would likely be affected by Griffey's ability to reject trades.

During the final homestand of the '98 season, with Griffey and Rodriguez each having two full seasons remaining on their contracts, the Mariners invited the players to meet separately in the owners' box at the Kingdome to discuss contract extensions. Griffey, twenty-eight at the time and having hit fifty-six home runs for a second consecutive season, received a five-year offer for $65 million, with the contract to begin when his existing contract expired at the end of the 2000 season. The twenty-three-year-old Rodriguez, who had his first forty home run season in 1998, was offered a seven-year deal for $63 million, also to begin after the 2000 season.

Neither player seriously considered the Mariners' overtures. It was rare for any player, let alone superstars of their magnitude, to agree to contract extensions when they didn't know what salaries would look like two and a half years into the future. There were also two other factors for the players to consider: how the M's new ballpark would play out for home run hitters and whether the Mariners could get back to contention.

Rodriguez offered hints late in the dismal '98 season of what he thought of staying long-term in Seattle. "I don't know what their (the Mariners') business strategy is," Rodriguez said. "I know only one thing. It is no fun getting kicked night after night like we did this season. I don't want that for my team anymore. I have to have a team committed to winning."

Another stumbling block arose when Griffey and Rodriguez were invited by the team to take batting practice at the unfinished stadium about a year before it opened; they reportedly came away concerned with how the new park would affect their offensive numbers. An unnamed Mariner employee described the decision to have the players hit at the new park as "the worst mistake we ever made."

Another critical blunder occurred toward the end of the '98 season, when several frustrated Mariners players met with management and were assured there would be changes for the '99 season. The players knew the team's window of opportunity to win would not last forever and expected management to do what it took to put a winning team on the field in 1999. While Safeco Field was not scheduled to open until mid-July, 1999, the Mariners had MLB backload their schedule so that a majority of the team's home games that season would be played in the final two and a half months of the season.

Even with a half season of increased revenues from Safeco Field and promises made to their key players, the Mariners seemingly had no intention of trying to contend in 1999. They kept the player payroll at $53 million, the same as the '98 payroll and refused to make adjustments in the offseason when the free agent market unexpectedly exploded.

If the Mariners thought that they could keep Griffey and Rodriguez just by offering tons of money, they were sadly mistaken. Both players had to wonder how the team would possibly compete with their salaries taking up such a large percentage of the team's payroll. With the promises made late in the '98 season unfulfilled, it was reasonable for the two stars to assume that Seattle's commitment wouldn't be any greater in the years to come.

The situation with the two superstars came to a head after the '99 season. For the second consecutive season, the M's finished under .500, and the team's plan, later revealed by Lou Piniella in Art Thiel's book, was to "tear down" and build back up once the new stadium was open. With the contracts of both superstars expiring at the end of 2000, the Mariners were anxious to find out if Griffey and Rodriguez wanted to stay. While they hoped to keep both players, privately they had to fear that neither player would sign a long-term contract.

That fear turned to reality when Griffey forced a trade to Cincinnati after the '99 season and Rodriguez left as a free agent a year later. Yet Mariners Chairman Howard Lincoln seemed perfectly happy to have a team without superstars. In spring training of 2001, he told the *Seattle Times*, "The more I see, the more I am convinced there isn't a connection between superstars and winning," adding, "I'm quite pleased with the team we have. More than any other, baseball is a team sport. We want to continue to approach it that way."

What followed, of course, in the first season after Rodriguez's departure, was the Mariners' record-setting 116-win season. In some ways the remarkable '01 season was the worst thing that could have happened to the Seattle franchise, as Lincoln, in his mind proven right that a team didn't need superstars, became more and more arrogant because of it. In 2002, he chased off his "superstar" Manager Lou Piniella, and Hall of Fame GM Pat Gillick quit the following season. They were replaced by a manager without any managing experience and a general manager who would prove to be one of the worst in baseball.

Thanks to Lincoln's brilliant "no-superstars" policy, the Mariners would never be the same.

Chapter 17

A MAGICAL SEASON

With the 2000 season over, talk turned to whether the Mariners could keep shortstop Alex Rodriguez. Heading into free agency, Rodriguez said all the right things about the possibility of staying with the Mariners.

Just a few days after the ALCS ended, Rodriguez attended the World Series between the Yankees and Mets and told the media in New York, "If I have to say something, I'd say I'm leaning toward Seattle because that's the known. It's my responsibility to get all the data, make the unknowns a known, and make my decision. I'm definitely apprehensive about the situation, because my comfort level is so high in Seattle."

While the M's were waiting on Rodriguez, they began to make other moves to improve the team for 2001. On November 8 they won the right to negotiate with Japanese outfielder Ichiro Suzuki with a sealed bid of $13.125 million, which was the posting fee to be paid to Suzuki's Japanese team, the Orix Blue Wave. The Mariners had thirty days to reach agreement with Suzuki on a contract or his rights would revert to Orix. Suzuki called Seattle's bid "an unbelievable number."

It took just nine days for the Mariners to reach agreement with Suzuki on a three-year, $14 million contract. Suzuki's agent, Tony Attanasio, said his client was filled with "absolute, complete, unadulterated elation at the satisfaction of a lifelong dream to play in the U.S. with the Seattle Mariners."

In mid-November the New York Mets pulled out of the Rodriguez sweepstakes. Their general manager, Steve Phillips, said Rodriguez's agent, Scott Boras, had made extraordinary demands for billboards, office space, and private jets. In a conference call with the media, Phillips explained why the Mets backed off.

"It's about twenty-five players working as a team," he said. "The twenty-four-plus-one-man structure really doesn't work."

On November 19, Rodriguez spoke with ESPN's Peter Gammons for damage control, telling Gammons, "I'm not a selfish player. I want to be one player on a good team that has a chance to win a ring. When I sign, people will see that there are no big side deals and they may find out that I took a little less to play for the team I want to play with."

However, in the end Rodriguez took the highest offer, a staggering $252 million in a ten-year deal with the Texas Rangers, who had finished in last place in the A.L. West in 2000. The deal, agreed to on December 11, included an opt-out clause for Rodriguez to end the contract after seven years to become a free agent, presumably if he wasn't happy with the Rangers team he was playing for or felt he could get more money from another team.

Beyond the dollars, the opt-out clause likely appalled the Mariners most and made re-signing Rodriguez impossible. Howard Lincoln told the media that Boras' insistence on the opt-out clause was "silliness." Since the team signing him would be obligated to pay the player an extraordinary amount of dollars for a very long period of time, regardless of the player's performance, Lincoln expected the player to be obligated to the team for the entire term of the contract. Lincoln called Texas owner Tom Hicks "a fool" for offering Rodriguez much more money than "the Seattle Mariners or any sane person" would offer.

Reports differed on how long of a contract the Mariners offered Rodriguez. While some said the offer was five years and $94 million, others said Seattle's offer included an option for the team to decline the final two years, making it essentially a three-year contract. Either way, the M's offer was for far shorter than what other teams proposed for Rodriguez.

"Seattle was the only team out of eight that didn't offer me ten years," Rodriguez said. "It was hard walking away from the team, but it wasn't hard walking away from that." Rodriguez expressed dismay that the Mariners had offered him less money than they'd offered him the year before — before he became a free agent.

Gammons reported that the Mariners "didn't make an effort" to keep the shortstop, disclosing that neither Howard Lincoln nor Chuck Armstrong traveled to Miami for a critical meeting the team had with Rodriguez and Boras in early December. Both were vacationing in Hawaii.

While the Mariners couldn't be faulted for not matching the Rangers' offer of $252 million, they certainly could have made more of a serious offer. It's true that Rodriguez was intent on becoming the highest-paid player in baseball, but the Mariners had to know that offering a contract in the three- to five-year range for a twenty-five-year-old superstar was not going to get this deal done, especially not when several other teams were offering ten-year contracts. Rodriguez was rightly chided for signing with a losing team in Texas, but the Mariners' short-term contract offer didn't leave him a legitimate option to stay in Seattle.

Moving on, the Mariners signed second-baseman Bret Boone, a free agent who'd hit .251 with 19 home runs and 74 RBI with San Diego in 2000. Because the thirty-one-year-old Boone was coming off knee surgery, the M's were able to sign him to a one-year deal for $3.25 million. That contract became one of the greatest bargains in team history when Boone hit .331 with 37 home runs and 141 RBI — all career highs — in 2001.

Another off-season addition was relief-pitcher Jeff Nelson. Foolishly traded away to the Yankees after the '95 season, Nelson had enjoyed his five years in New York, during which he won four World Series rings, but was happy to return to Seattle for a three-year, $10.65 million contract.

"I think it's probably the best bullpen in the league," Nelson said. "I'm just adding to it. We proved with four world championships in New York that a bullpen is really important. They had a good bullpen here last year, now Lou (Piniella) will have a better one."

With a week to go in spring training of 2001, Piniella wasn't happy with the M's sloppy play in exhibition games and called a team meeting. The M's had the worst record in the Cactus League. Piniella said the players were missing signs, throwing to the wrong bases, and generally had been lackadaisical.

"Basically, I told them we have to tighten things up this week," Piniella said. "You can't turn it on and off like a faucet."

The Mariners went 13-19 in spring training games, but most considered it a good omen. No Mariners team had reached the playoffs after finishing over .500 in spring training.

A crowd of 45,911 came to Safeco Field for Opening Night of the '01 season, the largest crowd to date for a regular-season game at the stadium. But it wasn't just any Opening Night — it was also the highly anticipated major-league debut for right-fielder Ichiro Suzuki. The Mariners fell behind 4-0 in the first four innings of a game played in 46-degree weather, and it looked to be a long, cold night for the M's and their fans. But Seattle rallied late, tying the game at 4-4 with two runs in the seventh and winning it with a run in the eighth.

Ichiro, who preferred to be identified by his first name only, was in the middle of both rallies, leading off the seventh with a line drive to center for his first big league hit and putting down a perfect sacrifice bunt in the eighth.

Ironically, because of the new, unbalanced schedule introduced in 2001, the Mariners played each of their A.L. West rivals nineteen times, including the Texas Rangers, who now had Rodriguez. Prior to 2001, Seattle typically would play division rivals twelve times each. League officials believed that increasing games between division rivals (such as the Red Sox and Yankees) would generate more fan interest, increase attendance figures, and bring in more revenue.

Thanks to that unbalanced schedule, Seattle played its first nineteen games against the other three A.L. West teams. The M's got off to an incredible start, the best in franchise history, winning fifteen of those games. On April 6, the Mariners played their first road game of the season, in Texas; Rodriguez was overshadowed by Ichiro who went 4 for 6 with a game-winning home run in the top of the tenth inning.

Ten days later, on the eve of his first trip back to Seattle as a visiting player, Rodriguez was asked what kind of reception he thought he'd get from Mariner fans. While initially he was coy, finally he told the *Seattle Times*, "They're going to boo the crap out of me. I guess I'm the villain there now. If it means being hated because I'm well paid, then it's a fact of life. I'm not dreading going back; I'm looking forward to it.

As expected, Rodriguez was booed vociferously by a sold-out Safeco crowd of 45,658 in all five of his at-bats in his first game back. Afterward, he said he hadn't noticed the fans throwing Monopoly money at him near the on-deck circle.

"I didn't see anyone," Rodriquez said. "I just heard them. I was expecting it. I've been expecting it for a while. It was pretty cool. The first one's always hard. I knew it would be a challenge."

Fans brought signs to the park that night that read "Who Let the Dog in?" and "Go Home, Pay-Rod" and "A-Rod Lost His Mojo." Rodriguez said he believed the Mariners had the opportunity to win "110, 115 games, the way they're going right now. They're really hard to beat. Top to bottom, they have a great lineup, with perhaps the best bullpen that's been assembled in the last twenty years, plus a great manager."

While most believed Rodriguez was being disingenuous, his prediction of the M's win total turned out to be pretty close to the mark.

In late April the Mariners swept a three-game series against the Yankees in New York to improve their record to 18-4 and increase their division lead to eight games. After the second of the three wins, Piniella said the team's focus was not on sweeps, just winning series — and the Mariners had won their first seven series.

"You don't play to win every game," Piniella said. "You play to win series. You keep winning series and things like leads and the standings take care of themselves."

An eight-game win streak in mid-May improved Seattle's record to 31-10 and increased its division lead to twelve games. On April 29 and May 1 Seattle had its first two-game losing streak of the season, but the M's wouldn't lose three games in a row until late September, after they had clinched the A.L. West title.

2001 TOP PERFORMERS

Bret Boone, .331, 37 HR, 141 RBI

Ichiro Suzuki, .350, 8 HR, 69 RBI, 56 SB

Edgar Martinez, .306, 23 HR, 116 RBI

Freddy Garcia, 18-6, 3.05 ERA, 238.2 IP

Jamie Moyer, 20-6, 3.43 ERA, 209.2 IP

A club-record win streak of fifteen games put Seattle's record at 47-12 and increased its lead in the A.L. West to seventeen games. The M's staggered a bit from June 9 until the All-Star break, going 16-12, but still maintained a nineteen-game lead. The All-Star Game was held at Safeco Field and the Mariners were well represented with eight Seattle players making the squad. Ichiro, Bret Boone, John Olerud, and Edgar Martinez all started the game, with Ichiro receiving the most fan votes, 3.4 million. Freddy Garcia, Kazuhiro Sasaki, Mike Cameron and Jeff Nelson were selected as reserves. Garcia pitched a perfect third inning and got the win in the American League's 4-1 victory, while Sasaki picked up the save with a 1-2-3 ninth.

The Mariners resumed a torrid pace after the All-Star break, going 41-16 in the following weeks to improve their record to 104-40. Following a win in Anaheim on September 10, Seattle was poised to clinch the division the next night with a win over the Angels and an Oakland loss.

However, there would be no game the next night, or for another week. The world woke up on September 11 to shocking terrorist attacks in New York and Washington, D.C. The attacks caused the baseball season to be interrupted for a week.

The Mariners resumed play on September 18 with a 4-0 win over the Angels, but Oakland also won, so clinching of the A.L. West would have to wait another night. The M's officially won the division title in the fourth inning of their game against the Angels when the A's lost to Texas. Shortly afterward, "2001 A.L. West Champions" appeared on the Safeco Field scoreboard, causing the sellout crowd of 45,459 to give the M's a standing ovation. After the final out of the M's 5-0 win over the Angels, an A.L. West Championship banner was unveiled in center field.

However, with the nation in mourning in the aftermath of the terrorist attacks, there was no big celebration on the field or in the Mariners clubhouse. Instead, after the final out, players hugged on the field, then circled the pitching mound, knelt, and bowed their heads in prayer. Finally, Mark McLemore, in an impromptu display of patriotism, carried the American flag around the field while the team followed.

"We are entertainers, we're baseball players, but before everything else, we are human beings," McLemore said after the game. "We have suffered this week like everyone else in the country. It was tough for us to take the stage and perform."

As the end of the regular season neared, the Mariners faced another challenge. Carlos Guillen, who'd done an admirable job at shortstop in place of Rodriguez, was diagnosed with tuberculosis. M's players and staff were tested for the disease, and Guillen spent a week in the hospital, missing the division series against Cleveland, but returned to play in three of the five games of the ALCS. McLemore capably filled in for Guillen at shortstop, but the injury limited Piniella's flexibility for the postseason with McLemore, who was a capable infielder and outfielder, not being available to fill in at other positions he'd played during the season.

On October 6, Sasaki recorded a team-record forty-fifth save by striking out Rodriguez for the last out of the ninth inning as the M's beat Texas 1-0 for their 116th victory of the season. The win tied a major-league record set by the 1906 Cubs, who had gone 116-36. The M's lost to the Rangers the next day, and remained tied for the most wins, but a magical regular season was over with Seattle finishing 116-46.

The Mariners' team and individual accomplishments were numerous. The team finished seventy games over .500 — fourteen different Mariner teams (nine before 2001, five after), had failed to win seventy games in an entire season! The team's 59-22 road record was the best in A.L. history, surpassing the 1971 A's mark of 55-25. Seattle also became the first team to win the unofficial Triple Crown since the 1948 Indians, leading the league with a .288 team batting average, 3.54 ERA, and .986 fielding average.

Ichiro won the batting title with a .350 average and was named MVP and Rookie of the Year of the American League; Boone led the league in RBI, Garcia had the lowest ERA in the league (3.05), and Jamie Moyer became just the second twenty-game winner in franchise history.

While the Mariners were disappointed at not winning a 117th game, they knew a bigger prize waited. After the season finale Piniella told the media, "Yeah, we wanted it … Who wouldn't? But what we want more is a World Series, and we're going to do all we can to get it. The true test of a quality team having a quality year is proven over the six months of the regular season, not the playoffs. But it would be nice to cap it right."

The postseason, however, began in disappointing fashion. The M's were shut out in Game 1 of the division series at Safeco Field by Cleveland's Bartolo Colon, who struck out ten in a 5-0 win. In Game 2, however, it took the M's just fourteen pitches to jump out to a 4-0 lead on Indians starter Chuck Finley, who gave up two-run homers to Mike Cameron and Edgar Martinez in the first inning. The M's won 5-1 and evened the series.

The best-of-five series headed to Cleveland where the Indians beat up on Aaron Sele and the M's bullpen in a 17-2 drubbing. Sele, a career 0-4 in postseason action, didn't make it past the second inning. Despite their incredible 116-win season, the Mariners faced elimination. They had to win the next two games, one in Cleveland and one in Seattle, to avoid elimination in the first round. To win Game 4, the M's had to go through Colon.

A rainstorm delayed the start of the game by two hours and twenty minutes but the Indians quickly took a 1-0 lead in the second inning on a home run by Juan Gonzalez. That one run looked like it might be enough because Colon held Seattle to just three hits over the first six innings. But the Mariners broke through in the seventh, loading the bases on a single by Stan Javier sandwiched between walks to Olerud and Cameron. David Bell drove in the tying run and Seattle went ahead 3-1 on singles by Ichiro and McLemore.

Cleveland scored a run in the seventh to make it 3-2, but the Mariners added a run in the eighth on Cameron's double and two more in the ninth on Martinez's home run to bring the series back to Seattle.

In a quick turnaround, Game 5 was an early-afternoon start the next day. The M's took a 2-0 lead on a second-inning single by McLemore. The Indians got a run back in the third and were threatening to tie or take the lead, but Moyer got Robbie Alomar to hit into a 5-4-3 double play to end the inning. The only other baserunner allowed by Moyer in his six innings came on a first-inning error. Since Moyer was working on three days' rest, he departed after just eighty-six pitches. The one-run lead was in good hands as Nelson, Sasaki, and Rhodes allowed just one baserunner over the final three frames. Seattle won 3-1 to take the series and would face the Yankees in the American League Championship Series for the second consecutive season.

The Yankees had been lucky to reach the ALCS, having become the first team in history to win a five-game postseason series after losing the first two games at home. But if the Yankees were weary from a tough series against the Oakland A's, they didn't show it. New York took the first two games of the series at Safeco Field, jumping out to early leads, winning 4-2 and 3-2. Seattle hitters went 0-for-10 with runners in scoring position in the two games.

After Game 2 an angry Piniella told reporters waiting outside the Mariners clubhouse that his team would be back in Seattle for Game 6; to do so, the M's had to win two of the next three games at Yankee Stadium.

"I want you all to hear this." Piniella said. "We're going to be back here to play Game 6. Print it. I've got confidence in my club. We've gone to New York and beaten this team five out of six [this year] and we're going to do it again."

However, there would be no Game 6 because New York took two of the three games in its home park, losing only Game 3, 14-3. Game 4 was the turning point in the series, a battle that was scoreless through the first seven innings. When Boone broke the tie in the top of the eighth with a home run, Seattle was six outs away from evening the series at two games each. After Rhodes struck out David Justice, who'd hit a crucial home run off Rhodes in the previous year's ALCS, to start the bottom of the eighth, it looked like the Mariners' luck had turned. But the next batter, Bernie Williams, tied the score with a home run to centerfield. Mariano Rivera came on for the top of the ninth and three M's hitters, Olerud, Javier, and Cameron, all made outs on the first pitch from Rivera.

Alfonso Soriano's two-run homer off Sasaki in the bottom of the ninth ended the game and put New York up three games to one. Game 5 wasn't close, as Sele allowed four runs in the third inning in what became a 12-3 blowout.

Piniella, in an unusual move, put Gold Glove right-fielder Ichiro in left for the start of Game 5 so that Jay Buhner, in what would be the last game of his career, could play rightfield, the position he'd played most of his career. Buhner had started just two games all year in right, so the move made little sense, except for sentimental reasons. In Game 2 of the series Piniella had explained his reason for starting Buhner in left: "In a way I owe it to him," Piniella said. "He's been a mainstay for this organization and all my years here. I've got a sense of history.

Seattle's dream season, which began six months before with twenty wins in its first twenty-four contests, ended with a whimper.

To this day, some believe the Mariners' spirited drive for their first World Series title was blunted by the events of 9-11. John McLaren, the Mariners bench coach that season, recalled a visit to Ground Zero upon the team's arrival in New York.

"…It was the only thing to do, to go and show tribute to those people," McLaren told *The Grand Salami*. "But it might have been the worst thing that we did, because I think it choked the team up. They took us out the back way and there was a memorial there, with teddy bears and rosaries. I had tears in my eyes. We all did. Then we saw the Statue of Liberty and it was like someone slugged you in the gut. So then we go to the stadium and they had an eagle fly in from center field and it lands on the mound.

"The guys were still choked up from Ground Zero and we weren't ready to play," he said.

Chapter 18

TEN ALL-TIME BEST PLAYERS

H ere are the best of the best Mariners over the years:

1. Ken Griffey Jr.

Griffey is undoubtedly the best player in Mariners history and the player most responsible for the building of Safeco Field. He hit forty or more home runs in six of his final seven seasons before being traded to Cincinnati, the exception coming in the '95 season when he missed three months after breaking his wrist crashing into the Kingdome outfield wall. The only one of the Mariners' Big Three not to win a World Series ring after leaving Seattle, it's expected that Griffey will be wearing a Mariners cap when he goes into the Hall of Fame in 2016.

2. Randy Johnson

Johnson was the most dominant pitcher of the 1990s, but also pitched well for several years into his forties. History proved that Chuck Armstrong and the Mariners were way off base when they ushered him out the door midway through his career — Johnson went on to win 170 games over the next eleven and a half years. I'll always wonder how many World Series the M's might have won if Armstrong hadn't let his ego get in the way of putting the best team on the field. A five-time Cy Young Award winner, Johnson was worth every penny of the "Maddux Money" he sought, and then some.

3. Edgar Martinez

Martinez is a Mariners icon after playing his entire eighteen-year career in Seattle and having a street outside Safeco Field named for him. A seven-time All-Star, he hit over .300 ten times and retired in 2004 with a career .312 average and .418 on-base percentage. If the M's had been smart enough to make him a regular player a couple of years sooner, his case for Cooperstown would be much stronger. His 2,247 hits, 309 home runs and lack of a World Series ring haven't wowed Hall of Fame voters outside the Northwest.

4. Alex Rodriguez

One of the all-time greats of the game, Rodriguez will forever be reviled in Seattle for chasing every last dollar in free agency. He'll also be remembered for becoming a superstar much quicker than Griffey did; A-Rod hit thirty-six home runs in his first full season in the bigs, while Junior didn't top twenty-seven homers until his fifth year in Seattle. The one regret is that because of service time earned in brief stints in the majors in 1994-95, the M's got only five seasons out of Rodriguez as a regular instead of the usual six. The M's paid him a shade over $11 million total for those five seasons, a little more than a third of what he gets per season now.

5. Ichiro Suzuki

Ichiro's first ten years in Seattle were remarkably consistent, a .300 average and 200 hits each year, while receiving All-Star and Gold Glove honors each season. He'd probably be a lock for the Hall of Fame even if he retired right now. It's a little troubling that he doesn't seem all that concerned that he hasn't played in a postseason game since his rookie season.

6. Jay Buhner

A fan favorite at the Kingdome, Buhner's best seasons were from 1995 to 1997, when he hit forty or more home runs each year, and he ranks third all-time on the club, belting 307 homers in fourteen seasons with the M's. He also had a rifle arm and was a defensive force in right field; the phrase "where triples go to die" was first uttered in Seattle about the man known as "Bone," not Ichiro. Buhner, a presence in the Mariners clubhouse and a born leader, would make a great manager someday if he were willing.

7. Jamie Moyer

The franchise leader in victories, Moyer won some big games during his ten seasons in Seattle, none bigger than Game 5 of the 2001 American League Division Series. He pitched six innings of one-run ball on three days' rest to beat Cleveland and send the Mariners to the ALCS against the Yankees. He missed the entire '11 season after having elbow surgery, but at this writing might not be finished, even at age forty-nine.

8. Felix Hernandez

Anointed "King Felix" before throwing a pitch in the major leagues, Hernandez has lived up to the lofty expectations of fans and media with a nineteen-win season in 2009 and a Cy Young Award in 2010. With Hernandez signed through 2014, the Mariners had better contend soon or consider trading their ace, who completed six full major-league seasons before turning twenty-six.

9. Freddy Garcia

While he couldn't completely fill the dominant shoes of Randy Johnson, Garcia was the undisputed ace on some of the Mariners' best teams and won sixteen or more games three times, pitching more than two-hundred innings in four of his five full seasons in Seattle. His late hours and fascination with the nightlife in Seattle's Belltown District probably kept the M's from signing him long term, but it didn't seem to affect his performance on the mound. Entering his fourteenth big league season, Garcia is still going strong, coming off a twelve-win season for the Yankees in 2011.

10. Dan Wilson

In a spirited battle for the last spot on this list, Dan Wilson won out over Bret Boone, Alvin Davis, Kazuhiro Sasaki, and Mark Langston. Wilson, whose Mariner career lasted twelve seasons, was a rock behind the plate and delivered his share of clutch hits. More important, he could catch the ball — he allowed just one passed ball in 144 games in 1997 and didn't have any in 101 games behind the plate in his last full season, 2004.

Chapter 19

"IT'S NOT OUR GOAL TO WIN THE WORLD SERIES"

While the Mariner players were dejected at not reaching the World Series with their record 116-win season, work on building the '02 team began shortly after the team was eliminated from the ALCS.

Several key players from the '01 team were free agents, including Bret Boone, Mark McLemore, Aaron Sele, and David Bell. Most important was Boone, who'd finished third in A.L. MVP voting. He'd played on a one-year, $3.25 million contract in 2001 and was expecting a big raise and a multi-year contract.

The Mariners made an offer to Boone for a reported three-year, $22 million deal, in late October before he filed for free agency, but it wasn't deemed strong enough by the second-baseman so he decided to test the market. Howard Lincoln said the team was prepared to let Boone leave as a free agent.

"We've made what we think is a competitive offer to Bret," Lincoln said. "He's decided he wants to go out and shop the market. That's fine. We're going to continue to have discussions with him, but the Alex Rodriguez case shows us we're prepared to let players go, regardless of how popular they are, if we simply can't put something together that makes business sense."

Figures released after the '01 season revealed that the Mariners had revenue in the neighborhood of $170 million that year, second only to the New York Yankees. The Mariners led MLB in attendance that year, drawing more than 3.5 million fans, a franchise record, yet Lincoln's concern seemed to be less about keeping the team intact than turning a profit. He told the *Seattle Times* that the Mariners were "absolutely determined" the player payroll would not exceed fifty percent of the team's projected revenues for 2002.

"We have to operate at a profit," Lincoln said. "And we have to make decisions with that in mind."

While the possibility of losing Boone loomed, the M's focused on upgrading at third base and contemplated trades for Philadelphia's Scott Rolen and Colorado's Jeff Cirillo. Rolen, who'd hit .289 with twenty-five home runs and eighty-seven RBI in 2001, was far more likely to be the better player, but Seattle was not prepared to give up the package of young pitchers demanded by the Phillies. Rolen had just one year remaining on his contract and the M's didn't think Rolen, an Indiana native, wanted to play on the West Coast.

Not so with Cirillo. He had spent his eight-year career playing for Milwaukee and Colorado, but made his offseason home in the Seattle suburb of Redmond. Additionally, Cirillo had already signed a four-year, $29 million contract extension with the Rockies that was set to begin in 2002. More important, the Rockies were looking to cut payroll, so the M's could acquire Cirillo for a group of second-tier pitchers and wouldn't have to give up Joel Pineiro, their top pitching prospect at the time.

The thirty-two-year-old Cirillo, a two-time All-Star and a solid defensive third-baseman, had a career batting average of .311 and was coming off a season in which he'd hit .313 with 17 home runs and 83 RBI for the Rockies. Overlooked was the fact that his numbers in 2001 were largely a product of the high altitude of Colorado's Coors Field, which has been reputed for years to enhance most hitters' statistics. Cirillo had hit .362 with 31 extra-base hits at Coors, but a pedestrian .266 with just 16 extra-base hits on the road.

Unconcerned, the Mariners completed the trade for Cirillo on December 14, sending pitchers Denny Stark, Brian Fuentes, and Jose Paniagua to the Rockies. Asked by a reporter about his ability to hit at Safeco Field, a tough park for hitters, Cirillo said, "I guess I have something to prove. I want to show I can hit, whether I'm playing in Safeco Field or on the moon."

Unfortunately the M's weren't scheduled to play any games on the moon in 2002. Cirillo hit just .217 with two home runs in seventy-two games at Safeco that year. He fared a bit better on the road, hitting .278 with four home runs in seventy-four games, but it was a far cry from the Mariners' expectations when they acquired Cirillo and the obligations of his pricey long-term contract.

The Boone negotiations carried over into the new year, and the second-baseman agreed to the Mariners' offer of arbitration, which came as a surprise to the M's. But Boone didn't get the multi-year offers he expected from other teams, so he agreed to arbitration, hoping to push the Mariners into a compromise. Faced with the prospect of having to pay Boone a $12 million salary on a one-year deal for 2002 if an arbitrator ruled in Boone's favor, the M's agreed to a three-year $24 million contract with a club option for a fourth year that would be guaranteed if Boone made 450 plate appearances in 2004.

"IT'S NOT OUR GOAL TO WIN THE WORLD SERIES"

Starting pitching was one area the M's didn't improve for 2002. With Sele leaving as a free agent, Seattle pursued Longview, Washington native Jason Schmidt of the Giants. Schmidt, who had won thirteen games in 2001, had said it was his boyhood dream to play for the Mariners. Yet San Francisco offered a four-year, $31 million deal, while Seattle held the line at a lesser three-year offer, and Schmidt stayed put, averaging fifteen wins a season for the Giants the next four years.

This was one instance where Gillick's conservative nature hurt the Mariners. Gillick, on record against contracts longer than three years, believed deals longer than that would create situations in which the player or the club would become disappointed at some point during the term of the contract. During his four years as Mariners GM, Gillick signed just one player to a contract of more than three years: reliever Arthur Rhodes.

A record crowd of 46,036 at Safeco Field saw the M's lose 6-5 to the White Sox on Opening Day of 2002. But the M's soon got off to a sizzling start and were well over .500, winning ten in a row and fourteen of fifteen by late April to keep pace with the '01 team at 17-4. While nobody thought it possible that the M's could repeat their 116-win season, another one-hundred-win season didn't seem out of the question.

On May 2, Mike Cameron accomplished an incredible feat: he hit four home runs in a game in Chicago against the White Sox. Cameron became the thirteenth player in baseball history to pull off this feat. Of the previous twelve, five were Hall of Famers, including Willie Mays, Lou Gehrig, and Mike Schmidt. In fact, Cameron, who homered in his first four at-bats, nearly became the first player to hit five in a game, flying out to deep right field in the ninth inning.

Thanks to an 18-8 April and a stretch in early May in which the M's won eight of nine and eleven of fourteen, Seattle built up a six and a half game lead in the A.L. West over the second place Angels. But the '02 team had flaws, one of which was starting pitching. With Sele lost to free agency and Paul Abbott, a seventeen-game winner in 2001, missing most of the season with a shoulder injury, the M's struggled early on to get decent starts out of any of their starters beyond Freddy Garcia and Jamie Moyer. Joel Pineiro was shifted from the bullpen to the rotation and did an adequate job, but former White Sox hurler James Baldwin, signed on the cheap two weeks before the start of spring training, did not.

On May 4, Gillick told Bob Finnigan of the *Times* that the team was trying to trade for help for Seattle's struggling rotation. "We need a starting pitcher," Gillick said. "Lou [Piniella] has been kind of shuffling around to get the right mix for the rotation." While Gillick said he hoped to make a trade, he also dropped a bombshell that day: the M's were $1.5 million over their $89 million budget and unlikely to add payroll to acquire a pitcher, or any other player.

As the '02 season progressed, it became clear the M's most pressing need was for an additional bat for the team's sputtering offense. The team would lose twenty-five one-run games, more than twice as many as they had in 2001. More important, thirty-nine-year-old designated hitter Edgar Martinez, a key component of the team's offense, ruptured his hamstring and missed half of the '02 season and was never adequately replaced.

During the first half of the season, Piniella complained, almost on a nightly basis, that his club was a bat short. But with less than a month to go before the July 31 trading deadline, the Mariners hadn't made any moves, nor were they expected to, according to Finnigan, who described Howard Lincoln's budgets for the Mariners player payroll as "sacrosanct."

As the deadline approached, Piniella was mum, reportedly silenced by a gag order imposed by Lincoln, forbidding the manager from complaining to the media about the team's need for midseason help. Sources said Piniella had expressed his frustration in internal talks and gotten nowhere.

A week before the trade deadline Gillick told Finnigan, "We probably could use a starting pitcher, but from the standpoint of budget, we are more than maxed out."

Gillick said he was looking for a deal he could make, but cautioned not to expect the team to make any significant moves before the trade deadline. "I don't want to mislead our fans," he said. "We are right up against our payroll. The door to a deal is more closed than open. Howard [Lincoln] has said over and over, the goal is to run the club on a self-sufficient basis, that if we put a competitive product on the field consistently and everything falls into place, we'll win."

2002 TOP PERFORMERS

John Olerud, .300, 22 HR, 102 RBI

Bret Boone, .278, 24 HR, 107 RBI

Jamie Moyer, 13-8, 3.32 ERA, 230.2 IP

Freddy Garcia, 16-10, 4.39 ERA, 223.2 IP

Joel Pineiro, 14-7, 3.24 ERA, 194.1 IP

"IT'S NOT OUR GOAL TO WIN THE WORLD SERIES"

With the M's having lost their lead in the A.L. West by late July and the team's main competition for a playoff spot making major trades to fill their holes (Oakland acquired Ray Durham, Ted Lilly, and Ricardo Rincon; Anaheim added Alex Ochoa; Boston traded for Cliff Floyd and Bobby Howry, and the Yankees acquired Raul Mondesi in July deals), pressure to make a trade began to mount. But ownership wouldn't budge.

On July 24, seven days before the trade deadline, Lincoln told Blaine Newnham of the *Seattle Times*, "If you don't operate as a business, all sorts of bad things happen."

Then Lincoln made a shocking admission: "The goal of the Mariners is not to win the World Series. It is to field a competitive team year after year, to put itself in a position to win a World Series, and hope at some point that happens. People want us to do something exceptional, but what we want to do is have the discipline to stick with our plan."

When Lincoln was reminded that the team had made exceptional profits in each of the previous two seasons, Lincoln replied, "We absolutely have to make money. No question, end of story."

Word of Lincoln's comment about the World Series soon reached the Mariner clubhouse. One unhappy player asked a reporter, "How would he [Lincoln] like it if we said we had no interest in going to the World Series, that we were only in it for the money?"

Reached for a response, Lincoln said, "We will not do a deal just so we can say to fans or players, 'Look at us, we did a deal.' This is not the way I operate a business."

Asked if a trade might provide an emotional lift for a struggling team, Lincoln replied sharply, "I'm in the baseball business, not the feel-good business. Everyone thinks he's a GM, just like everyone thinks they can hit a ball like Tiger Woods."

Asked how it felt for him to be a lightning rod for disappointment by Seattle fans, players, and a certain Mariners manager, Lincoln replied, "I feel great. I feel the Mariners are going to be super the balance of the season, that they are going to bring joy to the fans."

However, the Mariners weren't "super" the rest of the '02 season. The team, which had won sixty-one percent of its games before July 31 (66-42), faded in the second half with a .500 record (27-27). Two teams in the division, the A's and Angels, climbed over the Mariners, and the Angels went on to win their first World Series.

A disgruntled Edgar Martinez, nearing the end of his career and with dwindling chances to win a championship, spoke out the day after the trade deadline, telling Larry Stone of the *Seattle Times*, "I see every other team getting their team ready for the last couple of months. They're getting some help to make it to the playoffs. Sometimes it is a little frustrating when our team can be improved, and we don't make a move."

The only acquisitions Gillick made at mid-season were three players unwanted by their existing teams. Relief-pitcher Doug Creek (who had a 6.82 ERA at the time he joined the M's) was added on July 24 after being placed on waivers by Tampa Bay, the worst team in the majors. Utility-man Jose Offerman and pitcher Ismael Valdes were acquired in August, but neither provided much help. When Offerman was acquired from the Red Sox, Gillick sarcastically referred to the acquisition as *"an Oakland deal,"* meaning it wouldn't add much salary because Boston was paying nearly all of Offerman's contract.

While Lincoln would tell the media again and again that he owed it to the team's shareholders to make a profit, not once did he address his obligations to the team's fans, who were filling up Safeco Field like never before in 2002. The club set an attendance record that season, averaging 43,740 fans for the team's eighty-one home dates. Were the Mariners taking those fans for granted? It sure seemed like they were, especially when the team raised ticket prices for the fourth consecutive year at the end of the '02 season despite missing the playoffs.

Ownership's refusal to add payroll in 2002 was curious for another reason: Wouldn't the Mariners have earned more money if they made the postseason, not only from playoff and possible World Series games, but also from additional tickets sold the following year? The Mariners had reaped more than $2 million in extra revenue from reaching the postseason in 2001 and stood to make two or three times that in extra revenue if they made it to the World Series in 2002.

Instead, the Mariners ownership announced loudly to the team's fans, players, and staff that it was more important that their billionaire owners make a profit than it was to spend the money needed to have a shot at reaching the playoffs.

Within months the Mariners would lose the best manager the franchise ever had, but the franchise would lose much, much more in the years to come.

Chapter 20

SOMETIMES FREE AGENTS AREN'T FREE

The low budget Mariners of the 1970s and 1980s didn't dabble much in the free-agent market, so virtually all of the significant signings in club history have taken place in the past twenty years.

Signing free agents can be a crapshoot; the contract a player receives is usually more a byproduct of his past performance than an indicator of how the player will perform during the term of the new deal. Cincinnati Reds Manager Dusty Baker once said of free agency, "You're taking a chance on the transmission going bad or that the car was in a wreck. Or you can get an outstanding car with low mileage."

While all that is true, it helps to have a competent general manager making the decisions for your ballclub. Five of the top seven free-agent signings in M's history were made by Pat Gillick before the 2000-01 seasons — and that doesn't include Ichiro Suzuki, who technically was not signed as a free agent, but rather was signed by the Mariners in late 2000 after Seattle won his rights through the closed-bid international posting system. If Ichiro were a true free-agent signing, he'd jump to the top of the list of the best in M's history.

Bill Bavasi, thought of in most quarters as the worst general manager in Mariner history, was the anti-Gillick, signing five of the seven worst free agents for the M's.

BEST FREE-AGENT SIGNINGS

1. Bret Boone, 2001

Having lost Alex Rodriguez as a free agent, the M's replaced much of his production from the 2000 season by signing second-baseman Bret Boone to a one-year, $3.25 million contract for about an eighth of Rodriguez's annual salary with Texas. Boone, who was coming off a knee injury that cut his 2000 season short, had career highs in all three Triple Crown categories in 2001, batting .331 with 37 home runs and a league-leading 141 RBI.

2. Kazuhiro Sasaki, 2000

While there were questions whether Sasaki's success in Japan would translate to the American League, he quickly seized the closing duties from Jose Mesa and won A.L. Rookie of the Year honors in 2000. Sasaki still holds the team record for saves with 129 in his four seasons in Seattle.

3. Joey Cora, 1995

Signed as a free agent when the baseball strike ended in April of 1995, the veteran second-baseman hit .297 with eighteen stolen bases and helped the M's make the playoffs for the first time. Cora quickly became a fan favorite and was an All-Star in 1997, when he hit .300 with eleven home runs.

4. John Olerud, 2000

Olerud, a graduate of Interlake High School in Bellevue, Washington, returned home in 2000 and averaged 100 RBI per season and an on-base percentage over .400 in his first three years with Seattle.

5. Norm Charlton, 1995

Charlton, released by the Phillies in mid-July with a 7.36 ERA, took over the M's closer's job from Bobby Ayala in August of 1995 and was nearly perfect down the stretch. Charlton converted fourteen of fifteen save opportunities, allowing just twenty-three hits in 47 2/3 innings and posting a 1.51 ERA.

6. Arthur Rhodes, 2000

Left-handed setup man Arthur Rhodes gave the M's four solid seasons out of the bullpen, winning twenty-six games in relief and striking out ten batters per nine innings.

7. Jeff Nelson, 2001

Nelson returned to the M's after winning four rings in five seasons in New York. Nelson gave the M's two and a half solid seasons after his return, but was traded away in August of 2003, five days after making critical comments about management at the '03 trade deadline.

8. Russell Branyan, 2009

Branyan was signed to a $1.4 million contract by first-year GM Jack Zduriencik, and while it was hard to imagine how few runs the offensively challenged M's might have scored if not for Branyan's thirty-one home runs in 2009, it became obvious the following year, when Seattle's historically bad offense scored just 513 runs after not re-signing Branyan.

9. Raul Ibanez, 2004

Originally drafted by the Mariners in the thirty-sixth round of the 1992 draft, Ibanez never got much of a chance to stick with Lou Piniella's M's and was released in 2000. He had solid seasons as a regular in 2002-03 for Kansas City, prompting Seattle to bring him back as a free agent. While the M's unnecessarily lost their first-round pick in 2004 for signing Ibanez before the Royals had a chance to offer him arbitration, Ibanez was the most consistent hitter on the Seattle team for the next five seasons before leaving for Philadelphia.

10. Ken Griffey Jr. 2009

Griffey's return to Seattle after nine years away excited a fan base, boosted clubhouse morale and, because he could still hit the occasional long ball, he even helped the M's win a few games. Griffey's Hall of Fame career would have ended on a high note had he retired in 2009 after being carried off the field by his Mariner teammates on the last day of that season; unfortunately he chose to return for another season despite having batted just .214 in 2009.

WORST FREE-AGENT SIGNINGS

1. Carlos Silva, 2008

Bill Bavasi handed Silva, one year removed from a season in which opposing hitters had pounded him at a .324 clip with a .539 slugging average, a four-year deal for $48 million. Even naysayers expected Silva to be a serviceable innings eater for the first couple of years of the deal, but he had a 6.46 ERA in his *best* season in Seattle. The M's swapped bad contracts with the Cubs two years into the deal, taking on Milton Bradley's contract and paying the difference in the players' salaries, but that arrangement fizzled, too. Not only is the Carlos Silva signing the worst free agent signing in Mariners history, it ranks as one of the worst free-agent signings in baseball history.

2. Chone Figgins, 2010

After seven productive seasons in Anaheim, Figgins signed a four-year, $36 million contract with Seattle and somehow became one of the worst players in the league. A .291 hitter with the Angels, Figgins hit .236 in his first two seasons with the M's, including an abysmal .188 in 2011, when he saw his playing time severely reduced before landing on the DL for the final two months of the season.

3. Scott Spiezio, 2004

While Spiezio's contract wasn't for a ton of money, $9 million over three years, he was an abominable failure, hitting a career low .215 in his first year in Seattle, and was released after batting .064 in forty-seven at-bats in 2005.

4. Greg Colbrunn, 2003

The M's paid Colbrunn big bucks to bat just sixty-two times in 2003, but their biggest loss was surrendering a first-round pick that year, the nineteenth overall pick, to Arizona for the privilege of signing the backup first-baseman. Worse, they traded Colbrunn back to the D-Backs after the season for Quinton McCracken and sent Arizona $375,000 to cover the difference in the players' salaries. No word on whether the M's asked for the draft pick back.

5. Rich Aurilia, 2004

In their haste to run Carlos Guillen out of town, the M's didn't properly check out the thirty-two-year-old Aurilia, who'd lost most of his range at shortstop; he'd been able to get by in the National League, where he knew the hitters, but he was a disaster switching to a new league and was discarded half a season into his Mariner career.

6. Jarrod Washburn, 2006

After the Spiezio debacle, one would think the M's would have forbid Bill Bavasi from signing any more of his Anaheim buddies, but somehow Scott Boras convinced the M's to hand over $37.5 million to the mediocre southpaw, who was paid $1,171,875 for each of the thirty-two wins he delivered in his four seasons with Seattle.

7. Jeff Weaver, 2007

Spiezio reportedly warned his former Angels teammate to stay away from Seattle, but there probably weren't many teams offering Weaver more than $8 million after he'd been discarded the previous summer by the Angels with a 3-10 record. Weaver's improvement as a Mariner was marginal; he lowered his ERA from 6.29 to 6.20 after relocating to Safeco.

8. Greg Hibbard, 1994

The left-handed Hibbard went 1-5 with a 6.69 ERA in '94 after signing a three-year, $6.75 million deal with the M's. A torn rotator cuff ended his career prematurely.

9. Richie Sexson, 2005

Sexson, owner of the largest contract on this list, actually did fairly well his first two years with the M's, driving in more than one-hundred runs in both the '05 and '06 seasons. Unfortunately, Seattle had signed him to a four-year, backloaded contract, so they had to pay him $31 million in his final two seasons, when he hit .205 and .221. He never played again after 2008.

10. Ken Griffey Jr., 2010

While Junior's return was the feel-good story of 2009, he should have retired after that season. He made the mistake of returning for one last hurrah, but hit just .184 without a homer in 108 trips to the plate. For their part, the M's made the mistake of not signing an alternative DH so Griffey wouldn't have to play regularly. His Hall of Fame career ended badly; he slinked away into retirement eight weeks into the season with nary a word to his teammates or to Manager Don Wakamatsu, who was fired two months after Griffey's departure.

DISHONORABLE MENTION: Pete O'Brien, 1990; Jose Mesa, 1999; Jack Cust, 2011; Milt Wilcox, 1986; Pokey Reese, 2005; Chris Bosio, 1993.

Chapter 21

IF AT FIRST YOU DON'T SUCCEED, DO THE EXACT SAME THING AGAIN

As the '02 season wound down and it was clear that the lack of mid-season additions would doom the Mariners to miss the playoffs, Lou Piniella no longer could hold in his frustration.

Despite the gag order imposed by Howard Lincoln, Piniella spilled out his frustrations to ESPN's Peter Gammons and to *Sports Weekly*.

"We're not a deep team and we're not a power team," Piniella told Gammons. "*We need a bat*. I know Pat [Gillick] is trying, but I don't know what there is, or what we can take on [in salary]. But we need a bat in left field." He told *Sports Weekly*, "I've been telling these people [upper management] all year, but no one listened."

While Piniella's comments no doubt angered Lincoln, innocuous comments Piniella made to a writer from a Houston newspaper seemed to anger the Mariners chairman even more, leading to a confrontation between the two men. When the Mariners played the Astros in Houston in late June, Piniella was asked by a Houston reporter about the trade deadline deal that sent Randy Johnson to the Astros four years before.

"They were trying to win the World Series, and they thought Randy would be a major factor," Piniella said. "I think if you have a team that's one piece short, you owe it to your fans to give it a go — and to your players. How many teams get in position that way?"

Lincoln fumed when he read Piniella's quotes. He was certain that Piniella was speaking, in veiled terms, about the situation in Seattle, where Lincoln hadn't allowed Gillick to add payroll at the '02 trade deadline. Even though most contending teams in baseball operated with a philosophy contrary to Seattle's, adding players at midseason when needed and adding payroll if necessary, Lincoln took Piniella's quotes as a direct shot at him.

The philosophy employed by most of the other teams in the majors seemed foreign to Lincoln, whose primary goal appeared to be making money for the Mariners' ownership group. Instead of appreciating a long-time baseball man passionate about winning, Lincoln was more concerned about what he believed to be insubordination on Piniella's part. He sent a memo to Gillick and asked Gillick to share it with Piniella. The memo detailed Lincoln's concern that there was a communication breakdown since, in Lincoln's mind, Piniella had violated Lincoln's gag order.

Piniella marched up to Lincoln's office and in a tirade not unlike some of those he'd had on the baseball field during his managing career, let Lincoln know exactly how he felt about the memo. The two men agreed to disagree, but the conflict set into motion the possibility that Piniella might leave the Mariners at the end of the season, a year before his contract was due to expire.

Lincoln discussed that meeting with Piniella in Art Thiel's book, in which he was quoted as saying, "This was one of the few times in Lou's life when somebody was pissing him off and didn't back down. Lou wasn't used to somebody taking him on. My strong feeling was that nobody was bigger than the organization. Everybody needs to follow the rules. That's the way of any successful business. You can't have prima donnas."

Unfortunately for the Mariners and their fans, Lincoln and Armstrong had done a great job of ridding the team of so-called prima donnas Johnson, Griffey, and Rodriguez, and Lincoln was now on the verge of running another so-called prima donna, Piniella, out of town.

That left the M's with just two prima donnas, Lincoln and Armstrong. These two executives could not pitch, hit, or catch like the three Hall of Fame players they'd chased off, nor could they successfully manage a team or charm free agents like Piniella could. While Lincoln and Armstrong may have won the power struggles with Piniella and various players, they were Pyrrhic victories that would seriously damage the franchise for years to come.

As the '02 season drew to a close, the Mariners announced that Piniella would manage the M's in 2003. Club spokesman Matt Roebuck said, "He's our manager. We want him back." Despite that statement, Piniella already had informed team officials on the last weekend of the season that he was retiring, but the Mariners asked him to go home and think over his decision.

On October 11, Lincoln, Armstrong, and Gillick flew to Tampa to meet with Piniella, who told them he wanted out of the last year of his contract. Piniella said he wasn't retiring after all, that he was interested in taking one of the managerial jobs that had opened with the New York Mets or the Tampa Bay Devil Rays. Lincoln realized how badly Piniella wanted out when Piniella said that he would consider managing Tampa, a team that had never won even seventy games in a single season in its five-year history and had won only fifty-five games in 2002.

While Piniella's preference seemed to be New York, where the Mets' wealthy ownership likely would give him the opportunity to contend quickly, the Mariners preferred to make a deal with Tampa Bay. The reasons were never stated, but it seems likely that the Mariners wanted to avoid the embarrassment of having Piniella win in New York when he should have been managing in Seattle, forcing him to take the job with lowly Tampa Bay. Piniella never got the opportunity to talk to the Mets. The Mariners reached agreement on compensation from the Devil Rays for letting Piniella out of the last year of his contract: Seattle would receive outfielder Randy Winn, who had been Tampa Bay's lone All-Star in 2002.

Piniella took one final poke at the Mariners, saying he found it ironic that the Mariners had acquired a left-fielder as compensation for him, saying "In my ten years in Seattle, the Mariners never got a left-fielder for me."

With Piniella gone, the Mariners had to hire a new manager for the first time in ten years. It became a complex process, complicated by the fact that Lincoln and Armstrong, who insisted on meeting each and every candidate with Gillick, were off vacationing in Spain in the middle of the search. Ten initial candidates were interviewed and two "mystery candidates" were added late. Ultimately the M's whittled the competition down to four finalists: Buddy Bell, Sam Perlozzo, Jim Riggleman, and one of the mystery men — Arizona Diamondbacks bench-coach Bob Melvin, who was hired for the job despite having no previous managerial experience.

While it was somewhat surprising that the M's would turn to a man with no managing background for Piniella's successor, it was more of a surprise that Seattle didn't interview Dusty Baker, who had just taken an aging San Francisco Giants team to the World Series and was named National League Manager of the Year in three of his eight seasons with the Giants. Baker's contract in San Francisco had expired and he was interested in the Seattle job. Gillick was asked regularly by the Seattle media about Baker, but offered little comment until about a week before Melvin's hiring, when he told a reporter, "There is no possibility of him [Baker] coming here."

The Mariners never commented publicly on why they didn't bring a top candidate in for an interview, while focusing exclusively on managers with little or no experience or managers with track records of failure, but it's likely the M's considered Baker's style to be too close to Piniella's. Baker had good motivational and communication skills, but he liked to have a say in personnel decisions and he might challenge management or question its priorities, like Piniella had. Further, Baker would have been an expensive hire, costing more per season than the $2.5 million the team would have paid Piniella had he come back for the '03 season. Baker accepted the Chicago Cubs job and took the Cubs to the 2003 National League Championship before being derailed by a previously unknown Cubs fan named Steve Bartman.

Baker told the *Times*' Larry Stone at the winter meetings in December 2002 that it bothered him the Mariners hadn't called him for an interview. "Sometimes you don't fit into the plans; I never found out," he said. "I never talked to anybody. I thought I might have gotten a call. I heard it could have been attitude. I heard it could have been I didn't get along with management. I heard it could have been about the amount of money I never requested."

The Mariners met with heavy criticism in some circles, especially from the *Times*' Blaine Newnham, for having the arrogance not to give Baker the courtesy of a meeting before handing off their veteran team to a neophyte manager. Newnham wrote:

> The Mariners were willing to give Al Martin $5 million to play left field, but they won't spend $3.5 million on Baker? The club has got to be alert to the perception that it is cheap at all costs, that star-quality people only leave Seattle. Baker would engender tremendous excitement for next season, especially in the wake of Piniella's departure. Instead of ticket sales flagging, they might increase. All the Mariners have to do is spend some of that money they've collected as the second- or third-highest revenue-producing team in baseball, especially if they want to stay that way.

In Melvin, the Mariners had hired a "yes man" who was grateful to have a major-league managing job, would do his best with the players he was given, and wouldn't question or challenge management. The M's could be sure a rookie manager wouldn't complain if the team decided for a second straight year to cry poor at the trading deadline. After ten years dealing with the brash personality of Lou Piniella, this was the type of manager Seattle's management team wanted, but it was a big risk. Could the team continue its winning ways under Melvin?

Now that the M's had a new manager, there was more work to be done; Moyer, Olerud, and Dan Wilson were free agents and the team hoped it could come to a new agreement with Edgar Martinez. Martinez had played in just ninety-seven games in 2002 and the team wasn't going to exercise its $10 million option for 2003.

Meanwhile, as Gillick talked big, teasing fans about his desire to sign a No. 1 starter, a Mariners insider told the *Seattle Times*, "We're still trying to sign Jamie Moyer, and if we do that, we won't have any money left for one of those guys."

Moyer filed for free agency and, for a time, it appeared the M's might lose him because of management's insistence on limiting the contract to two years, but ultimately the deal got done. Moyer and the Mariners reached a compromise on a three-year, $15.5 million deal with a low base salary in the third year. The Mariners also re-signed Martinez (one year, $6 million), Olerud (two years, $15.4 million) and Wilson (two years, $8 million). Yet keeping all four veterans — with an average age of thirty-seven — came at a high price. They left little room in the team's budget for Gillick to acquire that No. 1 starter or help at other spots around the diamond.

If anyone thought the second-half collapse of 2002 would have an effect on Lincoln and how he chose to set the Mariners' budgets, he or she would have been mistaken. Despite that second-half collapse in a year when the club set a new attendance record, Lincoln increased the club's payroll by just $2 million for 2003. To top it off, the team decided to hike ticket prices for 2003 despite missing the playoffs in 2002. It would be the fifth consecutive season that ticket prices had gone up.

While the acquisition of Randy Winn upgraded the left-field spot, which had been a dead zone for much of the Mariners' history, it seemingly eliminated a couple of intriguing options for the '03 season. Hideki Matsui, nicknamed "Godzilla," a twenty-eight-year-old, power-hitting outfielder who'd hit .334 with fifty home runs for the Yomiuri Giants in 2002, was a free agent. Seattle could have used his big bat, but the M's normally reclusive owner, Hiroshi Yamauchi, announced in Japan on November 22 that the Mariners were not considering Matsui.

"We have already reinforced our outfielders, so we are not interested in Hideki Matsui," Yamauchi told the *Hochi Shimbun*. "We will not make him an offer." Matsui signed with the New York Yankees, where he hit .297 the next three years, averaging twenty-three home runs and 110 RBI per season.

Even with Winn in the fold, the M's could have found a spot for a power hitter like Matsui, but Ichiro's status with the team was likely a factor. Ichiro and Matsui had a feud dating over ten years back to their high school days, and Ichiro wasn't keen on sharing the Seattle spotlight with Matsui. Yamauchi rarely made announcements on behalf of the Mariners, but he knew of Ichiro's dislike for Matsui and perhaps wanted to send a message to the M's right-fielder that the owner had his back — that if Ichiro did not want his rival on the team, the owner would embarrass Matsui publicly by announcing that the Mariners had no interest in him.

Another outfielder the M's could have acquired that winter was Ken Griffey Jr. He'd battled injuries in his three years in Cincinnati and the Reds reportedly had called Seattle to see if the M's were interested in having him back. A reunion with Griffey, then thirty-three and still a productive hitter, might have added much needed power to Seattle's lineup and excited the team's fans. But Lincoln made it clear the Mariners had no interest.

Calling it "the story that wouldn't die," an annoyed Lincoln told the *Times* that he couldn't conceive of any circumstance in which Junior could return to the Mariners.

"We're very, very happy with the outfielders we've got. You can't have any better outfielders than the guys we have now," Lincoln said. "We wish Kenny well. He was instrumental in the Mariners getting in Safeco Field, and was a tremendous player for ten years. But he made a decision to play closer to home, and we moved on."

Without a significant increase in the team's budget, Gillick wasn't able to do much to improve the team for 2003, and Seattle went into the season with a club that was arguably weaker than the season before.

"The Mariners got spare parts this winter, but they needed more." Steve Kelley wrote in the *Times*. "They won more than ninety games again last season, but they didn't make the playoffs. They needed to spend more money to get better, and they didn't. The Mariners are still contenders. This is a veteran team that knows how to win. But the Mariners are getting older and the budget is as tight as Ebenezer Scrooge's fists. Mariners fans deserve more. The magic of SoDo Mojo makes for a great advertising campaign. But a roster shouldn't be built on a devout belief in magic."

Kelley wasn't excited, but new Manager Bob Melvin was. After his first meeting with Ichiro, he said "The first thing I noticed is how smart he is. He's very calculated, but easy to talk to. He was very receptive to what I had to say. Boy, it's going to be a pleasure to manage a guy like this. The expectation for this team is that the time is now. It's been that way for the last three or four years."

For the first time since 1994, the Mariners opened a season on the road. The M's originally were slated to open the '03 season in Japan, but that trip was canceled because of the war in Iraq. Since the M's were supposed to be in Japan, a WrestleMania event had been booked into Safeco Field for March 30. Seattle was shut out by Oakland ace Tim Hudson 5-0 as the M's lost for the fifth time in seven road openers.

The Mariners got off to a quick start in Melvin's first two months on the job, breaking off five different win streaks of four games or more, including an eight-gamer in early June. On June 5, after beating up on ex-Mariner Jose Mesa for three runs in the ninth inning of a 5-4 comeback win in Philadelphia, Seattle's record stood at 40-18. That was good enough for a winning percentage of .690 and a seven-game lead over Oakland in the A.L. West.

Howard Lincoln must have felt good at the time. All of the so-called prima donnas he could not tolerate were gone, but the Mariners owned the best record in baseball — despite having a rookie manager and a budget that hadn't allowed for impact additions for the '03 season.

It's likely that Lincoln never would feel quite so satisfied about the state of the Mariners again. From June 6 until July 28, three days before the annual trade deadline, the M's lost more games than they won and saw their division lead wither to three games.

2003 TOP PERFORMERS

Bret Boone, .294, 35 HR, 117 RBI

Ichiro Suzuki, .312, 13 HR, 62 RBI, 34 SB

Edgar Martinez, .294, 24 HR, 98 RBI

Jamie Moyer, 21-7, 3.27 ERA, 215 IP

Joel Pineiro, 16-11, 3.78 ERA, 211.2 IP

Fans and media cried out for the Mariners to make a trade to improve the club's struggling offense, which had hit the third-fewest home runs in the American League. But the Mariners cried poor once again, despite another season of incredible support at the box office. While attendance dipped slightly from 2002, the M's were still averaging more than forty-thousand fans a night. With all that cash coming in, surely Lincoln could have found a spare million or two just in the cushions of his couch.

Yet it was the same old story, with one slight change — Lincoln kept his mouth shut in 2003. While the team's chairman continued to rule the team with an iron fist, the comments of 2002 about needing to make a profit and not wanting to win the World Series weren't repeated. Perhaps someone convinced Lincoln that he sounded arrogant making such statements in a year in which the Mariners made a profit of $10.6 million. Regardless, nobody, not Pat Gillick and certainly not Melvin, was able to persuade Lincoln to authorize spending for a trade deadline acquisition in 2003.

A man much wiser than Lincoln, Albert Einstein, once said, "The definition of insanity is doing the same thing over and over again, and expecting different results." Was Einstein stating a general definition or prognosticating the path of the Seattle Mariners of the next millennium?

On July 20, Larry Stone of the *Seattle Times* interviewed Paul Beeston, who had been Gillick's boss in Toronto. Beeston said: "Pat would always make a trade to put the team over the top and he was making a statement. You're telling the team, 'We [the front office] are trying, too.'"

Stone wrote:

> "The players aren't the only group that sometimes needs to receive that message. The fans do, too. Especially fans who have paid increasingly hefty prices to fill Safeco Field...
>
> The Mariners, under the watch of Howard Lincoln, chairman and chief executive officer, cling zealously to their budgets, which is good business. But it's not such good business to leave fans with the impression they are unwilling to pay the price for a championship-caliber club, which Lincoln has done, rightly or wrongly, with various comments about the sanctity of the bottom line. In business, perception is reality. The Mariners, in the next few weeks, have a golden opportunity to change that perception. More important, however, they have an opportunity to give the team a boost heading into the stretch drive."

However, Lincoln wasn't listening. While the Mariners said all the right things in July of 2003 about trying to make a deal, the trade deadline revived an old refrain; Gillick made it clear that for the M's to pick up any salary, they'd have to trade equal salary in return. Seattle was reportedly looking to move its No. 1 starter, Freddy Garcia, who was making nearly $7 million that year, in order to add offensive help, but Garcia was having a miserable season, sporting an ERA over 5.00 in late July. No team was going to take on that kind of salary and give up the impact bat Seattle needed, making the possibility of a trade remote.

IF AT FIRST YOU DON'T SUCCEED...

Melvin said all the right things too. Six days before the July 31 deadline, he told a reporter, "I'm comfortable with the guys I have. We'll play the cards they give us."

A week before the trade deadline, Steve Kelley of the *Times* wrote: "This year, for the sake of the season, for the sake of their credibility in this town, for the sake of the forty-thousand loyalists who expect more, the Mariners have to learn from their history and make a move. The window is closing on the club's World Series potential. This surprise season shouldn't merely be about winning the West. The Mariners have to go for broke before their veteran team breaks. This season can't be Déjà Lou. The M's won't make the same mistake two seasons in a row? Will they?"

As the deadline neared, the players in the M's clubhouse wondered if management would make a move to get some help for the struggling team. Relief pitcher Jeff Nelson, asked by the *Times'* Larry Stone if the team needed a player for the second half, said, "I think we need one, if we have any thoughts of making the playoffs, and going further."

However, the Mariners didn't make an impact move at the trade deadline. They claimed to have tried to make a deal, but how hard they actually tried is questionable. Gillick wasn't even in Seattle on July 31; he was in Toronto packing his house for a move. It seemed to be strange timing for a baseball GM to be away from the office on what is typically the busiest trading day of the entire year. But Gillick knew what others didn't and probably realized without the authorization to add payroll, he wasn't likely to be active on July 31. Reading between the lines, Gillick appeared to be sending a message to the Mariner higher-ups: If they wouldn't let him take on payroll to make a trade, what was the point of even being in Seattle on the day of the trade deadline?

The M's three main rivals for a playoff spot in 2003 — Oakland, Boston and New York — all made aggressive acquisitions in the final forty-eight hours before the trade deadline, while Seattle again failed to make a move. The inaction didn't sit well in the Mariners clubhouse, and Nelson was the most vocal player.

"They tried? I'm sick and tired of 'tried,'" Nelson said. "They always say they tried, but other teams seem to do it. That's what the Yankees and Red Sox do. And we have the money, too. Heck, even Kansas City and Oakland and the White Sox do things, and they're smaller-market clubs than us. If I was a fan and having to pay these outrageous concession prices, I'd feel frustrated ... They deserve more than just, 'OK, we stood pat again.' Every year they say they're going to go out and get someone and they never do. I want to do everything we can to get in the playoffs. I care about right now, tonight and the rest of the season."

Mariner fans were angry too; fans behind first base at the August 1 game against Chicago held up a sign that read "Gillick Refuses to Lose," with "Lose" crossed out and replaced with "Win."

While the Mariners were never known for being quick to take action, they showed they could move quickly when they felt like it, shipping Nelson off to New York just five days after his critical comments. While the M's denied the move was meant to punish Nelson, claiming the trade was "a baseball move," it made little sense for the Mariners to strengthen a team they might have to face in the playoffs — if they could manage to get there.

Predictably, there were no playoffs for the Mariners in 2003, as the team faded in the second half, just as it had done the season before. A four-game sweep in Boston by the Red Sox in late August didn't help matters. While Seattle played .500 ball (27-27) after the trade deadline, the Oakland A's, buoyed by the July 30 addition of outfielder Jose Guillen, went 34-20 over the final two months to overtake the M's and win the A.L. West for the second straight season. Boston went 32-23 after the trade deadline to edge out Seattle for the Wild Card by two games.

It would be another long winter for Mariner fans.

Maury Wills managed just eighty-two games in the majors, all with the Mariners in 1980 and 1981.

Rene Lachemann led the 1982 Mariners to the team's best record, 76-86, in their first ten seasons, but it was his only full season managing in Seattle.

Dave Niehaus, the Mariners' radio and TV announcer for the club's first thirty-four seasons, was inducted into the broadcaster's wing of the Baseball Hall of Fame in 2008. He called 5,284 M's games before his passing in November 2010.

Rick "The Peanut Man" Kaminski tossed peanuts and entertained fans at the Kingdome and Safeco Field during the Mariners' first thirty-five seasons.

The Mariner Moose, shown here out of costume before a 2004 game, was introduced in 1990 as the M's first mascot.

Chuck Armstrong has been president and chief operating officer of the Seattle Mariners for most of the last thirty years.

Ken Griffey Jr., the Mariners' all-time leader in home runs, with 417, was named to the A.L. All-Star team for ten consecutive seasons before he was traded to Cincinnati in February 2000.

Ken Griffey Jr. and his dad high-five after Senior's home run against the Angels' Kirk McCaskill on September 14, 1990. Junior followed with a home run as the pair became the first father-and-son combo in major-league history to hit homers back to back.

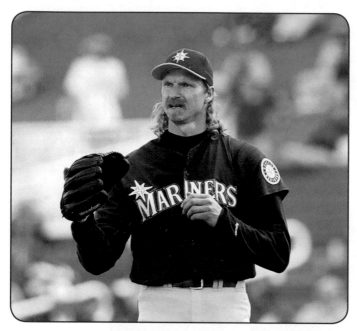

Randy Johnson, known to Mariner fans as The Big Unit, was the M's first Cy Young Award winner and won 130 games in his ten seasons in Seattle.

A seven-time All-Star who hit .300 in ten seasons and played his whole career in Seattle, Edgar Martinez had the biggest hit in Mariners history, a game-winning double that put the M's into the American League Championship Series in 1995.

One of the most popular players in M's history, Jay Buhner hit 307 home runs during his fourteen seasons in Seattle and was inducted into the Mariners Hall of Fame in 2004.

Lou Piniella compiled a record of 840 wins and 711 losses while managing the Mariners from 1993 to 2002.

Bobby Ayala, who pitched for Seattle from 1994 to 1998, is a lasting symbol of the Mariners' recurring bullpen failures of the mid to late 1990s.

Jeff Manto played in just twenty-one games with the Mariners in July and August 1996, but lives on in infamy as one of the worst players in club history.

Entering the 2012 season, Alex Rodriguez had hit 629 career home runs, sixth most all-time and one fewer than his retired former teammate, Ken Griffey Jr. Just 189 of Rodriguez's home runs came during his seven seasons (1994 to 2000) with Seattle.

Woody Woodward, the longest-tenured Mariners' general manager, acquired pitchers Randy Johnson and Jamie Moyer via trade, but also made three of the worst trades in M's history, dealing away Tino Martinez, David Ortiz, Derek Lowe, Jason Varitek, and Jeff Nelson for little in return.

Tino Martinez was traded to the New York Yankees in a cost-cutting move just fifty-one days after the Mariners' miracle 1995 season ended. Martinez averaged twenty-eight home runs and 115 RBI the next six seasons for New York, helping the Yankees win four World Series titles.

Catcher Jason Varitek, the Mariners' first-round pick in the 1994 amateur draft, was traded to Boston on July 31, 1997 and spent the next fourteen seasons with the Red Sox, seven as the team's captain.

In just the sixth game in Safeco Field history, Randy Johnson pitched a complete game shutout of the Mariners on July 20, 1999 as a member of the Arizona Diamondbacks. Johnson won Cy Young Awards in each of his first four seasons with Arizona. He retired after the 2009 season with 303 career victories.

The Mariners averaged ninety-eight wins per season in Pat Gillick's four years (2000 to 2003) as Seattle's general manager.

Mike Cameron, one of four players acquired in the February 2000 trade that sent Ken Griffey Jr. to Cincinnati, capably filled Junior's shoes in center field and hit eighty-seven home runs and drove in 344 runs in four seasons with the Mariners.

First-baseman John Olerud was the Mariners' biggest free-agent signing when the M's lured him away from the New York Mets with a three-year, $20 million contract in December 1999. Olerud averaged nineteen home runs and one-hundred RBI in his first three seasons with the Mariners.

Kazuhiro Sasaki was A.L. Rookie of the Year in 2000, when he saved thirty-seven games in his first year with the Mariners. He was an All-Star in 2001 and 2002 and holds the team's all-time saves record, saving 129 games in his four seasons with the M's.

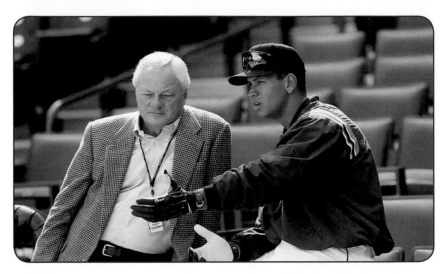

Alex Rodriguez emphasizes a point to team president Chuck Armstrong at Safeco Field in 2000, Rodriguez's final season with the Mariners.

Alex Rodriguez high-fives with Rickey Henderson after Henderson homered in his first at-bat as a Mariner in May 2000

Lou Piniella and veteran utilityman Mark McLemore hug after the Mariners clinched the A.L. Wild Card in Anaheim on the final day of the 2000 regular season.

Jay Buhner and Mike Cameron greet Rickey Henderson at home plate after Henderson scored the deciding run of the American League Division Series against the White Sox on October 6, 2000.

Ichiro Suzuki, pictured here in an M's uniform from the 1970s during a Turn Back the Clock game, was named Rookie of the Year and Most Valuable Player in 2001 and was named to the A.L. All-Star team in each of his first ten seasons with the Mariners. He set a new major league record for hits in a season in 2004, with 262.

Ichiro averaged thirty-eight stolen bases per year in his first eleven seasons (2001 to 2011) with the Mariners.

Bret Boone had the best season of his fourteen-year career in 2001, batting .331 with thirty-seven home runs and leading the American League with 141 RBI.

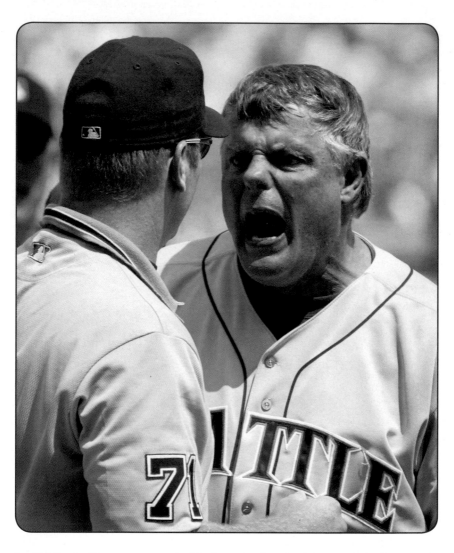

Lou Piniella takes his anger out on umpire Brian Runge just days after the 2002 trade deadline passed without the Mariners adding the hitter Piniella had asked for all season. Piniella left the Mariners at the end of the 2002 season.

Howard Lincoln has been chairman and CEO of the Seattle Mariners since late 1999.

Dan Wilson caught the most games, 1,287, in Mariner history during his twelve seasons in Seattle (1994 to 2005). His best year with the bat was 1996 when he batted .285 with eighteen home runs and eighty-three RBI and was named to the A.L. All-Star team.

Jamie Moyer posted a 145-87 record and a 3.97 ERA for the Mariners from 1996 to 2006, with his 145 wins the most in team history as of 2012 .

Freddy Garcia, one of three players acquired from Houston in the July 1998 trade that sent Randy Johnson to the Astros, went 76-50 with a 3.87 ERA in five and a half seasons with the Mariners.

Bill Bavasi is considered by many to be the worst general manager in Mariners' history. His ill-advised trades, free-agent signings, and draft selections set the franchise back for years. The M's finished in last place in four of his five years in Seattle.

Third-baseman Adrian Beltre signed the biggest free-agent contract in franchise history prior to the 2005 season, a five-year, $64 million deal. The slick-fielding Beltre won two Gold Gloves with the Mariners, but was not a good fit for Safeco Field, averaging .266 , twenty home runs, and seventy-nine RBI per year in his five seasons in Seattle.

In one of the worst trades in M's history, twenty-year-old shortstop Asdrubal Cabrera was traded to Cleveland in June 2006. Cabrera went on to become an All-Star with the Indians, smacking twenty-five home runs and driving in ninety-two runs in 2011.

Mike Hargrove won 192 games and lost 210 in two and a half seasons as Seattle's manager before abruptly resigning on July 1, 2007 with the Mariners in the middle of a seven-game winning streak.

Felix Hernandez, nicknamed King Felix before he reached the big leagues, pitched six full seasons in the majors before turning twenty-six. He won the A.L. Cy Young Award in 2010, but his best season probably came in 2009, when he went 19-5 with a 2.49 ERA.

Jack Zduriencik, hired as Mariners general manager in November 2008, was named Major League Executive of the Year in 2007 for his work as the Milwaukee Brewers' director of amateur scouting.

Ken Griffey Jr., who hit nineteen home runs in his return to the Mariners in 2009, is carried off the field by his Seattle teammates on the final day of the 2009 season.

Upon being hired to manage the Mariners in October 2010, Eric Wedge was reunited with Milton Bradley, a player he'd clashed with when he'd managed in Cleveland. The troubled Bradley was traded by the Indians shortly after showing up in the team's clubhouse wearing a T-shirt that said "Fuck Eric Wedge." Bradley would last just five weeks with the 2011 Mariners; he was released in early May after hitting .218.

Dustin Ackley, selected by the Mariners with the second overall pick in the 2009 amateur draft, reached the major leagues in mid-June 2011 and hit .273 with six home runs and thirty-six RBI in ninety games as a rookie.

The Mariners acquired twenty-two-year old catcher Jesus Montero from the Yankees in January 2012 in a four-player trade that sent right-handed starter Michael Pineda to New York.

Chapter 22

TEN ALL-TIME WORST MARINERS

1. JEFF MANTO (1996; .185 in 54 at-bats)

Manto, acquired from Boston in July of 1996, was supposed to be the solution to the M's third-base problems that season.

Lou Piniella had been searching for a fill-in since Russ Davis had gone down for the season in June with a broken leg. Piniella had even started Edgar Martinez at the hot corner in one game, but Martinez collided with catcher John Marzano and landed on the disabled list with broken ribs.

Manto, who arrived in Seattle sporting a heavy knee brace that Mariner scouts were unaware of, was so bad, with both bat and glove, that within a couple of weeks, right-fielder Jay Buhner offered to switch positions. "I could play over there," Buhner said. "I can pick it up. I'm not afraid to go over and try it if it will help the team."

Piniella didn't take Buhner up on the offer, but the desperate M's instead sent a twenty-year-old minor-league slugger, David Ortiz, to the Minnesota Twins for Dave Hollins, who would solidify the position for the final month of the '96 season.

2. STEVE TROUT (1988-89; 8-10, 7.40 ERA)

Trout came to Seattle from the Yankees in a trade prior to the '88 season. For $990,000 the M's got perhaps the wildest pitcher in team history. At the time, Trout was the team's highest-paid player.

Trout didn't make it out of the first inning of his Seattle debut, walking five batters, throwing two wild pitches and making an error. And he didn't improve much after that, posting a 7.40 ERA over the next year and a half. Trout's poor command prompted the *Seattle Times* to invite fans to call in with advice for the struggling pitcher.

M's pitching coach Billy Connors told the *Times:* "I'd call myself except I'm looking for ideas. Never mind calling the newspaper; if anyone has any good ideas, call me."

3. MACKEY SASSER (1993-94; .214, 1 HR in 192 at-bats)

While Sasser had once been a good-hitting catcher with the Mets, he'd developed an anxiety disorder and couldn't make the routine throw back to the pitcher.

The Mariners, figuring the problem would go away once Sasser was away from the bright lights of the big city, signed him to a two-year, $1 million contract. The problem didn't improve and Sasser played in the outfield instead, but he could no longer hit and was released one month into the '94 season. That $1 million would have been much better spent on Omar Vizquel, who was traded after the '93 season because the M's couldn't fit his $2.35 million salary into their budget for 1994.

4. CARLOS SILVA (2008-2009; 5-18, 6.81 ERA)

Silva, the lucky recipient of the largest free-agent contract ever given to a pitcher by the Mariners, rewarded the M's with a 4-15 record and a 6.46 ERA in the first year of the contract, leading the team to suggest that he might lose some weight off his 285-pound frame in the offseason. Silva complied, coming to spring training thirty pounds lighter in 2009, prompting the first-year Manager Don Wakamatsu, to say, "He looks like somebody cut him in half."

The slimmed-down Silva would suffer shoulder inflammation and make only eight appearances in 2009, and managed to put up worse numbers than he had the year before. Silva was traded to the Cubs for Milton Bradley the following winter in a swap of bad contracts that didn't work out for either team. It was a complete waste of $48 million.

5. SCOTT SPIEZIO (2004-2005; .198, 11 HRs in 414 at-bats)

Bill Bavasi's first big signing as Mariners GM was a disaster. Spiezio hit just .215 in the first year of a three-year contract. He was much worse in the second year, hitting poorly enough (.064) to get released with more than a year left on his contract and more than $4 million owed to him.

The Mariners should probably avoid signing former Angels in the future; in addition to Spiezio, Jarrod Washburn, Jeff Weaver, and Chone Figgins have all been disasters in Seattle.

6. HORACIO RAMIREZ (2007; 8-7, 7.16 ERA)

The soft-tossing Ramirez cost the M's stud reliever Rafael Soriano in an offseason trade because GM Bill Bavasi was desperate for starting pitching in 2007, but nobody should be this desperate.

Bavasi, unable to admit his mistake, tendered Ramirez a contract for 2008, costing the M's another $500,000 when he was released during spring training. Even worse, with the club needing to replace Soriano in its bullpen in 2007, they rushed their first-round pick from the previous June's draft, Brandon Morrow, to the majors instead of allowing him to develop as a starter in the minors.

7. ROB JOHNSON (2007-2010; .200, 5 HR in 474 at-bats; 18 passed balls).

The M's had high hopes for Johnson, the club's fourth-round pick in the 2004 draft, but he probably shouldn't have ever made the big leagues. He couldn't catch the ball, piling up big passed-ball numbers at every minor-league stop, including twenty-one in ninety games at Tacoma in 2008. Worse, he couldn't hit either, batting a dismal .188 as Seattle's regular backstop in 2010.

8. LEE TINSLEY (1993, 1997; .191, 0 HR in 141 at-bats)

Tinsley hit .158 in nineteen at-bats for Lou Piniella's Mariners in 1993. Duly impressed, the M's brought Tinsley back to be their starting left-fielder four years later, but he was released in September 1997 after hitting just .197. Continuing their Tinsley obsession, the club hired him as a coach for the 2009-10 seasons, but he probably wasn't very good at that either.

9. ANTHONY VASQUEZ (2011; 1-6, 8.90 ERA)

I'm not sure what the Mariners were thinking when they gave Vasquez seven late-season starts in 2011. While the twenty-five-year-old left-hander had put up decent numbers in the minors, he wasn't ready for prime time.

His fastball topped out at 85 mph and he didn't have the command to get away with it. He was hammered again and again, allowing forty-six hits, thirteen of them home runs in twenty-nine innings and infamously became the first major-league pitcher in seventy-two years to give up more than ten home runs and allow as many home runs as the number of batters he struck out.

10. BOBBY AYALA (1994-1998; 27-26, 4.88 ERA)

It's simply unexplainable how the Mariners gave Ayala as many chances, as they did, keeping him around for nearly three years *after* he'd punched out a window at the Chicago Westin in April 1996. He spent the next two months getting paid to be on the disabled list for his self-inflicted injury. At the time Ayala was facing drunk-driving charges.

While the M's traded away or lost better relief pitchers in Jeff Nelson, Mike Jackson, and Bill Risley during this period, they stuck with Ayala. Ayala was traded to the Expos in spring training 1999, but the M's had to pay two-thirds of his $1.8 million salary. Ayala, who'd stopped talking to the media in Seattle, didn't talk to the media in Montreal either and quickly wore out his welcome in a second country.

Chapter 23

QUICK DESCENT INTO LAST PLACE

As the disappointing '03 season came to a close, change was in the air in Seattle. Just two days after the last game of the year, GM Pat Gillick resigned his post after four seasons on the job. At the news conference announcing his departure, Gillick said, "I've had four kicks at the cat, and we couldn't get over the hump. Maybe it's time for someone else to give it a try and see if they can get over the hump."

While Gillick acted the part of the good soldier, not outwardly disparaging his bosses for failing to provide the funds necessary to make trade-deadline additions in his final two seasons, his frustration was evident. If ownership wasn't interested in doing what it took to win a championship, there was little sense for him to remain with a team whose core players were aging. Gillick knew it was time to move on and let someone else preside over the team's inevitable decline.

While his departure was called a retirement, those close to the sixty-six-year-old Gillick knew he wasn't the retiring type. Surely he'd resurface with another team when the right opportunity came along. After two years as a "consultant" for the Mariners, Gillick took over as the Phillies general manager after the '05 season. The championship that had eluded him in Seattle became reality in 2008, his third season in charge of Philadelphia's baseball operations. It was his third World Series title as a general manager, cementing his status as a Hall of Fame executive. Gillick would be enshrined in Cooperstown in 2011.

But what of the Mariners? They'd had significant success during Gillick's four seasons, but hadn't given him the resources to get "over the hump." Would the team give its next general manager the necessary resources? More important, would the team's next general manager be as sharp as Gillick and be able to maximize the resources he'd be given?

The Mariners interviewed several candidates to replace Gillick, including Mike Port, Omar Minaya, and in-house candidates Lee Pelekoudas and Benny Looper. One candidate the M's didn't talk to was Oakland GM Billy Beane; Seattle asked for permission to interview Beane, but the M's division rival quickly shot that down in a formal statement: "The A's have no interest in permitting Beane to speak to the Mariners about the position, for obvious reasons, nor does he have interest in pursuing the position."

The Mariners ultimately hired Bill Bavasi, son of legendary Brooklyn Dodgers GM Buzzie Bavasi, on November 7, 2003. The forty-five-year-old Bavasi had spent sixteen years with the Angels, including an undistinguished six years as their general manager, before resigning under pressure at the end of the '99 season. Since then Bavasi had worked as the farm director for the Dodgers.

While nobody knew it at the time, the hiring of Bavasi would set the Seattle Mariners franchise back for years.

Even before Bavasi came on board, the organization had two moves it was anxious to make: signing free-agent outfielder Raul Ibanez and jettisoning shortstop Carlos Guillen. Ibanez, released by Seattle in 2000 after two seasons as a part-timer, had become a solid hitter with Kansas City, averaging twenty-one home runs and ninety-six RBI with the Royals in 2002-03. But the Mariners were so eager to bring Ibanez back that they signed him on November 18, three weeks before the deadline for Kansas City to offer him arbitration. The Royals had indicated they weren't going to offer Ibanez arbitration, so by not waiting, the M's lost their first-round pick in 2004.

While Guillen had done an adequate job in three seasons since taking over for Alex Rodriguez, he wasn't a star and the team was down on him for off-field reasons. The team reportedly believed that Guillen was a bad influence on fellow Venezuelan Freddy Garcia. In June 2002, Guillen had gotten a drunk-driving citation in Clyde Hill, a Seattle suburb, and the feeling of Seattle's management was that with Guillen gone, Garcia might not spend as many nights in the bars in Belltown. While Garcia didn't need Guillen around to stay out late drinking and carousing, the Mariners were determined to rid themselves of the shortstop anyway.

Seattle's ideal plan was to sign free-agent shortstop Miguel Tejada and trade the skilled but fragile Guillen. Tejada, who later revealed that Seattle was his first choice, had averaged thirty-one home runs and 116 RBI from 2000 to 2003. The Mariners' initial offer of three years and $24 million was far from a winner; Tejada wanted more dollars and more years. While the M's eventually increased their offer to Tejada to four years, $40 million, they were outbid by the Baltimore Orioles, who signed Tejada to a six-year deal for $72 million.

Days later, the team turned to the trade market for a shortstop and had a deal completed that would have sent Guillen to Cleveland for thirty-six-year-old former Mariner Omar Vizquel. Vizquel, a nine-time Gold Glove winner who had last played for the M's in 1993, wanted to return to Seattle and told the Indians the only team he'd waive his trade clause for would be the Mariners. But he failed Seattle's physical and the deal was called off.

Still anxious to be rid of Guillen, Seattle signed free-agent shortstop Rich Aurilia in early January and traded Guillen to Detroit the same day. The two players the M's received from the Tigers, utilityman Ramon Santiago and minor-league infielder Juan Gonzalez, combined to play in just twenty-seven games with Seattle. Swapping out Guillen for Aurilia turned out to be a disaster. Aurilia was shaky in the field, hit just .246, and was discarded halfway through his first season in Seattle. Meanwhile, Guillen, who essentially had been given away, became a three-time All-Star with the Tigers, reaching career highs in average (.318), home runs (20) and RBI (97) in '04.

While the shortstop issue had seemingly been figured out, Bavasi had a lot more work to do to put together the 2004 team. Center-fielder Mike Cameron, utilityman Mark McLemore, and relievers Arthur Rhodes and Armando Benitez, who had been acquired from the Yankees that August in the trade that sent Nelson back to New York, all were allowed to leave as free agents. Additionally, third base was a major issue; Jeff Cirillo had been a bust in two years in Seattle, hitting .234 with just eight home runs. The M's needed to find a new third-baseman and they needed to find a team to take Cirillo. Even though Cirillo was owed nearly $14 million for the next two seasons, the M's were determined to trade him, even if they had to pay all of his salary.

Bavasi made his first signing on December 19 and it was a player he knew well from Anaheim, third-baseman Scott Spiezio. The deal appeared reasonable at the time, three years for $9 million, but Spiezio didn't manage even one solid season for Seattle, hitting .215 in 2004 and losing his starting job. He batted just fifty-one times for the M's in 2005 (and hit .064) before being released midway through the season, still owed about $4 million.

Soon after, Bavasi sent Cirillo to San Diego for two overpaid Padres, pitcher Kevin Jarvis and catcher Wiki Gonzalez, also acquiring pinch-hitter Dave Hansen in the deal. While the M's managed to rid themselves of Cirillo, they wouldn't save any of the $13.7 million he was owed, as they took on the pricey contracts of Jarvis (paid $4.25 million to post an 8.31 ERA in eight games in 2004) and Gonzalez (paid $2 million to spend all of 2004 in the minors and another $2.1 million to bat forty-seven times for the M's the next year) and sent the Padres about $5 million to even out the difference in the players' salaries.

The status of two key members of the Mariners' pitching staff, No. 1 starter Garcia and closer Sasaki was up in the air in mid-December. Garcia, who'd earned $6.875 million in 2003 had had a subpar season (12-14 with a 4.51 ERA), but he'd defeated the M's in arbitration the previous season and the club didn't want a repeat. The Mariners' plan was to non-tender him (not offer him a contract for the '04 season, which would have made him a free agent) if a deal could not be struck before the date to offer arbitration. While non-tendering Garcia would free up some cash, it would also have left a gaping hole in the M's starting rotation. Fortunately the M's and Garcia were able to reach agreement on a contract — for the same $6.875 million salary he'd played for in 2003 — about two hours before the arbitration deadline.

Sasaki's status was muddy because the team wasn't happy with him. The thirty-four-year-old reliever had averaged forty saves a season his first three years in Seattle, but had missed more than two months of the '03 season with broken ribs. The official explanation was that the injury had occurred when he fell while carrying a suitcase up a flight of stairs. Nobody really believed that story. It was learned later he'd hurt himself practicing pro wrestling moves while drinking. A rumor surfaced that Sasaki would go back to Japan and forfeit the $9.5 million remaining on his contract for 2004, but was denied by the Mariners and Sasaki in December. Regardless, the M's felt they needed some insurance and signed left-handed reliever Eddie Guardado to a three-year, $13 million contract that month. Guardado had saved eighty-six games the previous two seasons for Minnesota.

Sasaki's departure became reality when the closer announced the following month that he would forego the last year of his contract and return to Japan. The move should have freed up $9.5 million in payroll flexibility for the Mariners, money that could have been spent on a free agent still on the market. Two such free agents were available in future Hall of Famers Ivan "Pudge" Rodriguez and Greg Maddux, but the Mariners didn't get involved in bidding for either player, nor did they make serious efforts at trading for Chicago's Magglio Ordonez or Kansas City's Carlos Beltran, two impact hitters whose salaries might now fit into the team's '04 budget. But according to Bavasi, the M's could not spend the dollars saved by Sasaki's departure until Sasaki was officially an ex-Mariner and the procedural maneuvers to finalize the termination of Sasaki's contract might take weeks.

Another big bat the Mariners could have acquired early in 2004 was their former shortstop, Alex Rodriguez. After three years in Texas, A-Rod was on the trading block, with Rangers owner Tom Hicks willing to pay millions of dollars of Rodriguez's salary for him to play elsewhere. A deal that would have sent Rodriguez to Boston for Manny Ramirez fell through and he ended up landing in New York on February 16, traded for Alfonso Soriano, with Texas paying $67 million of the $179 million remaining on the superstar shortstop's contract.

Reached for comment after Rodriguez had been traded to the Yankees, Chuck Armstrong told the *Times'* Bob Finnigan that the Mariners would have tried to reacquire Rodriguez, "but we had no idea Tom Hicks would take on that much money. It's not even $16 million a year … for the best player in the game."

The Mariners could certainly have gotten involved, but why hadn't they? Seattle needed a shortstop that winter and they could have afforded A-Rod's contract with the money saved from Sasaki's departure. All it might have taken was a phone call or two to find out that Hicks was willing to pay that much of Rodriguez's salary. Surely Armstrong (or Bavasi) had the Rangers' number. But a Rodriguez return never had a chance because the Mariners top executives couldn't be bothered to do their due diligence and make that phone call.

The *Times'* Blaine Newnham wrote that Sasaki's decision to go back to Japan presented the Mariners with "a wonderful and unique opportunity" to improve the team.

"For Mariners management, this is a dream come true," Newnham wrote. "If, of course, they don't turn it into a nightmare. Beware. We're all counting, keeping track of the $9.5 million, not happy if it simply extends a contract here and there, or is held over for a trade this summer that never gets made."

Armstrong told Newnham, "This will get us flexibility," presumably referring to the ability to add payroll at the '04 trade deadline.

Newnham countered, "The fans don't want flexibility. They want hope. They want a bat in the lineup that energizes them and strikes fear in the opposing pitcher. They are looking for something that will neutralize the signing of Vladimir Guerrero by the Anaheim Angels." The twenty-eight-year-old Guerrero, who the Mariners claimed they couldn't afford, had signed a five-year, $70 million deal that winter with the Angels, who'd also signed two other impact free agents, Bartolo Colon and Jose Guillen.

There would be no need for flexibility at the '04 trade deadline though, as the Mariners quickly fell out of the A.L. West race and were twelve and a half games out of first place by mid-May. While most fans assumed that the M's could take the money saved on Sasaki's contract and add it to the payroll for 2005, the team made it clear that the payroll savings would not carry over from year to year.

The poor start didn't stop the M's from giving Manager Bob Melvin a one-year contract extension on May 4. The timing was odd, since the team wasn't playing well and Melvin didn't seem to have the fire necessary to inspire his players to perform better. But the M's apparently thought the extension would ease the pressure on the team, as Howard Lincoln told the media, "This sends a strong signal of support from us. This should silence any murmurs. He's our horse, and we're riding him all the way."

Regardless of Lincoln's unwarranted show of support, the horse (Melvin) would be sent to the glue factory at the end of the season, with the M's having to pay him $550,000 not to manage the team in 2005.

2004 TOP PERFORMERS

Ichiro Suzuki, .372, 8 HR, 60 RBI, 36 SB

Bret Boone, .251, 24 HR, 83 RBI

Raul Ibanez, .304, 16 HR, 62 RBI

Bobby Madritsch, 6-3, 3.27 ERA, 88 IP

Eddie Guardado, 2-2, 2.78 ERA, 18 saves

After a 1-0 loss to Minnesota in early May, a frustrated Bavasi told John Hickey of the *Seattle Post-Intelligencer*, "They (the Mariner players) don't play offense. They either don't know how to play offense or they can't." But insulting the players wouldn't work either, and the M's lost nine of ten from May 9-19 to fall to 13-26, the second-worst record in baseball.

With hopes for contention virtually over, attention turned to whether Melvin would survive the season (one betting service had installed him as a 6-1 favorite to be the first manager fired in 2004) and when the M's might trade Garcia, who was pitching like an ace again, going seven or more innings in six of his first seven starts of the '04 season.

How could a team that had averaged ninety-eight wins the previous four seasons turn into one of the worst teams in baseball overnight? The biggest factor was the change in general managers from Gillick to Bavasi. Gillick was one of the top GMs in the game, while it's likely that Bavasi would never have gotten a top job in baseball if not for his family connections.

Virtually every decision Bavasi made following the '03 season turned out to be a disaster, but the decision not to make a serious effort to keep Gold Glove center-fielder Mike Cameron hurt the M's more than they expected. The thirty-one-year-old Cameron, a fan favorite in Seattle, wanted to stay, but the best deal the M's would offer him was one year for $5 million, a significant pay cut from the $7.4 million he'd earned in 2003. The loyal Cameron would spurn the advances of division rival Oakland A's and sign a three-year deal with the New York Mets for $19.5 million.

"I wanted to be back. I tried hard to get back," Cameron told the *Seattle Times*. "In the end, it was kind of crazy, really different than I expected; it's like your dad tells you to get the hell out of the house."

In addition to his defense, Cameron was a solid run producer, driving in eighty-six runs per year from 2000 to 2003. But the M's were obsessed with his strikeouts, which averaged 153 a year those four seasons, and decided they'd be better off without him. But the team's new center-fielder, Randy Winn, didn't have the same tools as Cameron; he couldn't cover the ground, often got off to bad jumps, and had a poor throwing arm. He also didn't have the power of Cameron, who smacked twenty or more home runs in five of the next six seasons.

The deals for Spiezio and Aurilia hampered the club. Neither player produced at even a minimally acceptable level nor did the team have young players ready to step in at those positions. The M's other starting infielders similarly declined. Olerud hadn't had a good year in 2003 (.269 with 10 HRs) and fell off more in 2004 before being released in late July. Boone's numbers also dropped significantly from 2003. Meanwhile, the skills of forty-one-year-old Edgar Martinez had eroded. After hitting .294 with 24 homers and 98 RBI in 2003, he hit just .263 with 12 homers and 63 RBI and retired at the end of the season.

The struggles of these five aging players (average age thirty-five) contributed to the M's producing some of the worst offensive statistics in the American League in 2004. The club scored just 698 runs, the fewest in the league and fewest by a Seattle club in a full season since 1992. The Mariners' total of 136 home runs was also the fewest in the league.

With the M's out of contention early, they didn't have to wait until late July to trade Garcia, dealing him to the White Sox on June 27. Four other teams — the Yankees, Mets, Dodgers, and Red Sox — all made bids for Seattle's ace, with the Mets dropping out after refusing to part with third-base prospect David Wright. The M's were thought to be seeking second-base prospect Robinson Cano from the Yankees, but ultimately made the deal with Chicago and received catcher Miguel Olivo and two minor-leaguers, outfielder Jeremy Reed and infielder Mike Morse.

Attendance at Safeco Field dropped by more than three-hundred thousand in 2004, but nearly three million fans still came out to see a team that lost thirty-six more games than they won. While there would be no pennant race in Seattle in 2004, at least there was a good reason for fans to come to Safeco that September; Ichiro was challenging the all-time record for hits in a season, 257, set by George Sisler in 1920. Ichiro would break Sisler's record on October 1 at Safeco and finish the season with 262 hits. He also won his second batting title, hitting .372.

With the Mariners suffering through their worst season since 1983, some crucial decisions would need to be made in the offseason. Those decisions would shape the team's path for the remainder of the decade.

Chapter 24

THE MAN AT THE TOP

Mariners Chairman and CEO Howard Lincoln, who operates as the de facto owner of the team, had a critical decision to make in July 2002. His team had been in first place continuously since the first week of the season. But the team had issues.

Edgar Martinez, the team's thirty-nine-year-old designated hitter had missed most of the first half of the season with a serious hamstring injury and the club's new third-baseman, Jeff Cirillo, wasn't making the adjustment to Safeco Field.

Manager Lou Piniella and General Manager Pat Gillick had told Lincoln repeatedly in the first half of the '02 season that the Mariners offense was a bat short and the team needed help to withstand the challenge of A.L. West rivals Oakland and Anaheim. Piniella and Gillick were both baseball lifers, each having spent more than thirty-five years in the game. Both had won multiple World Series titles.

By contrast, Lincoln was in his third year running the Mariners. He'd been appointed chairman and CEO in late 1999 largely because he had run the Nintendo Company's U.S. operations for many years and was trusted by the company's president, Hiroshi Yamauchi. Lincoln had no World Series titles on his resumé.

The Mariners were flying high at the time. The club had made the playoffs in each of the previous two seasons, setting an American League record in 2001 with 116 wins. The team had achieved unprecedented success despite the departures of Griffey, Rodriguez, and Johnson from 1998 to 2000. The overconfident Lincoln must have been feeling pretty good about the job he was doing.

However, the '02 team had already started to fade. Its six-and-a-half-game division lead had shrunk to a single game by late July. The baseball professionals kept telling Lincoln that the team needed help before the July 31 trade deadline to stay in the race. The other teams competing with Seattle for a playoff spot that year were expected to add players and the M's were likely to miss the postseason if they didn't improve the team. But

Lincoln kept telling Piniella and Gillick that the team had no room in its budget to acquire an additional player at the trade deadline.

Piniella knew his team and he knew the team needed another bat. He pushed and pushed, and Lincoln pushed back. One meeting between Piniella and Lincoln was said to have gotten "loud."

Lincoln wasn't afraid to deal with the payroll issue head on in the Seattle media. He had dealt with many challenges in his years at Nintendo and he'd deal with these baseball challenges the same way, as if it was a decision about video game equipment. He'd handle Piniella and Gillick as he'd enforced his will on managers at Nintendo. They'd have to respect him because he was the boss. If they didn't like it, they could quit — and they soon would.

Yet the baseball business is different than any other business. When questioned about the budget and the team's need for offensive help, Lincoln would lecture the media that he needed to run the team as a business and that the business needed to make a profit.

But how much profit did the team need to make? In 2001, the Mariners had the second-highest revenue in baseball, reporting a profit of $15.47 million. Piniella and Gillick weren't asking for an additional $10 million or even $5 million at the trade deadline. Two million dollars probably would have been sufficient, with the team responsible for only the last two months of the new player's salary. Slugging outfielders like Brian Giles, Carlos Lee, and Cliff Floyd all were available on the trade market that summer.

Lincoln's answer was still a resounding "no." One of his recurring themes was "like any good business we stick to a budget." But what "good business" would do nothing of substance when a $10 million asset like Edgar Martinez was hurt and unable to produce? If a factory had a $10 million machine that broke down and couldn't be repaired for three months of critical production, wouldn't "any good business" do what was necessary to replace that machine's production by renting or purchasing a replacement, even if it were a less costly model?

Just days before the 2002 trade deadline, Lincoln made his infamous comments about it not being the team's goal to win the World Series. Much to his chagrin, those comments would follow him for the next decade. Years later he would have the nerve to question the Seattle media as to why it was so difficult for Mariner fans to believe that he really did want to win the World Series. It's as if Lincoln thought he could change the fans' perceptions merely by insincerely claiming that he hadn't really meant what he'd said in 2002. Or maybe he was just hoping the fans would have forgotten the comments with time. But Mariner fans will probably never forget.

Lincoln couldn't have made his point much clearer to the team's customers had he screamed it from the rooftops near Safeco Field. His message was loud and clear to the Mariner fans who were filling the stadium night after night in 2002. The message was this: the Seattle Mariners don't care about you. We're here to make money. While winning the World Series might be the goal of our customers, that's not of primary importance to us. We're not in the baseball business. We're in the business of making money.

What Lincoln hadn't realized was baseball was much different from the video game business. In baseball, your customers are the team's fans, the people who spend their hard-earned dollars buying expensive tickets, pricey concessions, and overpriced beer. The fans that live and die with every win and loss could see, just as Piniella and Gillick did, that the team needed help. These fans didn't want to hear that a team that had reported a profit of more than $15 million the year before couldn't spend a little extra to make sure the team was ready to compete in the second half of the season.

As July 31 neared, predictably, the M's main competitors all made major trades to fill holes. Pressure to make a trade began to mount, from the M's clubhouse, the local newspapers, and angry baseball fans on local sports radio station, KJR 950. One anonymous Mariner player told Bob Finnigan of the *Times*, "Maybe our owners have to realize what it feels like to sit and do nothing, while Oakland and other contending teams go out and do things." A National League scout told Finnigan, "Seattle looks a bit tired. The offense has been inconsistent, with little depth for patching up, so the pitching has had to work in thin-edge situations too much, and you may see that taking a toll, too."

The pleas fell on deaf ears. Lincoln had made his decision.

Predictably, the Mariners faded in the second half in 2002 and watched as Oakland and Anaheim jumped over them and made the playoffs, with the Angels winning the World Series for the first time.

After the '02 season, Piniella, who'd been called out by Lincoln for innocuous comments he'd made to a Houston reporter about trade deadline moves, had had enough of Lincoln and left to manage the lowly Tampa Bay Devil Rays. Lincoln had now managed to remove another "superstar" from the Mariners mix in Piniella, who was considered among the best managers in the game.

Lincoln and his executive team made a classic blunder in replacing Lou; they picked the single attribute they liked least in Piniella — a willingness to disagree with ownership's decrees — and chose a replacement who, if nothing else, would be submissive. Submissive management rarely makes for strong results, and the M's choice, the intelligent, but inexperienced and pliant Bob Melvin, would preside over the team's hasty decline on the field.

The decline, as Lincoln would point out, was not yet in the bottom line. Even with the second-half fade, the Mariners set an attendance record in 2002, averaging 43,740 fans per game that year. The team reported a profit of $10.6 million for 2002. The team could have acquired midseason help and still made a profit. And if the team had made the playoffs and possibly the World Series, there'd be millions more in 2002 profits and increased ticket sales for years to come.

Most people who own sports teams don't expect to make an operating profit running the team. They know the big money is made when they sell the franchise. The Mariners' current ownership purchased the team in 1992 for $100 million. The last valuation by *Forbes* magazine occurred in March 2011, with *Forbes* estimating that the M's were worth $449 million at that time. More recently, the judge in minority-owner Chris Larson's divorce case placed the value of the Mariner franchise at $641 million in December 2011. While that's not a guarantee that if the team went up for sale tomorrow they'd get that price, it's clear that whenever the current ownership group sells the team it's going to make hundreds of millions of dollars in profit.

Good leaders learn from their mistakes, but Lincoln didn't, and he refused to add payroll again at the '03 trade deadline. Once again the team spent much of the first half of the season in first place, but its lead, which was eight games in mid-June, had been cut to three games by late July. After the team did another second-half fade and finished out of the playoffs yet again, another superstar — Pat Gillick — departed at the end of that year. For Gillick's replacement, the M's hired someone with more experience than Bob Melvin, but again made sure to hire a man who wouldn't make waves.

That man, Bill Bavasi, didn't have the same eye for talent and wasn't very skilled at putting a roster together. Bavasi had figured prominently in Mariners history; he was the GM of the Angels team that blew a thirteen-game lead to the Mariners in 1995. Yet, despite year after year of terrible trades and awful free agent signings, Lincoln allowed Bavasi to keep his job for five years, all the while decimating the organization by trading away good young players and signing declining players to overpriced contracts.

When Bavasi was finally fired in June 2008 the Mariners were on their way to a record-breaking year — but not in a good way. That team was the first in baseball history to lose more than one-hundred games with a payroll over $100 million.

The budget issue arose again in 2010 when the GM who succeeded Bavasi, Jack Zduriencik, made a bold trade for Cliff Lee, one of the game's top pitchers. Lee had just one year left on his contract, so it seemed imperative that the team try to win in the one season they had him. Yet, after cutting payroll by nearly $20 million in 2009, the team cut payroll by another $10 million in 2010. Thus, Zduriencik didn't have the money for a suitable DH or a left-fielder; the team collapsed and finished 61-101, the worst record in the American League.

Unlike Bavasi, Zduriencik had a keen eye for talent, having drafted and developed several All-Star players as the scouting director for the rebuilt Milwaukee Brewers. But it seemed that Lincoln couldn't tell a skilled general manager from a bad one. Since Bavasi had spent the team's money on bad players, Lincoln apparently decided he wasn't going to allow Zduriencik to spend the money needed to put a solid team on the field.

The trouble with Lincoln and others who aren't baseball people is that in the non-baseball businesses they've run, success is all about image and perception. And while perception is important in baseball, it's not everything. The team's manager can't do a post-game interview after losing a game and tell the media that the team won. And he can't tell the media that a player hitting .180 is actually a .300 hitter. In baseball, the results are out in the open for everyone to see.

The biggest problem with the Seattle Mariners is accountability. Lincoln, unlike top executives with other major-league teams, has never been in danger of losing his job. This lack of accountability exists because the person who might make the decision to remove Lincoln, Hiroshi Yamauchi, is an absentee owner in Japan who's never attended a Mariner game. By all accounts, Yamauchi doesn't have much interest in baseball, so it doesn't necessarily concern him if the team loses as long as it makes money and supports the community. Yamauchi's apparent thought process: If the team makes money, if the M's are good-will ambassadors at local schools and hospitals, then it must be a good investment and the people running it must be doing a good job.

Based on those measures, Yamauchi must think Lincoln has done an incredible job — from 2001 to 2007 the team reported profits of $97.69 million. Yet the team has been one of baseball's biggest losers over the past eight years, finishing in last place six times from 2004 to 2011. Because Lincoln wasn't flexible with his budgets when he had a chance to make a difference, he's repeatedly led the Mariners into a deep hole, one which has proven difficult to escape.

But there is hope, even if it might be three or four years away. Lincoln turned seventy-two years old in February 2012 and should be thinking about retirement.

Chapter 25

SPENDING MONEY IS
NOT ALWAYS THE CURE

The final weeks of the '04 season were filled with media speculation about the status of Manager Bob Melvin, but Bavasi refused to comment. His standard reply was, "I refuse to entertain the question. I'm not about to discuss anyone's job status in public — Bob's, mine, or yours."

Melvin talked to the *Times'* Larry Stone during the last week of the season about his job status.

"What can I do by worrying about it?" he said. "It's such a negative situation. I understand when people write that (that he should be fired). And I understand that when there's a death like has happened here, someone's got to die. Whether or not I'm the guy that's going to be knocked out because of it, I don't really think it's in my control."

Melvin was correct. Less than twenty-four hours after the end of the '04 season, he was fired at a meeting at Safeco Field. At a news conference later in the day, Bavasi said "I think this is not to lay the blame for the number of losses right at Bob's doorstop. That's not our intention. But to go forward we thought a change was in order."

The Mariners didn't waste any time finding a new manager, hiring fifty-four-year-old Mike Hargrove on October 20, just sixteen days after firing Melvin.

Among the candidates interviewed at the time was Angels bench-coach Joe Maddon, who would be hired to manage the Tampa Bay Rays in 2006 and took that team to the World Series two years later.

The more experienced Hargrove had had significant success with the Cleveland Indians in the mid-90s, winning the A.L. Central five years in a row and taking that team to two World Series appearances. More recently, however, he had managed the Baltimore Orioles from 2000 to 2003 and finished in fourth place in all four seasons. In 2002, his penultimate season in Baltimore, the team collapsed, losing thirty-two of its last thirty-six games.

One of the first questions Hargrove faced at his introductory news conference was about Ichiro, the Mariners' perennial All-Star outfielder. Hargrove had managed a touring MLB team in Japan in 1998 and was asked at the time what he thought of the Japanese outfielder's chances to play in the U.S., and had infamously said "it would be impossible for him to be a regular player." Hargrove addressed the six-year-old quotes tersely, admitting that he had been wrong.

With an experienced manager hired, the Mariners organization now could focus on the future. After finishing with the third-worst record in baseball in 2004, the M's management team had a big decision to make. It had essentially two options.

One would be to rebuild, going with young players and trading veterans like Bret Boone and Jamie Moyer. That option would be designed to deliver greater long-term success, but the team's fans would have to be patient — the M's might not contend for a couple of seasons.

The second option was to go big on the free-agent market and try and buy their way back into contention. But the American League West, save for Seattle, was at its strongest during this period. While the M's were losing ninety-nine games in 2004, the other three teams in the division each won at least eighty-nine games. The Mariners had a lot of ground to make up, having finished at least twenty-six games behind each of the other three teams in the division. It would take more than a couple of expensive free agents to make up that difference.

The Mariners chose the second approach, diving head first into the free-agent market. It's not hard to figure out why the M's chose the path they did. Despite having the third-worst record in baseball in 2004, Seattle had the third-best attendance in the American League that year. The franchise had no stomach for a full-on rebuilding effort, like that undertaken by the Cleveland Indians following the '01 season. The Mariners had seen what had happened in Cleveland, when the team's attendance dropped nearly in half within two years. The fans in Cleveland never came back, even after the club came within a game of reaching the World Series in 2007.

With John Olerud released in July 2004, it wasn't surprising to see the Mariners try to sign first-baseman Richie Sexson, a native of Brush Prairie, Washington who had grown up a Mariners fan. The M's had had decent success over the years luring free agents such as Olerud and Aaron Sele who were originally from the region and Sexson was no different. What was surprising, almost shocking, was Seattle's chase of Adrian Beltre, the top third-baseman on the market that winter. Beltre's agent was Scott

Boras, who was disliked by the M's upper management for the way he'd handled the Alex Rodriguez negotiations.

Still, Seattle managed to sign both players in a two-day period in December, spending a combined $114 million. Sexson received $50 million for four years, while Beltre signed a five-year contract for a club-record $64 million. While fans were ecstatic that the M's had finally made a big off-season splash, there were issues involving both players. The twenty-nine-year-old Sexson, who had two forty-five home run seasons on his resume, was coming off an injury-shortened season with Arizona in which he'd played in just twenty-three games and was recovering from shoulder surgery. Beltre had finished second in National League MVP voting in 2004, when he hit .334 with 48 home runs and 121 RBI, but those numbers were not in line with what he'd done the first six years of his career. Prior to 2004 he'd hit higher than .275 just once and had never hit more than 23 homers in a season.

While these signings looked good at the time, by this point the M's had to overpay to attract free agents. When Piniella and Gillick were running the team, winning ballplayers would sign with the Mariners because they wanted to play for Piniella and trusted Gillick to build a championship contender. But after its ninety-nine loss season in 2004, Seattle was no longer seen as a prime destination for players who wanted to win.

Howard Lincoln spoke to the *Times'* Blaine Newnham about the signings, saying he believed there was a buzz in the community about the Mariners again. Lincoln might have spoken a little too soon; while Mariner fans were indeed excited about the expensive free-agent signings, they also wanted a winner and the M's had a lot of other holes to fill to compete in the A.L. West. Asked for comment, Jamie Moyer told a reporter that the signings were "a great start," but added: "I hate to be the one to look at the glass half empty, but what about shortstop, what about pitching?"

The forty-two-year-old Moyer, now the club's elder statesman with Edgar Martinez having retired in the offseason, was right. Despite backloading the contracts of Sexson and Beltre so the two would account for just $17 million of the team's 2005 player payroll, the Mariners claimed they didn't have enough money in their budget to acquire a decent shortstop or an above-average starter to add to a rotation that had lost Freddy Garcia and didn't have a starting pitcher win more than seven games in 2004..

The shortstop signed by the M's, the-often injured Pokey Reese, got hurt in spring training and never played a regular-season game for the team. The Opening Day shortstop in 2005 was career minor-leaguer Wilson

Valdez, who was claimed on waivers three days before the season opener. As for the pitching Moyer was concerned about, the four starters behind him in Seattle's rotation all finished the '05 season with ERAs over 5.00.

The Mariners were hoping for big contributions in 2005 from two twenty-nine-year-olds with long injury histories, DH Bucky Jacobsen and starting-pitcher Bobby Madritsch. Both had provided hope in the second half of 2004, with Jacobsen slugging .500 with nine home runs and Madritsch winning six games and posting a 3.27 ERA after joining the club in late July. But Jacobsen never fully recovered from offseason knee surgery, while Madritsch suffered a shoulder injury in his first start of the '05 season. Neither played in another major-league game.

Two young players, catcher Miguel Olivo and center-fielder Jeremy Reed, both acquired in the Garcia trade, also disappointed. The M's ended up tying a club record in 2005, using seven catchers as Olivo, who hit .151 and had problems catching the ball, was shipped off to San Diego in late July. Reed, a perennial .300 hitter in the minors, hit .251 with just three home runs.

The Sexson/Beltre era started well as the M's beat Minnesota 5-1 before an Opening Day crowd of 46,249 at Safeco. Sexson became the first Mariner in team history to hit homers in each of his first *two* at-bats with the team and drove in all five of Seattle's runs.

The M's hung tough in April, managing a 12-12 record. It was the first month since September 2003 that they didn't lose more games than they won, but it was the last time Seattle would see .500 in 2005.

2005 TOP PERFORMERS

Richie Sexson, .263, 39 HR, 121 RBI

Ichiro Suzuki, .303, 15 HR, 68 RBI

Raul Ibanez, .280, 20 HR, 89 RBI

Jamie Moyer, 13-7, 4.28 ERA, 200 IP

Eddie Guardado, 2-3, 2.72 ERA, 36 saves

The Mariners lost nine of ten games in early May and were six games behind the division-leading Angels a few days into the month. A big reason for the team's slow start was that Beltre wasn't hitting. He had typically been a slow starter throughout his career and 2005 was no different as his average sunk to .221 (with two home runs) after he went 0-for-12 and didn't reach base in an early May series against the Angels. The M's scored just four runs in the series and were swept by their division rivals. Making matters worse, Beltre didn't talk to the media after the final two games of the series.

On May 10, with the '05 season already slipping away, Bavasi expressed frustration with the M's early-season struggles, telling the *Seattle Times*, "We have expected some early-season adjustments, but not this many. We have to see the center-fielder [Reed] play more. We expected Beltre and Sexson to have to go through adjustments coming over to this league. The issues behind the plate [with Olivo, who was hitting .133 and alienating most of the pitchers on Seattle's staff] are more than we expected."

By the end of May the M's had sunk to 21-30 and had fallen nine and a half games off the pace in the A.L. West. The team's standing didn't improve in June, when the Angels went 17-9 and extended their lead over Seattle to fourteen and a half games. On June 25, when the M's lost 8-5 to San Diego and Oakland beat the Giants, the Mariners settled into last place, where they'd remain for the rest of the '05 season. Just as they had in 2004, the M's were out of contention before the school year was over.

The summer of 2005 featured the departure of two familiar faces, Bret Boone and Randy Winn. Boone, hitting just .231 with seven home runs and thirty-four RBI, was released on July 3, while Winn was traded to San Francisco on July 30 for catcher Yorvit Torrealba and pitching prospect Jesse Foppert.

Two other players, Moyer and Guardado, should have been traded that summer, but weren't. The M's actually had a deal struck with the Houston Astros in late July that would have made Moyer an Astro, but the left-hander had been in the majors more than ten years (with at least the last five with Seattle) and he had so-called "10/5 rights," which allowed him to veto the trade. Moyer used his veto, reportedly because Houston would not agree to extend his contract and then vetoed a trade to the Yankees in early August.

Guardado, in the second year of a three-year contract with Seattle, was having a spectacular season (twenty-four saves and a 1.50 ERA at the trade deadline). Several teams were interested in him, but the Mariners were said to be reluctant to part with the thirty-five-year-old left-hander because they valued his clubhouse leadership and didn't believe they had anyone ready to replace him in the ninth inning. Six teams were said to be interested, including the Red Sox. The M's matched up well with Boston, who had minor-league pitchers Jon Lester and Anibal Sanchez near ready for the majors. Besides the fact that Guardado was having a great season and had tremendous value to other teams, there was another reason to move him. He was pitching with a partially torn rotator cuff and could land on the disabled list at any time. The M's should have cashed in their Guardado trade chip when they had the chance and shifted the injury risk to another team. Instead, Seattle held onto him and had to pay him $6.25 million to save five games in 2006 before discarding him halfway through that season.

Two fresh faces arrived in the summer of 2005 in nineteen-year-old pitcher Felix Hernandez and twenty-two-year-old shortstop Yuniesky Betancourt. Hernandez, whose arrival in Seattle had been eagerly awaited since he'd signed with the M's out of Venezuela in 2002, joined the team in early August with a nickname earned in the minors, "King Felix." Betancourt, who had defected to the states from Cuba in 2003, had signed with the M's in January 2005 and, having impressed in the minors, was deemed ready to take over at shortstop for the major-league club.

The pair provided hope for the future in the final two months of the '05 season, with Hernandez going 4-4 with a 2.67 ERA in twelve starts and Betancourt smacking seventeen extra-base hits and making dazzling plays in the field. Still, with the team finishing the season 69-93 and becoming the first franchise since 1917 to follow two consecutive ninety-win seasons with consecutive ninety-loss seasons, there would be a lot of work to do in the offseason.

Chapter 26

JUST GIVE HIM THE GOLD WATCH ALREADY!

Chuck Armstrong, the Mariners' president and chief operating officer, is second in command in the organization and one of the club's longest-tenured employees, having served in his position for twenty-seven years as of this writing. Given that length of time and the amount of money he's been paid over that time, it is amazing how little useful baseball knowledge he appears to have absorbed in his nearly three decades of involvement with the game.

"One Buck Chuck," as some call him, joined the team as president in October of 1983. He had held a similar position with George Argyros' real-estate management company in California the previous three years. Naively, Argyros figured Armstrong could run a baseball team. Not only was Armstrong unqualified, he didn't want the job. At the time, he told the media that the position with the M's was his dream job, but he later testified under oath in a deposition in the Mariners' 1984 lawsuit against King County that "this was neither a job that I sought or desired," and revealed that he had counseled Argyros not to buy the team, that "the purchase of any sports team did not pencil out."

Armstrong likes to fancy himself an expert in baseball matters, but by all accounts, he remains unqualified to be involved in decisions regarding player acquisitions. By his own admission, he's meddled in numerous important personnel decisions over the years.

One horrifying example: In 2006, the Mariners traded elite relief-pitcher Rafael Soriano to Atlanta for Horacio Ramirez, one of the worst starting pitchers in team history. Soriano continued to be one of the best relievers in the game, while "Ho-Ram" flamed out after one brutal season in Seattle (7.16 ERA). A few months after the trade Armstrong told the media that he had told GM Bill Bavasi to trade Soriano for "whatever he could get," alluded to mysterious and never-identified issues the team supposedly had with Soriano, who'd never been arrested nor been an off-the-field distraction with the Mariners or other teams.

Or how about the Jarrod Washburn fiasco in August 2008? The team's GM had a trade worked out that would send the disappointing Washburn to the Minnesota Twins, but Armstrong killed the deal because he thought the M's weren't getting enough in return. The deal would have saved the team more than $10 million on Washburn's salary for the rest of 2008 and all of 2009 and given the team financial flexibility to sign better players; Armstrong claimed he thought the team could trade Washburn over the winter and get more value. He was wrong. No team wanted to trade valuable players and pay more than $9 million a season for a mediocre pitcher like Washburn, so the M's were stuck paying his salary.

Former Mariner Manager Dick Williams wrote in his 1990 autobiography, *No More Mr. Nice Guy*, that during his days with the Mariners, Armstrong was learning baseball "like a two-year-old learns not to drink from the toilet," but that Armstrong often claimed he knew baseball because he had played the game at Purdue. Williams countered that his daughter played softball at Duke and that she wasn't qualified to run a baseball team either.

Perhaps the biggest blunder in Armstrong's long tenure with the Mariners was his role in ushering future Hall of Famer Randy Johnson out of Seattle. Armstrong and the Big Unit had engaged in a nasty feud in the pitcher's last five seasons with the Mariners. While Johnson, who'd won his first Cy Young Award in 1995, had returned from back surgery to win twenty games in 1997 and finished second in Cy Young voting that year, Armstrong was still anxious to be rid of the giant with Hall of Fame skills and a personality that was sometimes petulant.

On the day Ken Griffey Jr. was named American League MVP for the '97 season, the first time a Mariner had been so honored, Armstrong ruined the mood by proclaiming that the team would not offer Johnson a contract extension past the '98 season. Armstrong said he believed that Johnson's back was too big a risk. Of course Johnson went on to win Cy Young awards in each of the next four seasons, winning 170 games after leaving Seattle and finishing his career with over three-hundred victories.

In most organizations, any executive who made such a foolish, ego-driven decision that so clearly damaged the franchise would have been fired or demoted. But not in the Mariners organization, where Armstrong had not only been allowed to remain in his position of power, he's been rewarded handsomely for it. Sources close to the Mariners say his salary as of 2011 was close to $1 million a year. Remarkably, it seems that no matter how bad his performance, Armstrong can keep his job as long as the current ownership group owns the team.

At least Jeff Smulyan, who sold the team in 1992 to the current ownership group, had the right idea. One of his first acts upon purchasing the team in 1989 was to relieve Armstrong of his duties. But when the new ownership group came in, Armstrong managed to weasel his way back into his old job.

In May 2000 Armstrong reportedly threatened to quit if the team signed outfielder Rickey Henderson, who'd been released by the New York Mets and was available for the major-league minimum salary. Thankfully, GM Pat Gillick ignored Armstrong's threat, as Henderson, who entered the Hall of Fame in 2009, posted a .362 on-base percentage as the M's leadoff hitter that year, stole thirty-one bases and was instrumental in the team's run to the postseason. We're not quite sure what Armstrong's beef was with Henderson, but it's probably no coincidence that two of the M's best base-stealing threats, Mike Cameron and Mark McLemore, improved their stolen base percentages after playing with the all-time steals leader for most of the 2000 season.

While Armstrong's desire to keep Henderson off the team was likely just as arbitrary as some of the other decisions he's made during his time with the Mariners, the M's employed malcontents Carl Everett, Milton Bradley, and Jose Guillen in subsequent seasons, presumably without protest from Armstrong.

In 2008, after some members of the Seattle media called for Armstrong's firing after the M's 101-loss season, Armstrong authorized spending money on focus groups to convince Howard Lincoln that the average Mariner fan cared more about the Safeco Field experience and the cleanliness of the stadium than whether the team won.

It's puzzling why Armstrong has remained in the employ of the Seattle Mariners for as long as he has. He's never been held accountable for his mistakes, he embarrasses the franchise every time he opens his mouth, and he's never been qualified to hold a high-ranking position of power in baseball.

Armstrong was seventy-one years old at this writing, grossly overpaid, and not an asset to the team. The time has come for Armstrong to retire or be retired by the Mariners.

Chapter 27

BILL BAVASI'S PATH
OF DESTRUCTION

Despite two miserable seasons under Bill Bavasi, a dissatisfied fan base and declining attendance, the general manager kept his job for the '06 season. None of the columnists in the daily newspapers had called for Bavasi to be fired yet, so the Mariners must have figured he was doing a good job. Part of the team's thinking may have been that Bavasi had been left with a team filled with old and unproductive players and that he just needed more time to get the franchise turned around.

The Mariners couldn't have been more wrong; a culture of losing had started to fester in Seattle. Bavasi had shown he wasn't much of a talent-evaluator, either of major-league players or minor-league prospects. His free-agent signings of Rich Aurilia, Pokey Reese, and Scott Spiezio had been disasters while his trades of Freddy Garcia, Carlos Guillen, and Randy Winn had failed to net the M's any young players the organization could count on as building blocks for the future.

Bavasi talked a good game. He was tall with a commanding presence, had contacts throughout baseball, and perhaps most important, he got along with his bosses, keeping them well informed while never complaining to the media about budgetary limitations.

Shortly after the end of the '05 season, Ichiro made critical comments about his Mariner teammates and Manager Mike Hargrove to the Kyodo News Service in Japan. Asked for his response, Hargrove admitted that he and Ichiro had had several disagreements about strategy during the '05 season, but expressed disappointment that the All-Star outfielder had gone public with his criticism.

The disconnection between Hargrove and the Mariners' star player was apparently much worse than reported in Seattle. Jon Heyman of *Newsday* wrote that Hargrove had tried to have Ichiro traded and that Bavasi was on board with the idea. Heyman spoke to a Yankees official, who said that New York would do "whatever it takes" to acquire Ichiro, including trading second-baseman Robinson Cano and pitcher Chien-Ming Wang, who both had excelled as rookies in 2005. But Seattle ownership quickly made it clear that Ichiro would not be traded.

When Ichiro learned that Hargrove had tried to have him traded, he, in turn, tried to have Hargrove fired. Eventually a truce was called, but it was clear that the two men didn't care for each other. They would co-exist for another season and a half until Hargrove shockingly resigned in the middle of the '07 season.

The Mariners added a second Japanese position player to their lineup for the '06 season, signing catcher Kenji Johjima to a three-year contract for $16.5 million. The twenty-nine-year-old Johjima had averaged twenty-five homers a year for the previous five seasons in Japan and regularly hit over .300. Johjima was said to be a workhorse behind the plate, but he faced a language barrier. No Japanese catcher had played in the majors. Would Johjima be able to communicate well enough with the Seattle pitching staff to be an asset?

One spot where the M's took a risk was at designated hitter. Traditionally, Seattle had avoided controversial figures as not fitting the Mariners' family-friendly image, but after two consecutive losing seasons, Bavasi was desperate for a power hitter. The team signed Carl Everett, whose explosive temper had led to a string of incidents, on and off the field, in the seven cities he'd played during his career.

While acknowledging Everett's history, Bavasi said the Mariners needed his "left-handed sock." The thirty-four-year-old Everett had hit twenty-three home runs for the White Sox in 2005. Bavasi said the M's had given Mike Hargrove his choice of several DH options and that Hargrove "went for Carl right away." Bavasi acknowledged that the Mariners clubhouse "probably just got a little more hectic," but claimed it was a good thing.

One of those other DH options was Frank Thomas, who had hit thirty or more home runs eight times in his career. Thomas didn't come with Everett's baggage and, because he was coming off an injury, wouldn't have required much guaranteed money. Thomas signed with Oakland for a base salary of $500,000, with the chance to earn another $2.6 million in incentives. And while Thomas earned all his incentives, hitting .270 with 39 home runs and 114 RBI and was paid a total of $3.1 million to help the A's win the A.L. West, Everett, who was paid a guaranteed $4 million by Seattle, hit a paltry .227 with 11 home runs before being released in late July, three weeks after a shouting match in Hargrove's office.

Bavasi made one more ill-advised decision that winter, signing former Angel hurler Jarrod Washburn to the largest contract the M's had ever given a pitcher — $37.5 million for four years. The contract terms were shocking since Washburn was hardly an ace, having gone 29-31 with a 4.10 ERA in his final three seasons with the Angels and had won more than eleven games once in his eight-year career. "We really felt we had to get a better pitcher into our rotation, along with making our pitchers a little better. This is the first step toward that," Bavasi said.

It apparently was the last step, too, as the Mariners didn't sign any other pitchers that winter. And while the M's talked up how a fly-ball pitcher like Washburn would benefit from pitching half his games at spacious Safeco Field, he actually pitched worse once he got to Seattle.

An Opening Day crowd of 45,515 saw the Mariners' bullpen give up two runs to the defending A.L. West champion Angels in the top of the ninth to break a 3-3 tie, leading to a 5-4 loss. One bright spot that day was Johjima's first major-league home run. The M's had a streaky April that featured two three-game winning streaks, but also included two four-game losing streaks and a three-gamer. By the end of the month, Seattle found itself four games under .500 at 11-15 and in the cellar of the A.L. West.

May wasn't any better for the M's, who went 12-17 that month. They were still mired in last place, but the first-place Rangers were still within view, just six games up on Seattle. While there was still hope, looking at things realistically, it appeared to be just a matter of time before the '06 Mariners, with a record of 23-32 entering June, would fall out of contention as they had the previous two years.

Another dismal season appeared at hand for the M's and their fans. Beltre was off to another poor start, hitting .230 with just two homers as the calendar turned to June. Sexson had started slow too, hitting an anemic .205 with six home runs. Reed was hitting just .227 with ten RBI. Guardado was 0-3 and had blown three of eight save opportunities and lost his closing job. Even twenty-year-old Felix Hernandez, expected to be the savior of the M's rotation, had disappointed, going 4-6 with a 5.78 ERA in his first eleven starts. The Mariners seemed destined for their third consecutive ninety-loss season.

A byproduct of another disappointing season was an alarming drop in Safeco Field attendance. Season ticket sales had fallen from 17,100 in 2005 to 15,000 in 2006 and a three-game series against Texas in April had drawn the three smallest crowds in the history of Safeco Field.

On May 21, Steve Kelley wrote in the *Seattle Times* about the M's struggles.

"Both the GM and the manager are in trouble, Bavasi apparently more so than Hargrove" Kelley wrote. "Fans are clamoring for both of their heads. Barring some magical turnaround, this season will look a lot like the past two and, in the fall, the owners will be looking for a new general manager and another new manager. The empty green seats at Safeco are screaming for change, and this franchise-at-a-crossroads had better listen."

However, just when it seemed like Bavasi and Hargrove might lose their jobs, things turned around. Suddenly, a team that hadn't had a winning month in three years had a winning month. And not just a winning month, but one of the best months in franchise history — eighteen wins and eight losses. It was quite a surprising turnaround, as the M's won seven of their eight series that month, including three-game sweeps of the Angels, Giants, and Diamondbacks. A team that seemed on the verge of collapse entering the month, Seattle's record stood at 41-40 as it closed out June.

With first-place Oakland just five games above .500 at the time, the M's found themselves only two games out of first and seemed to have a chance. But the team wasn't getting much production from its DH spot, especially against left-handed pitching. While Everett was a switch-hitter, he hit just .200 with two home runs against left-handers that season.

Thanks to one good month, Bavasi, the GM who seemed on the verge of losing his job weeks before, was still employed and in a position to make a trade that would haunt the Mariners and their fans for years. On June 30, Bavasi sent twenty-year-old shortstop Asdrubal Cabrera, who had reached Triple A in the Seattle organization, to Cleveland for a part-time designated hitter, thirty-six-year-old Eduardo Perez. An excited Bavasi told the media "This is the kind of a trade, I guess you can say, that our players made. They played well enough where we really have to get behind them and make this club a little bit better."

The trade didn't make the team better, not even a little, because Hargrove refused to write the new DH's name on Seattle's lineup card. In Perez's first four weeks with the M's he started just four games. It appeared as if Hargrove was afraid to sit the volatile Carl Everett on the bench for fear he might go off on the manager. That finally became a moot point when Everett was released on July 26 to make room for another player Bavasi had acquired from the Indians, left-handed hitting DH Ben Broussard.

For the second time in a month, Bavasi had traded one of the organization's top prospects, this time twenty-four-year-old outfielder Shin-Soo Choo, to Cleveland in hopes of improving the M's woeful production from the DH spot. Choo, who had put up good power numbers in the minors, hadn't been given much of an opportunity at the major-league level, batting just thirty-three times for Seattle in 2005-06 combined.

2006 TOP PERFORMERS

Raul Ibanez, .289, 33 HR, 123 RBI

Richie Sexson, .264, 34 HR, 107 RBI

Adrian Beltre, .268, 25 HR, 89 RBI

Felix Hernandez, 12-14, 4.52 ERA, 191 IP

J.J. Putz, 4-1, 2.30 ERA, 36 saves

A satisfied Bavasi spoke with Larry Stone after acquiring Broussard, telling the *Times* reporter, "Our division is wide open right now, and we'd like to take it. But we still see us as a developing organization and we're going to be careful. We're trying to rebuild this thing. But now we find ourselves in a position where we're still in it. Now we have to try to do both — rebuild and win. We're the only one in our division trying to do that. We're the only one trying to do some of both — serve two masters, if you will. It's a nice problem to have."

Broussard (.238 with eight HRs and seventeen RBI) managed a little better numbers than Perez (.195 with one home run and eleven RBI), who retired at the end of the season, but neither player was very good. Worse, while Bavasi claimed he was being careful and downplayed the significance of the players he'd traded, the two prospects sent to Cleveland, Cabrera and Choo, became a big part of a resurgence by the Indians. Cabrera developed into one of the top shortstops in baseball within a few years, making the All-Star team in 2011, when he hit .273 with 25 homers and 92 RBI, while Choo became a fixture in the middle of the Tribe's batting order, hitting .300 or better with good power in three consecutive seasons

The Mariners weren't graduating many players from the amateur draft to the major leagues during this period. However, thanks to a strong international presence, led by the club's international scouting director, Bob Engel, the team reaped more benefits from foreign-born players than any other team in baseball. Hernandez, Betancourt, and second-baseman Jose Lopez, who'd make the '06 A.L. All-Star team in his first full season in the majors, all had been international signings. So had Cabrera and Choo.

Years later, after seeing Cabrera and Choo become stars, Bavasi reflected on two of the worst trades in Mariners history. Naturally, he deflected some of the blame from himself, telling ESPN's Jerry Crasnick, "We were trying to get better fast. Believe me, in Seattle there was no taste for a five-year plan. The '06 club was sort of starting to get it together and we believed it was important for the players to see we were serious about ... maybe not winning ... but at least getting better *now*."

While Bavasi didn't address the Cabrera trade in detail, he admitted to Crasnick that he hadn't bothered to run the deal by Engle before trading away a prized player the international scouting director had signed as a sixteen-year-old out of Venezuela, presumably to avoid being talked out of making the trade. "It was a bad mistake," Bavasi said. "Bob was really upset as the year went on and Eduardo sat."

Looking back at the Cabrera deal, Bavasi was brutally honest, telling Crasnick that he thought to himself, "The GM of the Seattle club is a fucking idiot." Those were exactly the sentiments of much of the Mariners' fan base.

In early August the M's completed a sweep of lowly Tampa Bay to move into a tie for third place and improve their record to 56-57, pulling within five and a half games of first-place Oakland. The next day Seattle headed out on an eleven-game road trip, the longest of the '06 season. With games against all three A.L. West rivals, this trip would show whether this Seattle club would be contenders or pretenders.

The Mariners limped home from Anaheim on August 20, having lost all eleven games of the road trip. It was the worst road trip in franchise history and the team's longest losing streak since 1992, when Bill Plummer's M's lost a franchise record fourteen consecutive games. One Mariner who didn't return home with the club was Moyer, who was traded to Philadelphia for two minor-league pitchers on August 19. While Moyer had rejected two trades the previous year, this time he'd managed to secure a mutual option for the '07 season from the Phillies and their new GM, Pat Gillick.

All hope of a pennant race was gone when the M's returned home fourteen games out of first with thirty-eight games left to play. The team managed to go 22-16 in those games to ensure the club's best record (78-84) since 2003, but that meant little to a franchise that had now missed the postseason five years in a row.

M'S WHO GOT AWAY

The Mariners have traded away or lost more talent than any team in the major leagues. Following is an All-Star team comprised solely of former Mariners.

The numbers next to each of the players' names are the number of seasons each played in Seattle and the number of seasons each played in the majors after leaving Seattle (as of the end of the '11 season). Eight players played ten seasons or more after leaving the Mariners.

STARTING LINEUP

C, Jason Varitek (0, 14)

1B, Tino Martinez (5, 10)

2B, Asdrubal Cabrera (0, 5)

SS, Alex Rodriguez (5, 11)

3B, Adrian Beltre (5, 2)

LF, Adam Jones (0, 4)

CF, Mike Cameron (4, 8)

RF, Shin-Soo Choo (0, 4)

DH, David Ortiz (0, 13)

BENCH

B1, Omar Vizquel (5, 18)

B2, Carlos Guillen (4, 8)

B3, Raul Ibanez (8, 6)

B4, Jose Cruz Jr. (1, 11)

B5, Mike Morse (1, 2)

B6, Yorvit Torrealba (1, 6)

STARTING ROTATION

SP1, Randy Johnson (10, 11)

SP2, Freddy Garcia (6, 7)

SP3, Derek Lowe (0, 14)

SP4, Doug Fister (3, 0)

SP5, Joel Pineiro (6, 5)

BULLPEN

RP1, Rafael Soriano (2, 5)

RP2, J.J. Putz (4, 3)

RP3, Matt Thornton (2, 6)

RP4, Mike Jackson (5, 6)

RP5, Arthur Rhodes (5, 6)

Chapter 28

MIKE HARGROVE'S
MYSTERIOUS EXIT

With the '06 season winding down, fans and media in Seattle called for GM Bill Bavasi and Manager Mike Hargrove to be fired. Bavasi had been on the job for three years, Hargrove for two, and the team had shown little improvement during their tenures.

Steve Kelley wrote in the *Seattle Times* late in the season that it was time for the Mariners to clean house.

"This is a franchise that needs remodeling, and that means it needs a new architect," Kelley wrote. "In his three seasons as general manager, Bill Bavasi hasn't made the Mariners better. He's had his chance, and he hasn't delivered. The Mariners have slipped into a malaise, and the time for change is now."

Management stood fast. During the last week of the '06 season, Lincoln stepped up and defended Bavasi and Hargrove, saying he believed the pair were the right men to lead the Mariners to the next level and that the organization had "great confidence" in their abilities. Finally, Lincoln said that "continuity of leadership is extremely important at this point in time."

In a letter to the team's season-ticket holders, Lincoln said "Although this was our third consecutive losing season, there were a number of bright spots and several areas of improvement on the team this year. After reviewing all aspects of our organization and looking ahead, we believe that the Mariners are much better at both the major-league and minor-league levels than we were in 2004, when the rebuilding process began. The talent level is better and deeper and gives us the flexibility to make trades that will help us.

Regarding Bavasi, Lincoln said, "Under Bill's watch, we have seen a dramatic improvement in our scouting and player-development departments, which has already resulted in several top prospects climbing quickly up the minor-league ladder and playing key roles for us this year." Lincoln also had good things to say about Hargrove, who by then had failed to lead a team to a .500 season in his previous six years as a major-league manager. "Mike is uniquely equipped to lead a young team. His experience in developing and dealing with young players is one of the reasons we hired him in the first place," Lincoln said.

However, little of what Lincoln said was true. The Mariners weren't headed in the right direction. The drafts under Bavasi were horrible and failed to produce even one starting player. Bavasi didn't have a good eye for talent and worse, he was trading away some of the organization's best young talent for mediocrities. Not only had he parted with Cabrera and Choo in the middle of the '06 season, but during spring training that year he traded the M's first-round pick in 1998, left-handed pitcher Matt Thornton to the White Sox for an outfielder, Joe Borchard, who was discarded a month later after Hargrove started Borchard in just two of the team's first twenty-eight games. Thornton became a highly effective relief pitcher for the White Sox the next six years.

Lincoln was equally misguided when it came to Hargrove. The manager wasn't uniquely qualified to lead a young team, as he had always preferred veterans to inexperienced players. He'd never had any success during his managerial career guiding and developing young players and that wasn't going to change in Seattle.

What Lincoln was essentially telling Mariner fans was that disrupting a bad management team would do more harm to the franchise than allowing Bavasi and Hargrove to continue in their positions. He couldn't have been more wrong.

As the offseason began, the Mariners were looking to overhaul their starting rotation. While Hernandez and Washburn were set, poor planning by Bavasi had left the M's with three rotation spots vacant after 2007. The M's also had holes to fill in the outfield and needed a DH.

So, rather than firing the inept Bavasi, Lincoln decided he'd give him more money to waste, raising the payroll for 2007 to $111 million, a $16 million increase from 2006. It was a bizarre decision. Lincoln had pinched pennies for years with a Hall of Fame-caliber GM in Pat Gillick, but now was giving free rein to Bavasi, who hadn't proven to anyone that he knew how to spend money wisely.

It was one of the worst mistakes in franchise history. If the Mariners were prepared to open up the checkbook and allow their general manager to spend freely, they should have fired Bavasi and replaced him with a general manager who knew how to put together a team, instead of the GM that had put the team in such a precarious position in his first three seasons on the job.

The M's averted disaster when two of their top pitching targets that offseason, free-agent Barry Zito and Kei Igawa, a Japanese hurler available through the posting system, signed with other teams. The M's reportedly offered Zito a deal close to the seven-year, $126 million deal the pitcher signed with the Giants (he won only forty-three games in the first five years of that contract), while the Yankees paid a $26 million posting fee for Igawa and then signed him to a five-year, $20 million contract. For its $46 million, New York would get just two wins out of Igawa, who spent much of the five years in the minors.

Three other pitchers also spurned the M's that winter: right-hander Jason Schmidt, who had nearly signed with Seattle after the '02 season, left-hander Ted Lilly, and right-hander Adam Eaton.

An interesting rumor at the winter meetings had Seattle discussing a three-way trade with Atlanta and San Francisco that would have sent Richie Sexson to San Francisco and reliever Rafael Soriano to the Braves, with right-hander Tim Hudson and first-baseman Adam LaRoche (32 HRs, 90 RBI in 2006) coming to Seattle. That deal fizzled, but would have worked out better than the trade Bavasi made — sending Soriano to Atlanta for Horacio Ramirez, a soft-tossing left-hander who was likely to have become a free agent in another week. The oft-injured Ramirez, who'd only managed to pitch in fourteen games in 2006, was eligible for arbitration for the first time, and Atlanta wasn't expected to offer him a contract for 2007.

While the M's were desperate for starting pitching, with one free agent after another rejecting their advances that winter, trading one of their best chips in Soriano for a pitcher like Ramirez was folly. Pitchers like Soriano, who'd struck out sixty-five batters in sixty innings in 2006, were hard to find, but mediocrities like Ramirez could be found on the cheap every winter as minor-league free agents.

This deal was a disaster from the moment it was conceived, but became worse when Ramirez, whose salary increased from $370,000 in 2006 to $2.2 million, had the worst season of his career in 2007, posting a 7.16 ERA in twenty starts, allowing 139 hits in 98 innings. Meanwhile, Soriano continued to establish himself as one of the best relievers in baseball, first as a setup man and later as a closer for the Braves and Rays (72 saves in 2009-10).

Months later, after the swap of Soriano for Ramirez had proven to be a miserable failure, Chuck Armstrong admitted that he had ordered Bavasi to trade Soriano for "whatever he could get," due to unspecified issues the team had with Soriano. Despite that edict, a good general manager would have been able to obtain value for a prized asset like Soriano, but the Mariners didn't have a good GM at the time.

Bavasi's next move was to sign Jose Guillen to play right field, but that was a gamble on two fronts. While Guillen had three twenty-five-home-run seasons in his career, he was coming off an injury-plagued season in which he'd hit just .216. Despite that, Bavasi gave Guillen, who'd never made more than $4 million in any of his ten previous seasons, the richest contract of his career — a guaranteed $5.5 million and an opportunity to earn another $3.5 million in incentives if he stayed healthy the entire season.

Having given Guillen a player-friendly contract that put all the risk on the Mariners, Bavasi should have insisted on a team option so the M's could have retained the right-fielder for a second season if he had a productive season in Seattle. Instead, Guillen's contract included a mutual option for 2008, which the player quickly declined after hitting .290 with 23 homers and 99 RBI in '07.

The other risk in signing Guillen was that he was a temperamental player cut from the same mold as Carl Everett, who'd been with Seattle the previous season. Much like Everett, Guillen was well-traveled, having played for seven different major-league teams. One of those teams, the Angels, had suspended him for the final two weeks of the '04 season and the entire postseason after a dugout confrontation with Manager Mike Scioscia.

The Everett experiment had been a disaster, the team had traded Soriano that winter because of unspecified off-field issues, and now they were signing another troublemaker? Just two years before, Lincoln had praised Scioscia in a *Seattle Times* interview for having the backbone to discard a player who'd been the second-best hitter on the '04 Angels because he'd been a clubhouse cancer. Now Lincoln was allowing Bavasi to sign the same player!

The M's signed Guillen to play right-field because Ichiro had moved to center-field late in the '06 season and had agreed to play there in 2007 if the team wanted him to. It had taken months of coaxing to get Ichiro to agree to the move, but now that he had, the M's wanted to make sure they could fill the spot with a hitter who would produce enough runs to help their offense.

Bavasi signed thirty-six-year-old right-hander Miguel Batista to a three-year, $24 million deal, but still had the funds to make an ill-advised trade with the Washington Nationals for Jose Vidro, who'd be the team's new DH. Vidro had once been among the best second-basemen in the

National League, but by then his bad knees prevented him from effectively playing the field, he couldn't run, and he had a hefty contract. Without a DH in the N.L., the Nationals were stuck paying Vidro $16 million over the next two years to be an expensive pinch-hitter. Enter Bavasi, who agreed to trade for Vidro, take on seventy-five percent of the $16 million left on his contract and still trade two young players, outfielder Chris Snelling and pitcher Emiliano Fruto, to Washington.

None of these signings or trades was popular with Mariner fans, with Bavasi seemingly paying big money to the aged and infirmed that winter. Bavasi admitted in December that the M's had miscalculated how much pitching help they could acquire for the money they had to spend that winter.

"We're always wrong," he told Larry Stone. "But we've never been this wrong."

Asked by Stone if he was concerned about negative fan reaction, a defensive Bavasi replied, "I'm the one dealing in the market. I know what the market is. I know what's available. The reaction is probably a whole lot different if I drag you with me for a month, and you see what it's like. That's not an excuse; just a fact … to say I'm not concerned is just rude. That's not the way I am. But is it going to color the way we try to manage a payroll and try to manage a roster? God, no!"

Bavasi had two more money-wasting moves up his sleeve in January. While most of the big-name free agents had signed, the M's still had money to spend, so Bavasi, with his job on the line, spent that money, handing over $8.325 million to starting-pitcher Jeff Weaver and another $2 million to reliever Chris Reitsma.

Weaver was a veteran starter, but was coming off a poor season in which he'd gone 3-10 with a 6.29 ERA for the Angels before being shipped off to St. Louis in July. He wasn't much better in 2007 for Seattle, going 7-13 with a 6.20 ERA. The acquisition of Reitsma may have been worse. He'd posted an ERA of 8.68 for Atlanta in 2006 and missed half the season after needing surgery, but Bavasi claimed at the time that Reitsma was more consistent than Soriano and would more than make up for Soriano's loss. But that was hardly the case. While Soriano gave the Braves seventy-two innings with a 3.00 ERA in 2007, Reitsma was only available for twenty-six innings and put up a 7.61 ERA when he wasn't on the disabled list. Reitsma never appeared in another major-league game.

As spring training arrived, the Mariners were facing a major issue — Ichiro's contract was due to expire at the end of the season and there had been no talks about an extension. Ichiro told the Seattle media he was upset by the state of the team and that it was possible he would go to free agency. He made it clear that the performance of the '07 team would play a big part in his decision on whether to stay with the M's. The issue of Ichiro's contract lingered for much of the season, with most people assuming if the team was able to contend for the first time in four years it would help Seattle's chances of retaining the perennial all-star.

Seattle did contend for most of the '07 season, but it was apparently an off-field issue, a big one, that impacted his decision more than anything else. Ichiro's relationship with Seattle Manager Mike Hargrove had always been a frosty one.

When Hargrove joined the Mariners for the '05 season, one of the first things he did was try to change Ichiro's hitting style, wanting him to draw more walks. Ichiro had experienced a similar situation with an oppressive manager as a rookie playing for the Orix Blue Wave in Japan. That manager, Shozo Doi, had tried to get Ichiro to adopt a more orthodox hitting style. When Ichiro didn't make the appropriate adjustments, he was sent to the minors.

Since Ichiro was the biggest star on the Mariners, there was no chance he'd be sent to the minors. With free agency in view, Ichiro had all the leverage. The Mariners were anxious for him to sign a new contract and presumably made him offers that had not been negotiated. The team depended on him for millions of dollars in revenue each year, and the team's ownership didn't want to find out how much attendance at Safeco Field might drop without the club's most popular player.

And so it was that on the morning of July 1, 2007, the Seattle Mariners called a news conference to announce some shocking news: Hargrove was retiring after that day's game and would be replaced by the bench coach, John McLaren. The news might have been less astonishing if it had occurred in the middle of a losing Mariners season, but at the time the team had a 44-33 record and had won their last seven games.

While Hargrove claimed that the resignation was entirely his idea — that he hadn't been forced out — his words weren't very convincing when he denied a quote admitting that he had lost his passion for the game that the Mariners had inserted into a news release distributed to the media that day.

It's been whispered in back rooms, but never confirmed — until now, by a source close to the team - that Ichiro told the Mariners he would not re-sign with Seattle if Hargrove continued as manager. When the team told Hargrove he was going to be replaced at the end of the season, Hargrove chose to resign immediately. McLaren was close with Ichiro, having been a fixture on Lou Piniella's coaching staff when Ichiro first joined the Mariners. It was no mere coincidence that nine days after Hargrove's departure, word leaked that Ichiro and the Mariners had reached agreement on a contract extension. A five-year, $90 million deal was announced on July 13, three days after Ichiro was named MVP of the 2007 All-Star Game.

Despite all the attention focused on this strangely timed change in managers, the Mariners still had the second half of the season to play. The club performed well for the first seven weeks of McLaren's tenure, winning twenty-eight games and losing twenty. On August 24, with five weeks to go in the '07 season, Seattle was one game behind the division-leading Angels and three games ahead of the New York Yankees in the race for a Wild Card berth. Seattle appeared to be primed for its first legitimate pennant race since 2000.

The M's lost to Texas 5-3 on August 25 when journeyman Rick White, making his first appearance with Seattle after being released by Houston with a 7.67 ERA, allowed the winning runs to score. White was signed after Bavasi had failed to acquire any reliable help for a bullpen that was showing signs of wearing down after being heavily used in the first half of the season.

That loss began a slide that didn't end until the M's had lost nine consecutive games, four of them because of bullpen failures in the late innings. It was a total team collapse though; the M's starting pitchers, the team's offense and McLaren all contributed. The offense scored just twenty-nine runs, with just thirteen extra base hits in the nine games.

Perhaps the most frustrating element of the M's collapse was the role played by Jose Guillen. With left-fielder Raul Ibanez scuffling badly in midseason (he hit .184 and went homerless the entire month of July), the M's called up rookie Adam Jones, who had hit twenty-five homers and knocked in eighty-four runs at Triple-A Tacoma, with the idea of inserting Jones' bat into the lineup on a regular basis. When news of Jones' call-up reached the Seattle clubhouse, Guillen erupted, telling Geoff Baker of the *Seattle Times*, "I just hope they [Mariner executives] understand this is not Triple A. This is the big leagues. This is a totally different league. I understand he's a good prospect and they think he's ready. He's going to have to come here and prove that to us. Because this team has been good with what we have and I don't think that's what we need. I don't know what they're trying to do. I hope they don't do something stupid to mess with the lineup that we have. Because I believe we have a pretty good one."

Guillen's comments put the M's rookie manager in a tough spot. A veteran manager might have sat Guillen down and told him to keep his mouth shut, that the manager would decide which players gave the team the best chance to win. But McLaren, barely a month into his first job as a big-league manager, couldn't do that. If he did, he'd risk losing the veterans in the Mariners clubhouse. Unfortunately, it seemed McLaren let the situation affect his lineup decisions, because Jones got few starting opportunities down the stretch despite a team-wide slump that called out for some new blood.

2007 TOP PERFORMERS

Jose Guillen, .290, 23 HR, 99 RBI

Adrian Beltre, .276, 26 HR, 99 RBI

Raul Ibanez, .291, 21 HR, 105 RBI

Felix Hernandez, 14-7, 3.92 ERA, 190.1 IP

J.J. Putz, 6-1, 1.38 ERA, 40 saves

What became of that pennant race of late August? By the time the M's snapped the losing streak on September 9, they were eight games back in the A.L. West and five games behind the Yankees in the Wild Card race and all but mathematically eliminated from the postseason. Everything the Mariners had worked for during the '07 season had been destroyed by a losing streak at an inopportune time. While Seattle managed to win their final five games of the campaign, the victories were meaningless and only served to pad the team's win total in yet another disappointing season.

FIFTY HIGHEST SALARIES

Since starting *The Grand Salami* in 1996, I've listed the salaries for the Mariners and opposing players in each monthly issue.

Salary is an important tool in evaluating and comparing players. If a rookie making the major-league minimum salary hit .260 with twenty home runs and seventy-five RBI, he would be seen as having a great season. But if that were the performance of a marquee player making $15 million, it would be considered a disappointing season by most.

While baseball players' salaries are readily available on the Internet, people aren't used to seeing the salaries for entire rosters in one place. Over the years a handful of players, including Jamie Moyer, made it known they were unhappy that I was listing their salaries.

Another former Mariner, Mike Cameron, liked to tease me good-naturedly about listing player salaries. In 2000, in the visitors' clubhouse at Comiskey Park, I was interviewing Al Martin, who had been acquired by the M's the previous week, when Cameron said to Martin, "They list all our salaries in there."

Martin, unfazed, looked up Cameron's player profile in the magazine and said with a quizzical look, "You make that much?"

Following are the fifty highest single-season salaries in Seattle Mariners history.

Player	Year	Salary
Ichiro Suzuki	2011	$18 million
Ichiro Suzuki	2010	$18 million
Ichiro Suzuki	2009	$18 million
Ichiro Suzuki	2008	$17.1 million
Richie Sexson	2008	$15.5 million
Richie Sexson	2007	$15.5 million
Adrian Beltre	2009	$13.4 million
Adrian Beltre	2008	$13.4 million
Milton Bradley	2011	$13 million
Richie Sexson	2006	$13 million
Adrian Beltre	2007	$12.9 million
Adrian Beltre	2006	$12.9 million
Ichiro Suzuki	2007	$12.5 million
Ichiro Suzuki	2006	$12.5 million

Player	Year	Salary
Ichiro Suzuki	2005	$12.5 million
Carlos Silva	2009	$12.25 million
Felix Hernandez	2011	$11.7 million
Adrian Beltre	2005	$11.4 million
Milton Bradley	2010	$11 million
Jarrod Washburn	2009	$9.85 million
Jarrod Washburn	2008	$9.85 million
Jarrod Washburn	2007	$9.85 million
Chone Figgins	2011	$9.5 million
Miguel Batista	2009	$9.5 million
Miguel Batista	2008	$9.5 million
Cliff Lee	2010	$9 million
Bret Boone	2005	$9 million
Ken Griffey Jr.	1999	$8.76 million
Chone Figgins	2010	$8.5 million
Jose Vidro	2008	$8.5 million
Jeff Weaver	2007	$8.32 million
Carlos Silva	2008	$8.25 million
Ken Griffey Jr.	1998	$8.01 million
Jamie Moyer	2005	$8 million
Bret Boone	2004	$8 million
Bret Boone	2003	$8 million
Bret Boone	2002	$8 million
Kazuhiro Sasaki	2003	$8 million
Ken Griffey Jr.	1997	$7.87 million
Erik Bedard	2009	$7.75 million
John Olerud	2004	$7.7 million
John Olerud	2003	$7.7 million
Kenji Johjima	2009	$7.66 million
Jose Vidro	2007	$7.5 million
Aaron Sele	2000	$7.5 million
Ken Griffey Jr.	1996	$7.5 million
Ken Griffey Jr.	1995	$7.5 million
Jarrod Washburn	2006	$7.45 million
Mike Cameron	2003	$7.41 million
Felix Hernandez	2010	$7.2 million

Chapter 29

$117 MILLION FOR THIS?

As the end of the '07 season neared, media attention turned again to whether the Mariners would retain General Manager Bill Bavasi. The team had contended for most of the season, but that was expected given the significant increase in player payroll. However, the starting rotation Bavasi put together had been a major factor in the late-season collapse, with two of those starters, Weaver and Ramirez, failing miserably.

Once again, the Mariners decided the franchise couldn't afford to remove the worst general manager in the league, with Howard Lincoln again citing how disruptive a change would be to the organization. Lincoln told the *Seattle Times* during the final week of the '07 season, "Bill has produced a winning season. That was the first challenge. He didn't get us to the playoffs, but I think he deserves to continue on as the general manager. It's so disruptive to an organization to change general managers … It's not time to change horses in midstream."

For the second straight season, the Mariners seemingly recognized that Bavasi wasn't very good at his job, but chose not to fire him because of the damage they thought the franchise would suffer from the disruption. The M's didn't realize that *not* making a change and giving Bavasi more and more money to spend would do significantly more harm to the franchise, immediately and for the future.

While Lincoln claimed that changing general managers was too disruptive, he need only have looked back a few years into the Mariners' own history to be proven wrong. When Woody Woodward departed as GM and was replaced by Pat Gillick, the team went from a 79-83 third place finish in 1999 to winning ninety games and the Wild Card in 2000 and setting an A.L. record for victories in 2001.

The eighty-eight-win season not only gave management an excuse to keep Bavasi, it also gave the Mariners false hope that they were close to seriously contending in 2008 and only needed one key player to get back to the postseason.

While the team would lose Jose Guillen and the twenty-three homers and ninety RBI he provided in 2007, the Mariners' main focus that offseason was improving the starting rotation, which had been the weakest part of the team that season. The previous winter they sought three starters, and this time they were looking for just two, to replace Weaver and Ramirez.

Mid-November found Bavasi and McLaren in Japan hoping to recruit free-agent right-hander Hiroki Kuroda, a free agent. Kuroda was one of the premier pitchers in Japan, having compiled a record of 103-89 and a 3.56 ERA in eleven seasons with the Hiroshima Carp. But Kuroda signed with the Dodgers, accepting a three-year, $33 million deal instead of Seattle's four-year, $44 million offer.

Kuroda had been the centerpiece of the M's off-season plan, as Seattle had believed it could sign him before the competition amped up their efforts, as they'd managed to do with Johjima two years before. Having missed out on Kuroda, the Mariners had to refocus their efforts on other pitchers.

While Minnesota ace Johan Santana wanted to play on the East Coast, another left-handed starter available that winter was Erik Bedard of the Baltimore Orioles. The twenty-eight-year-old Bedard had finished fifth in Cy Young voting in 2007, when he went 13-5 with a 3.16 ERA and finished second in the A.L. in strikeouts. Bedard had two years left until free agency and Baltimore, in a rebuilding phase, was looking to trade him. The Orioles were said to be seeking a package of players built around young position players, with their initial asking price from Seattle reported to be a package centered on outfielder Adam Jones, catcher Jeff Clement, and pitcher Brandon Morrow. All three had been first-round picks of the Mariners in recent seasons.

Unwilling to meet Baltimore's initial asking price, the M's turned to the free-agent market, which didn't contain many quality starters that winter. The best of the crop seemed to be twenty-eight-year-old Carlos Silva, a middle-of-the-rotation starter who'd spent the previous four seasons as a solid innings-eater for Minnesota. The going rate for a starter of that ilk was typically $6 million or so annually. Bavasi, in his fifth year of building Mariner teams, knew if the team didn't win soon he'd be out of a job. Silva's best offer was from the Kansas City Royals (three years, $30 million), a team with an even worse record of recent ineptitude than the Mariners. Remarkably, Bavasi gave Silva a four-year contract for $48 million even though there were no other teams offering contracts of that type. While Silva was no ace, he was expected to be a league average starter for at least the first two seasons of his contract. But the Mariners didn't get even one decent season out of Silva, who proved to be one of the worst free-agent signings in baseball history, going 5-18 with a 6.81 ERA in two seasons in Seattle before he was shipped off to Chicago in a bad contract swap with the Cubs.

As the calendar turned to January, the Bedard trade talks between Baltimore and Seattle heated up. The trade discussions hit several snags, but when the Mariners signed outfielder Brad Wilkerson on January 31, it was a clear sign the deal for Bedard was imminent. The M's only needed Wilkerson if Jones was being traded. When the deal was finally completed, Jones, relief-pitcher George Sherrill, and three pitching prospects were headed to Baltimore.

Opinions were mixed in Seattle. Some thought this was the move that would push the Mariners over the top with Bedard and Hernandez giving the M's the best 1-2 punch in the league. Others thought the Mariners couldn't afford to give up Jones and several other players for two years of Bedard.

Early in spring training, Lincoln talked to Jerry Brewer of the *Seattle Times* about the state of the Mariners. Lincoln described the seasons from 2004 to 2006 as "a very difficult phase," adding "We had a lot of critics, a lot of people down on us. But I am very happy with how we've turned things around." With respect to the patience management had shown Bavasi, Lincoln replied defiantly, "Any fool can fire a general manager. It's a very easy way out. It makes some of the fans feel good."

By the same token, any fool could keep the same general manager for five years despite strong evidence that said general manager was over-matched in his job, taken advantage of by rival GMs and player agents in nearly every deal he'd made.

Once spring training started, it didn't take long for Bedard to make a lasting impression. After his first outing of the spring, he told reporters covering the Mariners that he'd answer just four questions.

"Why only four?" Bedard was asked.

"That's one," he replied.

The entire session lasted seventy-eight seconds, but it started the Bedard Era in Seattle off on the wrong foot. Bedard's interview should probably have been a sign that maybe 2008 wasn't going to be the season the Mariners and their fans hoped it would be.

Another bad sign came on the second day of the season when closer J.J. Putz went down with a rib injury after giving up a game-winning home run to the Rangers' Josh Hamilton. Seattle had won the season opener and was two outs away from being 2-0 when Hamilton went deep. Putz had been the most dominant closer in baseball in 2007, striking out eighty-two batters and allowing just fifty base-runners in 71 2/3 innings. While he'd return to action three weeks later, he wasn't nearly as effective as he'd been in 2007, blowing more than a third of his save opportunities after converting forty of forty-one in 2007.

On April 17 the Mariners defeated the A's 8-1 to sweep a two-game series in Oakland and improve their record to 9-8. It was the last time the '08 M's would be over .500. The team lost seventeen of its next twenty-one games, falling eight games back in the division by early May.

Wilkerson, who'd been given $3 million by Bavasi after hitting just .234 for Texas in 2007, was released after barely a month with Seattle. At the time, Wilkerson was hitting .232 without a home run in nineteen games. Wilkerson's signing was yet another case of Bavasi throwing away the Mariners' money.

Wilkerson wasn't the only Mariner hitter who underachieved. Sexson, who'd hit .205 and driven in just sixty-three runs in 2007, was again flirting with the Mendoza Line, but with the M's owing him $15.5 million that season, the team was much more patient with him than they were with Wilkerson. Vidro, paid $7.5 million, hit .211 in April, but he, too, remained in the lineup. Johjima hit .177 in April with no home runs and five RBI, but he not only received regular playing time, he was given a three-year, $24 million contract extension late in the month.

Johjima was in the last year of the original three-year contract he'd signed with the Mariners. While he'd put up decent offensive numbers in his first two seasons with the team, he'd had conflicts with some of the Mariners pitchers, with at least two, Hernandez and Washburn, going to the manager and asking to work with another catcher. It was revealed toward the end of the '08 season that the extension for Johjima was, as many suspected, a move ordered by Yamauchi, the team's owner in Japan.

The Mariners underachieved in April, but their 13-15 record at the end of the month kept them within four and a half games of the division-leading Angels. But May wouldn't be so kind to the M's. They went 9-20 that month, with three separate losing streaks of at least five games each, including a seven-gamer. By the end of the month, any illusions that the Mariners might contend in 2008 had been eradicated, and Seattle finished May eleven and a half games out of first place and seven and a half games behind third-place Texas.

With pressure mounting for the organization to take action and hold someone accountable for this epic disaster, Chuck Armstrong appeared on the Ian Furness Show on KJR 950 AM and blamed the team's underachieving players for the poor start. He said Bavasi was doing "an outstanding job" and would not be fired.

A few weeks later, on the morning of the finale of a three-game series with the Angels, in which the Mariners were swept, Armstrong was overheard yelling at several Mariner coaches about the team's inability to play up to its capabilities. Asked about the tirade, an angry Armstrong told John Hickey of the *Seattle P-I* that he believed his conversation with the coaching staff was "private" and shouldn't have been reported by the media. "I have conversations all the time with the manager and the coaching staff, every day and to me, they are privileged conversations," he said. After the Mariners lost that day's game, in either a misguided show of power or a futile attempt at embarrassing the players he felt were underachieving, Bavasi ordered clubhouse workers not to put out towels or the post-game food spread for the Mariner players until all the players had spoken with the media. Bavasi insisted in a post-game media briefing that he was not prepared to give up on the season — even though the M's had fallen fifteen and a half games out of first place.

McLaren had a tirade of his own when he spoke with the media after the game, but his words sounded contrived.

"We're playing our ass off every day and got nothing to show for it," McLaren said. "I'm tired of fucking losing, I'm tired of getting my ass beat, and so are those guys. We gotta change this fucking shit around and get after it. And only we can do it. The fans are pissed off and I'm pissed off, and the players are pissed off. And that's the way it is. There's no fucking easy way out of this, [and we] can't feel sorry for ourselves, we gotta fucking buckle it up and get after it. I'm tired of goddamn losing. It's fucking every night, we bust our ass. It's gotta be a total team fucking effort, turn this thing around, and that's it."

Five days later the first domino fell when hitting coach Jeff Pentland, in his third season with the team, was fired. The dismissal took place June 9, a Monday, an off day and traditionally a popular day for firings in the baseball world.

The following Monday, it was finally Bavasi's turn to get the ax, with a three-game weekend sweep at the hands of the lowly Washington Nationals seemingly providing the impetus for the move.

The general manager who had seemed invincible for five years, and who Armstrong had said was doing "an outstanding job" just weeks before, was finally relieved of his duties. Mariner fans from Aberdeen to Zillah rejoiced.

At the news conference announcing Bavasi's dismissal, Lincoln said the Mariners were going to make whatever changes were necessary to get the team turned around as quickly as possible, emphasizing that "nothing is off the table," which was taken to mean that nobody in the organization was safe, that any player, including Ichiro, could be traded.

Unfortunately, some things were off the table, notably that Lincoln and Armstrong might resign or be removed by the club's board of directors. These two were the ones who had hired Bavasi and who for five years seemed to be in denial about Bavasi's competence, while allowing him to decimate a once-proud franchise.

Lincoln had claimed after the '06 season that "the entire organization, *especially me*," was on "the hot seat." Yet, having made the fateful decision to stick with Bavasi for so long, Lincoln remained unscathed, still in his position as the Mariners' chairman and CEO.

2008 TOP PERFORMERS

Raul Ibanez, .293, 23 HR, 110 RBI

Jose Lopez, .297, 17 HR, 89 RBI

Adrian Beltre, .266, 25 HR, 77 RBI

Ichiro Suzuki, .310, 6 HR, 42 RBI, 43 SB

Felix Hernandez, 9-11, 3.45 ERA, 200.2 IP

Three days later, McLaren joined Bavasi on the unemployment line, and bench coach Jim Riggleman took over as interim manager for the rest of the season. In a bit of a surprise, it was revealed that Lincoln and Armstrong were prepared to have McLaren finish out the season, but Lee Pelekoudas, who had taken over for Bavasi on an interim basis earlier in the week, had pushed for McLaren's early termination. Pelekoudas told the media, "With ninety games left in the season, we thought we owed it to our fans and ourselves to win as many games as we possibly can."

The Mariners, 25-47 at the time, didn't show much improvement, finishing the '08 season with a 61-101 record. It was the first 100-loss season in Seattle in twenty-five years, but the Mariners had also made baseball history in an ignominious way. The M's were the first team ever to lose one-hundred games with a payroll over $100 million.

INFAMOUS QUOTES

I think we'll be competitive. I think this is the best time to be an expansion club. — Mariners announcer Dave Niehaus, days after his hiring in December 1976

I might have to start smoking a cheaper cigar, but everything is cool. — Mariners part-owner Lester Smith, after acknowledging in July 1977 that the expansion team was coming up short of expected revenue due to unsold advertising space on the club's TV and radio broadcasts.

It stinks. I would have been better off if they had released me. When the manager called me in, I was thinking of New York or Milwaukee. I don't even know who plays for Seattle. — Relief-pitcher Dick Drago, after hearing he'd been traded from the Red Sox to the Mariners in April 1981.

Another of those mob scenes watched the game, with 7,181 squeezing through the turnstiles, but the fifty-thousand empty seats were probably the best thing that happened to the Mariners. Empty seats don't boo. —Seattle P-I beat writer J Michael Kenyon in April 1978.

It's great to be going to a club like the Yankees, but the Mariners are not that far away from contention. outfielder Ruppert Jones, after being traded to New York in October 1979.

I think your play goes up thirty percent when you perform in front of a big crowd, and when it's not there, you still try, but it's not the same. — Mariners DH Willie Horton, after a three-game series against Oakland in April 1980 drew a total of 12,600 fans to the Kingdome.

I wouldn't be surprised if it was Leon Roberts. — Mariners Manager Maury Wills, when asked at a January 1981 press conference who would play center-field for the M's in the upcoming season. Roberts had been traded to Texas five weeks earlier.

Look, these days you've got to give credit to anyone who risks $13 million for a franchise. — Mariners President Dan O'Brien after George Argyros bought the team in 1981.

I was just trying to win a game. — M's third-baseman Lenny Randle, in May 1981, explaining why he got down on his hands and knees and tried to blow a ball bunted by Kansas City's Amos Otis into foul territory.

I don't think you can buy a winner. I want to build a true champion. You can't get a true champion when you have to buy one with money. It's completely irresponsible for some of our owners to be signing players at these rates. I think it's a sad day in professional sports every time it happens. — Mariners owner George Argyros, after the San Diego Padres signed Steve Garvey to a five-year contract for $6.6 million in December 1982.

I don't change my clothes in a phone booth, but I feel that I am a better manager than I was last year or than I was two weeks ago. I'll just take all the scrapbooks and the Boy Wonder stuff and see if I can come up with another job. — Rene Lachemann, after being fired as Mariners manager in June 1983.

I ain't coming to Seattle to fail. — DH Gorman Thomas, upon being acquired by the Mariners in December of 1983. He hit .157 the following season.

I keep hearing copouts, like the weather early in the year is too bad to stand in line for tickets. Then, later on, I'm told it's too nice to spend indoors at a game. Well, I've heard that movie attendance goes up in the summer. We gave out Robert Redford posters. And we've got some players that look like movie stars. What else can we do? — Mariners President Chuck Armstrong, complaining about Kingdome attendance in June 1984.

We're not going to do anything dumb, but I'd even like to work a trade for the talk factor, something for our fans to chew on, for the sports pages and the talk shows — something to make news. — Chuck Armstrong, December 1985.

I think we have too many players who think that if we lose that's the way The Lord meant it to be. — M's General Manager Dick Balderson, upon telling the media in October 1986 that he believed there was too much religion in the Mariners clubhouse.

There are a lot of players on this team who got paid a lot of money last year who didn't perform. The pendulum is starting to swing back and that is becoming obvious throughout baseball. — Balderson, in January 1987, explaining why the M's tried to cut the salaries of several Mariner players, including Phil Bradley, who hit .310 in 1986.

Fathers could be seen covering the eyes of their children every time a grounder was hit towards third. — *Seattle Times* columnist Steve Kelley after Edgar Martinez made four errors on Little League Day at the Kingdome in May 1990.

That was the most classless thing I have ever seen on a baseball field. — Tigers catcher Chad Kreuter in May 1993 after Ken Griffey Jr. grabbed his crotch twice and yelled an obscenity at Detroit Manager Sparky Anderson after hitting a home run one day after Tigers pitchers had walked Griffey four times.

We try not to be stupid. We're not anxious to take on Boras again, but we're not going to let him scare us off. I know some GMs who will not take a player because he is represented by Boras. — Mariners Director of Scouting Roger Jongewaard after the M's selected Jason Varitek in the first round of the 1994 amateur draft, the third straight year Seattle had picked a player represented by Boras in the first round.

We've got to get home and get a place to play at home. I don't care if it's Tacoma, the Kingdome, or some cow pasture. We can't continue on the road the rest of the year. The league has to force other teams to play in Tacoma if they have to. The American League can't keep us out there playing like a Barnum and Bailey show the rest of the year. — Lou Piniella, in July 1994 after falling ceiling tiles at the Kingdome forced the Mariners to play twenty straight games on the road.

I loved to hear that. There's nothing wrong with a little feistiness. Hey, back in my day we had an altercation about once a week. — Lou Piniella, after learning that Mariner pitchers Bobby Ayala and John Cummings had nearly come to blows on the team's lengthy road trip in August 1994.

Statistics are like bikinis — they show a lot but not everything. — Lou Piniella, date unknown

When I first got here, if you wanted to see a lot of people, feel a lot of emotion, you went to a Seahawks game. But those fans have come to help us now. Seattle used to be known for only grunge rock, Starbucks and Microsoft, but we're on our way to making it known for baseball, too. — Randy Johnson after pitching a complete game to defeat the Angels in a one-game playoff, sending the Mariners to their first-ever playoff series in October 1995.

I don't know what happened and I don't want to know. — M's closer Norm Charlton in April 1996 after learning that fellow reliever Bobby Ayala had punched out a window at the team's Chicago hotel.

Who is to say someone's wrong for doing it? I don't know if they're good or bad. If you abuse anything, there are going to be effects down the road. If steroids are done in moderation, done correctly and safely, it might be an option. — Mariners second-baseman Bret Boone in July 2002 after being asked his opinion on steroids in baseball

To tell the truth, I'm not excited to go to Cleveland, but we have to. If I ever saw myself saying I'm excited going to Cleveland, I'd punch myself in the face, because I'd be lying. — Ichiro, June 2007

He said, "Woof, woof, woof," which meant, "Stay, stay, stay," Of course, I listened. — Ichiro in July 2007, revealing that his dog Ikkyu had played a major role in his decision to sign a five-year contract extension with the Mariners.

Chicks who dig home runs aren't the ones who appeal to me. I think there's sexiness in infield hits because they require technique. I'd rather impress the chicks with my technique than with my brute strength. Then, every now and then, just to show I can do that, too, I might flirt a little by hitting one out. — Ichiro, August 2009

Chapter 30

"IN JACK WE TRUST"

A s the '08 season ended, the focus in Seattle was on who the Mariners' next general manager would be. While the job might have seemed like an attractive one with the team's revenue streams ensuring reasonably high payrolls, some candidates were likely scared off by the possibility of interference from upper management.

Chuck Armstrong had bragged about intruding in personnel matters, and there was also the interference from Japan. While the Kenji Johjima contract extension had been mandated by Yamauchi in Japan, the dollars paid to Johjima counted against the team's payroll budget like any other bad contract.

Several interesting candidates declined to be interviewed for the Seattle GM job, including assistant GMs Chris Antonetti (Cleveland), Jed Hoyer (Boston), and David Forst (Oakland). The Mariners interviewed eight candidates, including internal candidates Pelekoudas and Bob Engel, but settled on four finalists: Blue Jays Assistant GM Tony LaCava, Dodgers Assistant GM Kim Ng, D-Backs executive Jerry DiPoto and Brewers VP of Player Personnel Jack Zduriencik.

On October 22, Zduriencik was named as the new general manager. At fifty-seven, Zduriencik was the oldest of the four finalists. Having drafted most of Milwaukee's best players, he was seen as the main reason the Brewers had managed to turn things around and reach the postseason in 2008.

Zduriencik quickly set out to find a new manager for the Mariners and within a couple of weeks had whittled his list of candidates to seven finalists. Surprisingly, none of the finalists had major-league managing experience. While former Mariner second-baseman Joey Cora appeared to be the frontrunner to get the job, two Red Sox coaches, Brad Mills and DeMarlo Hale, were also in the mix, along with Cardinals third-base coach Jose Oquendo, D-Backs third-base coach Chip Hale, Padres Triple-A Manager Randy Ready, and Oakland A's bench coach Don Wakamatsu.

On November 19, Wakamatsu was named the M's new manager. The forty-five-year-old former catcher was familiar with the A.L. West, having worked for all three of the M's division rivals in the previous seven years.

At the annual winter meetings in Las Vegas, Zduriencik was hard at work and pulled off his first trade as Mariners GM, a three-team, twelve player deal with the Cleveland Indians and New York Mets. The key player traded away by Seattle was closer J.J. Putz, but the Mariners received seven players in return, including center-fielder Franklin Gutierrez, left-handed pitcher Jason Vargas, and first-baseman Mike Carp. All three became significant contributors to the Mariners over the next three years, while Putz lasted just one year in New York. None of the other players traded by Seattle in the deal (Jeremy Reed, Sean Green, and Luis Valbuena) did much with their new teams.

With the Mariners clearly in the early stages of a rebuilding movement, the team's payroll for 2009 was cut nearly $20 million from the $117 million that had been spent in 2008. The reduction in payroll was understandable since the team wasn't likely to contend in 2009. But it helped that the team had hired a GM in Zduriencik who was capable of finding reasonably priced players who could be productive.

Zduriencik was the first GM in the M's history to have *Moneyball* skills: the ability, popularized by Oakland A's General Manager Billy Beane to identify and acquire players who were undervalued by other teams and who could be acquired for less money. Under Bavasi, the M's had been the epitome of the anti-*Moneyball* approach, repeatedly signing and trading for expensive players who didn't produce to the level of their contracts. While Beane might sign a player for $2 million that ended up giving the club a $10 million performance (such as Frank Thomas in 2006), Bavasi and the Mariners did the opposite, acquiring players such as Vidro, Everett, Weaver and Sexson and overpaying them significantly.

In addition to adding Gutierrez, who played Gold Glove caliber defense and hit .283 with 18 home runs and 70 RBI in his first season in Seattle, the M's got big performances in 2009 from two other players who had been undervalued by their previous teams. Relief-pitcher David Aardsma, acquired from Boston for a minor-league pitcher, became the M's closer and saved 38 games, while first-baseman Russell Branyan, signed as a free agent for $1.4 million, led the '09 team in home runs, with 31, and drove in 76 runs.

A late addition to the team, Ken Griffey Jr. signed with Seattle after spring training had begun. This was a reunion that some thought would never happen as long as Howard Lincoln was running the Mariners. Lincoln was known to hold a grudge over the way Junior had forced the trade to Cincinnati following the 1999 season and Lincoln had on several occasions ruled out the possibility of Griffey returning to the M's. But a combination of factors led to Griffey rejoining the Mariners.

As a free agent, Griffey was acquired without having to trade any players; the Mariners needed a DH, and Junior was willing to play for a base salary of $2 million. It also seemed from his numbers that Griffey could still hit — he had hit eighteen home runs and drove in seventy-one runs in 2008 and he'd hit thirty home runs in 2007. More important though, Griffey's return was expected to stem the decline in attendance at Safeco Field after the 101-loss season.

On April 6, the M's opened the '09 season in Minnesota and defeated the Twins 6-1 with Griffey hitting the 612th home run of his career in the fifth inning. It was his eighth Opening Day home run, tying a major-league record. While few gave the '09 Mariners a chance to contend, Seattle surprised a lot of people in the first week of the new season, going 5-2 on the season-opening road trip, including a three-game sweep in Oakland. After one week of the season, Seattle held a one and a half game lead in the A.L. West. It was the first time in six years — since August 23, 2003 — that the M's had been in first place by themselves in the division.

On April 14, a crowd of 45,958 came to the home opener at Safeco to welcome Griffey back to Seattle. The crowd roared when Junior was introduced before his first-inning at-bat. He tipped his cap, then hit a single to right field. The M's delivered a 3-2 win in ten innings and remained in first place.

The surprising Mariners actually remained atop the A.L. West until early May when they lost six in a row. Griffey and another veteran DH, Mike Sweeney, helped create a loose environment in the Seattle clubhouse that hadn't existed in 2008. One reason is the pair helped integrate Ichiro back into the clubhouse. While Ichiro had felt a part of things early in his Mariner career, when players like Boone and Cameron welcomed him, Ichiro had become isolated from his teammates in recent years.

It helped that the M's were winning and it helped, too, that the Mariners now had a manager with some leadership skills in Wakamatsu. The first-year manager was firm when he needed to be, as evidenced by him challenging Felix Hernandez after a game in mid-May in which the M's ace allowed five stolen bases. Hernandez stepped up his game shortly afterward, winning A.L. Pitcher of the Month honors for June, a first in his career.

Actually, the Mariners' entire pitching staff performed well in 2009, producing the lowest ERA in the American League. Factoring in the pitchers' success was the team's defense, which was also rated tops in the league, with Gutierrez having the best defensive rating among all major-league outfielders that year. According to the most widely recognized defensive metric Gutierrez saved the Mariners 29.1 runs in 2009.

As the '09 trade deadline neared, the M's found themselves in a quandary. With the club just four games out in the A.L. West on July 19· it was close enough to consider adding a left-fielder to close the gap between itself and the division-leading Angels. The M's had lost their best left-fielder in mid-June when Endy Chavez, another player acquired in the three-team blockbuster deal that brought in Gutierrez, collided with shortstop Yuniesky Betancourt and suffered a season-ending knee injury.

That collision may have been the final straw for Betancourt in Seattle. The twenty-seven-year-old had looked like a future star when he came up in July 2005, but he'd shown little improvement over the years and had come to be seen as more of a liability than an asset, especially since he was owed a guaranteed $10 million on his contract. While Betancourt typically hit for a high average, he rarely walked; in his four seasons in Seattle, his highest annual walk total was seventeen. Wakamatsu and hitting coach Alan Cockrell spent countless hours trying to get Betancourt to change his approach at the plate. They wanted him to be more selective, take more pitches, and walk more. He'd go along for a couple of days, but then revert to his bad habits. He also had lost a significant amount of range in the field. Somehow Zduriencik was able to a find a team that valued Betancourt — the Kansas City Royals — which gave up two prospects and took on the bulk of Betancourt's contract obligations.

Betancourt's replacement was acquired two weeks later when Zduriencik traded five players, including catcher Jeff Clement, the club's first-round pick in 2005, to Pittsburgh for shortstop Jack Wilson and pitcher Ian Snell. While the Pirates agreed to pay the salaries of both players for the rest of the '09 season, their motivation in making the trade was to get off the hook for Snell's contract, which guaranteed him $4.25 million in 2010. The twenty-seven-year-old Snell was the Pirates' highest-paid pitcher in 2009, but had been demoted to the minors and strangely refused a promotion back to Pittsburgh.

2009 TOP PERFORMERS

Russell Branyan, .251, 31 HR, 79 RBI

Jose Lopez, .272, 25 HR, 96 RBI

Ichiro Suzuki, .352, 11 HR, 46 RBI, 26 SB

Felix Hernandez, 19-5, 2.49 ERA, 238.2 IP

David Aardsma, 3-6, 2.52 ERA, 38 saves

With the M's considering adding a bat to the lineup, they also had Bedard and Washburn in the last year of their contracts. Both left-handed starters were having good seasons and would be attractive to contending teams if the M's slipped farther back in the standings and decided to become sellers at the July 31 trade deadline.

When the M's were swept by the Cleveland Indians in a three-game series at Safeco Field the weekend of July 24-26, it became clear that the M's would be sellers. While Bedard landed on the disabled list on July 25 with a sore shoulder, ending the possibility of getting value in a deadline deal, the M's were able to trade Washburn. While he was having the best of his four seasons in Seattle, he was due to become a free agent at the end of the season, so Zduriencik took the best offer he could get — two pitching prospects from the Tigers.

The '09 season ended on a high note October 4 when Seattle defeated Texas 4-3 with Hernandez getting his nineteenth win, a career high. Griffey singled in his final at-bat and got a curtain call from the crowd of 32,260 at Safeco. After the game Griffey, who had not yet made a decision whether to play another season, was carried off the field by his Mariner teammates. A few minutes later, a red-eyed Griffey told the media at his locker, "This is probably the most nervous and emotional roller-coaster I've ever been through. If this is going to be the last one, it's tough."

Chapter 31

RANKING THE MARINER MANAGERS

1. Lou Piniella (1993-2002; 840-711; .542 winning percentage)

While Lou Piniella benefited greatly from having more talent than any other Seattle manager, Jim Lefebvre and Bill Plummer couldn't get the Mariners past the eighty-three-win mark with many of those same players. Piniella cared about winning more than anyone in the entire Seattle organization and he got the most out of his players.

The only Mariners manager with a career record over .500, Piniella is also the only manager to take the M's to the postseason. Piniella likely will remain as the top-ranked manager in club history until Seattle gets to a World Series.

2. Rene Lachemann (1981-83; 140-180; .438)

The club's third manager, Rene Lachemann was barely thirty-six when he took over from Maury Wills in May 1981. A former catcher, the outgoing "Lach" did wonders with Seattle's young bullpen in 1982, when the M's had their best season to that point. But when the magic wore off the following season, it took George Argyros less than half a season to fire Lachemann, a move described in a *Seattle P-I* editorial as the most unpopular with the team's fans in the M's first seven years.

While Lach managed only one full season in Seattle, he gets the nod as the second-best manager. It would have been interesting to see what he could have accomplished had he been given more talent to work with.

3. Eric Wedge (2011; 67-95; .414)

Since Eric Wedge had managed only one season in Seattle at this writing, it's hard to judge him on anything but his handling of the team. In 2011 he kept the M's in contention until July despite an offense that was the worst in the league for the third season in a row. Wedge did a good job developing young players in Cleveland and he's expected to do the same in Seattle if given enough talent to work with.

4. Darrell Johnson (1977-1980; 226-362; .384)

The M's first manager, Darrell Johnson, was an old-school type, having once played for Casey Stengel. Johnson had managed the '75 Red Sox to the World Series, but lost his job in Boston halfway through the following season, making him available to the expansion Mariners.

A master of the baseball chess board, Johnson might well be the best bench manager the Seattle franchise has ever had. Too bad it didn't have much talent in the three-plus years he led the charge.

5. Jim Lefebvre (1989-1991; 233-253; .479)

Jim Lefebvre's reward for leading the M's to their first winning season in 1991? A pink slip four days after that season ended. While he wasn't well liked by his players, they respected him as a manager. His ouster had more to do with his big mouth; then-owner Jeff Smulyan planned to move the team to Tampa and GM Woody Woodward didn't believe Lefebvre could keep a secret.

6. Don Wakamatsu (2009-2010; 127-147; .464)

It looked like the Mariners had a good manager in place when Don Wakamatsu led the 2009 Mariners to an eighty-five-win season, a twenty-four-game improvement from a disastrous '08 campaign.

Wak probably would have survived the disappointing '10 season if he didn't have Ken Griffey Jr., unhappy about being benched, turning the clubhouse against him. Look for him to get another managing opportunity down the road, and maybe get to a World Series before the Mariners.

7. Dick Williams (1986-1988; 159-192; .453)

When the fifty-seven-year-old Williams took over as Seattle manager in May 1986, he'd already taken three different teams to the World Series, so it was expected he'd make the Mariners winners too. But while the disciplinarian Williams got the M's farther than any manager had to that point, a 78-84 record in his only full season at the helm, some good young talent was traded away because of personality conflicts with Williams. He clashed with his Mariner bosses a bit too often and was fired in June of 1988.

8. Bob Melvin (2003-2004; 156-168; .481)

When Piniella left Seattle after the '02 season, the Mariners were so anxious to hire a manager who was the anti-Lou that they didn't even bother to interview veteran Manager Dusty Baker, who was interested in the job. They found their yes man in Melvin, who didn't make waves with the front office or with umpires on the field.

After Melvin won ninety-three games his first season, the team aged quickly and lost ninety-nine games the following season, with the ax falling on Melvin the day after the last game of the '04 season.

9. Mike Hargrove (2005-2007; 192-201; .478)

While Hargrove had been a successful skipper with a loaded Cleveland team, he finished under .500 in each of his last six full seasons as a big-league manager.

Hargrove made plenty of mistakes in Seattle, among them sticking too long with his veterans and not using his bench enough. But his biggest mistake was thinking he could win a power struggle with Ichiro. He hasn't managed since "quitting" the M's in the midst of a seven-game winning streak midway through the '07 season. At sixty-two, he probably won't manage again.

10. John McLaren (2007-2008; 68-88; .436)

The job of taking over the M's in the middle of the '07 season after Mike Hargrove's sudden "retirement" would have been a tough assignment for anyone, but it was especially difficult for McLaren, who had no previous major-league managing experience nor a spring training to prepare for the head job.

McLaren is not likely to get another chance at managing in the bigs, but it would have been interesting to see how the M's might have fared had he, instead of Melvin, taken over from Piniella after the '02 season.

11. Chuck Cottier (1984-1986; 98-119, .452).

Chuck Cottier was a nice man, but overmatched as a big-league manager. He's perhaps best known for a tirade at Yankee Stadium in 1985 when he picked up first base and threw it into right field.

Piniella, who hadn't yet become a manager, was New York's hitting coach at the time, so Cottier may well have provided some inspiration for one of Piniella's signature moves. Cottier was a players' manager, so naturally when the ax fell on him, he was replaced by a hard-ass in Williams.

12. Del Crandall (1983-1984; 93-131; .415)

While Del Crandall didn't even get to manage a full season in Seattle, he actually had the 1984 Mariners just five games out of first place in late July. But when the M's lost twenty of their next thirty games, he was replaced by Cottier.

Crandall wasn't much of a manager, but he holds the distinction of being the best player ever to manage the Mariners, having been an eight-time All-Star as a catcher with the Milwaukee Braves.

13. Bill Plummer (1992; 64-98; .395)

Bill Plummer, who'd been Lefebvre's third-base coach, replaced him as manager after the '91 season. Plummer was fired after one season when the team went in reverse, losing ninety-eight games a year after finishing over .500 for the first time. But at least all that losing in 1992 served a purpose — the M's were able to draft Alex Rodriguez with the first overall pick in the '93 draft.

14. Maury Wills (1980-1981; 26-56; .317)

It's quite possible that no manager in history made as many blunders as Maury Wills did during his brief eighty-two-game reign of error in 1980-81. He made numerous strategic mistakes, used a player he'd waived before the game, tried to alter the batters' box, and regularly blamed others for his mistakes.

While other teams are known for more prestigious things like multiple World Series titles, the Mariners are known for having arguably the worst manager in the history of baseball.

Chapter 32

BELIEVING BIG

While the '09 season had been an unqualified success for the Mariners, the club had a lot of work to do in the offseason, with several positions (left field, first base, third base, and DH) needing to be filled for 2010.

One issue was settled early in the offseason when Johjima decided to return to Japan and forfeited the final two years of his guaranteed contract. While Johjima's decision opened up another position, it was a spot the M's thought could be filled adequately by young catchers Adam Moore and Rob Johnson. More important, Johjima's departure freed up $15.8 million over the next two seasons. Johjima had been a part-time player in 2009 and had hit .247 with 9 home runs and 22 RBI, so he clearly was not worth the huge contract he'd been handed.

Another issue was solved in mid-November when the M's reached agreement to bring Griffey back for the '10 season. On the day of the signing, Griffey's agent, Brian Goldberg, said Junior would be ready for whatever role Wakamatsu had for him, "large or small." That made sense; since Griffey had hit .214 in 2009, most people expected the M's to sign a full-time DH, with Junior playing once or twice a week, but continuing to have a big role in the clubhouse.

The M's seemingly solidified two infield spots, re-signing shortstop Jack Wilson to a two-year deal for $10 million and luring the Angels' leadoff hitter, Chone Figgins to Seattle with a four-year, $36 million commitment. Wilson was considered one of the best defenders in the game, but wasn't much of a hitter. Five-million dollars a season for a good glove seemed like an extravagance the weak-hitting M's couldn't afford.

The versatile Figgins had played third base with the Angels in 2009, but had previous experience at second, so the M's decided to move second-baseman Jose Lopez to third and play Figgins at second. The experiment was a failure. The position swap and the move from the leadoff spot seemed to be Figgins' undoing. A .291 career hitter in seven seasons in Anaheim, Figgins hit under .200 for much of the first two months of 2010 and played poorly in the field.

Zduriencik pulled off a shocking trade in mid-December, acquiring Phillies ace Cliff Lee for a package of three minor-leaguers, none of whom could be considered top prospects or players the Mariners would miss. The best player sent to Philadelphia in the deal was the club's first-round pick in 2007, Phillippe Aumont, but he'd been shifted to the bullpen in 2009 and faced an uncertain future in Seattle.

Lee was one of the top pitchers in the game at the time, so it was not only a surprise that Seattle was able to acquire him, but also that the M's hadn't had to mortgage their future to do so. The price to Philadelphia in prospects was significantly less than Seattle had given up to acquire Bedard two years earlier. Even better, Lee was signed to a below-market salary of just $8 million for 2010, so the M's had the money to make more impact moves to try to win. The major reason the Phillies had traded Lee was they hadn't been able to get him signed long term and didn't want to let him leave as a free agent with just draft choices for compensation.

Logically, if Lee hadn't wanted to sign an extension with the Phillies, it seemed even more unlikely that he'd forego free agency to sign long-term in Seattle. When it became clear that Adrian Beltre was not going to return in 2010, most observers expected that the M's would use the money saved on his contract and that of Johjima's to fill their other holes.

Signing Figgins and trading for Lee seemed to be a good start to the offseason for Zduriencik, but the M's had other needs, specifically in left field and DH. First base also became a position of need when the M's decided not to re-sign Branyan due to concerns about a back injury that forced him to miss the last five weeks of the '09 season.

Zduriencik took a gamble in replacing Branyan, trading with Boston for Casey Kotchman, who'd hit .268 with seven home runs in 2009. Kotchman had never hit more than fourteen home runs in a season, but the M's were hoping for a breakout season from the twenty-seven-year-old, who'd been a first-round pick of the Angels several years before. However, unlike the bargain acquisitions of Branyan and Aardsma in 2009, Seattle would have to pay the arbitration-eligible Kotchman $3.5 million. Kotchman wouldn't produce as well as Branyan or Aardsma either, hitting just .217 with nine home runs in 2010.

Despite big holes remaining at the crucial spots of left field and DH, management seemingly cut off Zduriencik before he could finish building the '10 team. There were free agents available at both spots (DHs Vladimir Guerrero, Johnny Damon, Jim Thome, and Hideki Matsui and left-fielders

Matt Holliday, Jason Bay, Mike Cameron, and Mark DeRosa), but the M's wouldn't let Zduriencik spend the money to sign any of those players. When the offseason dealing was done, the Mariners' payroll for 2010 was more than $10 million less than it had been in 2009. There was no announcement that the M's had decided to cut payroll. What had happened to the money saved by Johjima's departure? Apparently the team had decided not to put that money into the 2010 team.

This decision was a curious one and extremely shortsighted. If you're only going to have a pitcher like Lee for one season, it seems the team should have made the moves necessary to give it the best chance to win. That $10 million would have gone a long way toward filling the holes in left field and designated hitter. A team that had had a $117 million payroll in 2009 was now down to an $86 million payroll.

Despite opportunities to improve the team at both DH and left field, the M's did little. That meant Griffey, who'd shown in 2009 that his days as a regular player were probably over, would be the team's primary DH. For left field, the Mariners had twenty-three-year-old Michael Saunders, but he'd hit .221 without a home run in a forty-six-game trial in '09 and couldn't be counted on to produce in 2010.

It seemed Zduriencik's only option for an experienced left-fielder was to make a bad contract swap with the Chicago Cubs. The Mariners still owed more than $24 million for the next two years to Carlos Silva, who'd pitched poorly while appearing in just eight games in 2009. Meanwhile, the Cubs were looking to dump Milton Bradley, who had been suspended and sent home with two weeks remaining in the '09 season. While Bradley had a disappointing season in 2009 (.257 with twelve homers and forty RBI), it was a more useful season than Silva had given the Mariners and, from the M's point of view, another team's trash looked much better than their own. The toxic-waste swap was consummated on December 18, with the Mariners sending $6 million to Chicago to cover the difference in the two players' salaries.

In late January the Mariners locked up staff ace Felix Hernandez with a five-year, $78 million contract through 2014. At the time, Hernandez was two years away from free agency and there had been rumors that Seattle might need to trade Felix if they couldn't get him signed to a long-term deal. At the news conference announcing the signing, Hernandez explained, "I just wanted to be here. I didn't care about free agency. I'm here for five more years. We're really close right now. I think we're going to make the playoffs this year."

Ichiro had high expectations for the '10 season, too, telling the *Seattle Times* at the beginning of spring training, "We made good moves and have bigger expectations and that's what we have to play to."

Mariners' management appeared to have high hopes for 2010 as well, even while cutting payroll significantly. The team unveiled a marketing campaign with the catchy slogan "Believe Big." While the campaign was intended primarily to sell tickets, with a slogan like that it would have been impossible not to raise the hopes of fans who had rooted for a team that hadn't made the postseason in nine years.

Despite the increased expectations of star players and fans, there were no playoffs for the M's in 2010; in fact, they didn't come close. In a carbon copy of the '08 season, Seattle again lost 101 games, with the atmosphere in the M's clubhouse turning toxic.

As spring training neared, Zduriencik talked about wanting to make some tweaks to the team, but the only additions were a couple of low-cost signings, first-baseman/DH Ryan Garko and outfielder Eric Byrnes. Neither was the answer, because the club waived Garko during spring training and Byrnes was released in early May, two days after he helped lose an extra-inning game against Texas when he inexplicably pulled his bat back on what was supposed to be a suicide-squeeze attempt.

Another move that didn't help the 2010 team was the trade that brought in Jack Wilson and Ian Snell. It seems unlikely that if Zduriencik had known the team's payroll was going to drop $10 million from 2009 to 2010 that he would have chosen to spend $9 million on Wilson and Snell because those funds could have been better allocated to improving the team's offense. In any event, it was money wasted, as the oft-injured Wilson played in only sixty-one games in 2010. Snell was worse; he went 0-5 with a 6.41 ERA in twelve games and was banished to the minors in mid-June.

It took less than a week into the '10 season for Bradley to show those unfamiliar with his act why the volatile outfielder had worn out his welcome with so many teams. After notching just one hit in his first seventeen at-bats with the M's, Bradley flipped off fans during a game against the Rangers in Arlington.

The Mariners didn't need this type of player in their clubhouse. While management believed that Griffey's presence would help Bradley grow up, they were wrong. But because management had cut payroll despite making a profit of $3.5 million in 2009, Zduriencik had little choice but to take a chance on Bradley.

Perhaps more important, the team's second-year manager, Waka-matsu, didn't need the distraction. Wakamatsu had done a good job in 2009 leading the team to a winning record and winning over the Mariner players. But he hadn't had to deal with such issues in 2009. Mount Bradley erupted again in early May, as the troubled outfielder, hitting .214 at the time, left Safeco Field in the middle of a game, angry over being pulled in the middle innings. He was placed on the restricted list and didn't play for the next two weeks while he sought counseling for "personal issues."

The '10 season began on the road, with the M's losing five of their first seven games before returning to Seattle for the home opener on April 12. But a capacity crowd of 45,876 left disappointed when the M's managed just two hits in a 4-0 shutout loss to Oakland. Seattle seemed to turn things around after the opener, winning seven of the eight games remaining on the opening homestand. With a 9-7 record, the M's headed to Chicago for a three-game series with the White Sox. Little did they know that it was the last time they'd be over .500 during the '10 season, as they lost each of the three games in Chicago on home runs in the Sox's final at-bats.

On April 30 the 11-11 Mariners returned home to Safeco for a nine-game homestand with reason for optimism. Lee, who'd missed the first month of the season with an abdominal injury, made his Mariners debut against the Rangers. Lee had a dominant debut, shutting out Texas for seven innings, but he got a no-decision when Seattle couldn't score in a 2-0 twelve-inning loss. The M's best opportunity to win the game came in the eleventh inning, when Ichiro was tagged out trying to score on the suicide squeeze play that fell apart thanks to Eric Byrnes. In a bizarre end to his career, Byrnes departed the Seattle clubhouse on his bicycle after-ward without talking to the media, nearly running over Jack Zduriencik. Byrnes refused to talk about the play the following day and was released with a batting average of .094.

The Byrnes fiasco may have doomed the M's; the team lost each of the next seven games of the homestand. More likely it was the fact that the Mariners couldn't hit; the team scored just nine runs in the first eight games of the homestand and after twenty-nine games of the '10 season, Seattle had scored a total of ninety-one runs, an average of barely three runs per game.

On May 3, Zduriencik addressed the Associated Press Sports Editors' regional meeting and admitted that, despite the great expectations for 2010, he had known before the season that "there were still other things we needed on this club to be a real, real good ballclub." Zduriencik, while claiming he was working the phones looking for ways to improve the Mariners' horrific offense, also admitted that it was not yet "hunting season," meaning that it was too early in the season to acquire offensive help because teams weren't ready to make trades. While Zduriencik seemed hopeful that things would improve, he made it clear that acquiring offensive help would not happen anytime soon.

The biggest weakness on the team was apparent to anyone who'd watched the M's in the early stages of the season. The forty-year-old Griffey could no longer hit. After collecting a double on Opening Day, he went the next month without an extra base hit, yet his name was on the lineup card nearly every day for the first six weeks of the '10 season. The man who had hit 630 career home runs had suddenly lost his ability to hit the long ball, as he couldn't even reach the warning track in his final season.

By the time a .190 hitting Griffey was reduced to occasional starts in mid-May, the M's were 14-26 and had little hope of turning things around and getting back in contention. On June 2, less than two weeks after having his playing time reduced, Griffey walked out on the Mariners, quitting without telling anyone, only alerting management that he had decided to retire after he had been in his car for several hours driving away from Seattle.

While Griffey was gone, he was not forgotten; the damage he caused to the Mariners clubhouse lived on for the remainder of the '10 season. On May 10, Larry LaRue, beat writer for the *Tacoma News Tribune*, who had covered the M's since 1988, the year before Griffey made his major-league debut, wrote on his blog that Griffey would retire or be released by the Mariners within the month. LaRue not only cited Griffey's poor performance at the plate, but also a piece of what he described as "anecdotal evidence" that indicated Junior was no longer the team leader he'd been in 2009. Two of Griffey's teammates, described as "younger players who didn't have an ax to grind," revealed to LaRue that Junior had been sleeping in the clubhouse in the late innings of a close game and had not been available for pinch-hitting duties.

Asked directly by the media whether he'd been sleeping in the clubhouse, Griffey didn't deny the allegation, instead saying, "I can't win this." That didn't stop teammates from coming to his defense. DH Mike Sweeney demanded that the two unnamed players come forward, saying he wanted to fight them for having the nerve to tell the media of Griffey's alleged transgressions.

Griffey, for his part, believed he had been betrayed not by any of his teammates, but by Wakamatsu, whom he thought was LaRue's source.

While Griffey later learned otherwise, the damage had been done — Junior told his teammates that he believed he'd been stabbed in the back by the manager. In a comical twist that showed the priorities of the Mariners' team president, Art Thiel wrote on seattlepi.com that Chuck Armstrong accompanied Griffey's agent to the *News Tribune* offices hoping to persuade the newspaper to retract the Napgate story, but because the story was true as written, the newspaper refused to back down.

The petty Griffey had been successful turning the Seattle clubhouse against Wakamatsu and Junior got the last laugh when one of his closest friends on the team, Chone Figgins, got into an altercation with the manager in the M's dugout in the middle of a game in late July. Within weeks the M's had no choice but to fire Wakamatsu. He'd lost the respect of the M's clubhouse and wasn't likely to get it back. The manager who had been such a big part of the team's turnaround in 2009 was fired on August 9 and replaced by interim Manager Daren Brown.

2010 TOP PERFORMERS

Ichiro Suzuki, .315, 6 HR, 43 RBI, 42 SB

Felix Hernandez, 13-12, 2.27 ERA, 249.2 IP

Cliff Lee, 8-3, 2.34 ERA, 103.2 IP

Jason Vargas, 9-12, 3.78 ERA, 192.2 IP

David Aardsma, 0-6, 3.44 ERA, 31 saves

Seattle made a curious move in late June. Already fifteen games behind the division-leading Rangers, it traded two prospects, including outfielder Ezequiel Carrera, who'd hit .337 at Double-A in 2009, to Cleveland to reacquire Branyan. While the Mariners were short on power, there was little point in trading prospects to add power to a team in the middle of a lost season. The move became even more of a head-scratcher when the M's declined Branyan's contract option for 2011 at the end of the season, even though he'd managed to lead the Mariners in home runs (fifteen) in just half a season in Seattle.

With another Mariners team out of contention in the A.L. West by July 1, attention turned to what Seattle might get in a trade for Lee. Despite missing the first month of the season, Lee had lasted seven innings in twelve of his thirteen starts with Seattle and had dominated American

League hitters like no pitcher in recent memory (8-3 with a 2.34 ERA with an 89:6 strikeout-to-walk ratio). He was clearly a pitcher in high demand; one who several teams thought might get them to the postseason or help them win the World Series.

While some thought the M's would make out best waiting until the July 31 trading deadline, as well as Lee was pitching, his value wasn't going to get any higher, and there was always the risk he'd sustain an injury. Several teams were said to be after Lee, but in the end Zduriencik chose a four-player package from the Texas Rangers, centered around slugging first-baseman Justin Smoak instead of a three-player package the Yankees were offering that would have netted the M's catching prospect Jesus Montero, a player Seattle would acquire in a separate trade early in 2012.

With five games left in the '10 season, the only drama remaining was whether the M's could avoid the fifth one-hundred-loss season in franchise history. With a record of 61-96 on September 29, the M's needed to win two of their last five contests of the season to avoid its second 100-loss season in three years. It wasn't to be, as the M's lost their last five games of the season, all at Safeco Field, including a season-ending four-game sweep at the hands of the Oakland A's, who managed to reach .500 and edge out the Angels for second place in the A.L. West.

Chapter 33

GOUGING THE MOST LOYAL
FANS IN BASEBALL

B etween 1996 and 2010 the Seattle Mariners enjoyed attendance of more than two million fans each season for fifteen straight years. That streak was broken in 2011, when attendance at Safeco Field fell short of the two million mark by some sixty-thousand fans.

That was pretty remarkable, considering the performance of the team on the field. As of this writing the M's had finished in last place in the American League West in six of the eight seasons.

However, the steady decline in attendance, from a team-record of 3,542,938 in 2002, began *before* the Mariners began finishing in last place on a regular basis — most likely because of increases in ticket prices.

Despite second-half fades that caused the team to miss the playoffs in the 2002-03 seasons, season ticket prices went up after both seasons. The club lost three-thousand season tickets after each season, which accounted for much of the declines of 275,000 (2003) and 327,000 (2004) in attendance those years.

While the M's didn't raise season ticket prices following the ninety-nine-loss '04 season, they instituted a new pricing scheme under which the cost of single game tickets increased year after year to the point a ticket that had cost $38 at the box office in 2004 might cost as much as $65 by 2011.

On top of that, after finishing above .500 in 2007 for the first time in four years, the Mariners raised season ticket prices for 2008 and added a "premium game" surcharge of $3 for Opening Day and games against the Yankees and Red Sox. After losing 101 games in 2008, the M's didn't raise their season ticket prices for 2009 but decided, with a nationwide recession going on, that it was as good a time as any to increase the premium game surcharge to $5 and expand the number of premium games from ten to eighteen. Not only were games against the Yankees and Red Sox worthy of a surcharge, but the M's felt games against two last-place teams, the Cleveland Indians and Arizona Diamondbacks, were also worthy of an extra $5 a ticket simply because those games were taking place on weekends in the summer.

The premium game pricing was expanded again in 2010, adding a $2 surcharge for every weekend game in the summer, with the "summer surcharge" added on top of the $5 surcharge for Yankee and Red Sox games so that Yankee and Red Sox games on summer weekends would then carry a $7 surcharge for every ticket in the ballpark.

Where once the Yankees and Red Sox drew sellout crowds each time they'd come to Seattle, by 2011, in large part due to the premium-game surcharges, a three-game series against the Yankees drew an average attendance of 20,220. Attendance at a series against last-place Kansas City in August 2010, which went up against Seafair, a popular annual festival, also seemed to be affected by the summer surcharge, as that series was the lowest attended weekend series in Safeco Field history.

None of those price increases were justified. In most seasons since 2003, the M's had not put a competitive team on the field. Sellouts became rare at Safeco, yet the Mariners seemingly weren't satisfied to sell out games against popular opponents like New York and Boston, believing they had to gouge their customers for those games, resulting in a significant drop in attendance.

Several other teams in baseball reacted to the recession by lowering ticket and concession prices. In 2009, the Los Angeles Dodgers, who had reached the National League Championship Series the year before, lowered some of their ticket prices and significantly cut some of their concession prices. Beer prices at Dodger Stadium were cut from $8 to $6, bottled water from $5.75 to $3.75 and soft drinks from $5 to $3.75.

Yet in Seattle, where the team hadn't made the playoffs in over a decade, management didn't seem inclined to make fan-friendly decisions; neither the ticket prices nor concession prices ever go down at Safeco Field. While attendance at Mariner games declined in eight of nine seasons from 2003 to 2011 and season ticket sales have dropped significantly (from a high of 27,500 in 2002 to fewer than ten thousand by 2011) somehow the M's still averaged twenty-three thousand fans per game in 2011.

Mariner fans are a loyal bunch, but that loyalty has been consistently tested over the past decade. What will the team do to keep its fan base interested in the years ahead?

MARINERS ATTENDANCE 1996-2011

YEAR	ATTEN-DANCE	AVG	A.L. RANK	W-L	FINISH
1996	2,723,850	33,628	4th	85-76	2nd
1997	3,192,237	39,410	3rd	90-72	1st
1998	2,651,511	32,735	5th	76-85	3rd
1999	2,916,346	36,004	4th	79-83	3rd
2000	2,914,624	35,983	4th	91-71	2nd
2001	3,507,326	43,300	1st	116-46	1st
2002	3,542,938	43,740	1st	93-69	3rd
2003	3,268,509	40,352	2nd	93-69	2nd
2004	2,940,731	35,863	3rd	63-99	4th
2005	2,725,459	33,648	4th	69-93	4th
2006	2,481,165	30,632	6th	78-84	4th
2007	2,672,223	32,588	6th	88-74	2nd
2008	2,329,702	28,762	7th	61-101	4th
2009	2,195,533	27,105	7th	85-77	3rd
2010	2,085,630	25,749	8th	61-101	4th
2011	1,939,421	23,088	8th	67-95	4th

This cartoon originally appeared in the August 2010 issue of *The Grand Salami*

Chapter 34

THE KIDS ARE ALRIGHT

The day after the '10 season ended, Howard Lincoln and Jack Zduriencik sent emails to Mariner fans preaching patience.

Zduriencik noted that eight of the M's nine minor-league teams had made the playoffs in 2010, with three of those teams, including the Triple-A Tacoma Rainiers, playing in their league's championship series. And while the M's had reached a new level of offensive futility in 2010, scoring 513 runs, the fewest in the majors since 1972, Zduriencik pointed out that Seattle's minor-leaguers had led baseball in runs scored and home runs in 2010, with the cumulative win-loss record of their nine teams at .544, second best in baseball.

Most of the hitters the Mariners were developing were in the lower levels of the minor leagues and weren't ready to play in the majors in 2011. While the Mariners preached patience, they couldn't expect their fans to go through another season of watching the worst offense in baseball. The team needed to add some offense for the '11 season if it expected to get back on the winning track.

While Zduriencik said in his letter to the fans that he wanted the Mariners to produce better results "sooner rather than later," it soon became apparent that Zduriencik would have even less flexibility to build the '11 team than he'd had in 2010. Management had not authorized an increase in the player payroll, leaving Zduriencik forced to shop the bargain bin for upgrades.

Before Zduriencik could begin his quest of acquiring better players to replace some of the failures of 2010, he had a major task at hand: hiring a new manager to lead the Mariners. It's often said that a team's managerial hires go in cycles — that when a players' manager like Wakamatsu were let go, the team would likely go the opposite route in choosing his successor, hiring a disciplinarian.

And that's what happened in Seattle when the Mariners hired former Cleveland Indians Manager Eric Wedge, choosing the forty-three-year-old Wedge over former Mets Manager Bobby Valentine, former Blue Jays

Manager John Gibbons, former Astros Manager Cecil Cooper and former Pirates Manager Lloyd McLendon. In contrast with the managerial search the M's had conducted when Wakamatsu was hired, Zduriencik only interviewed men with experience managing in the majors.

Wedge not only had that experience, but he'd had a good deal of success, winning ninety-plus games twice in seven seasons managing the Tribe, including an '07 season in which the Indians were one game from defeating the Red Sox in the ALCS and going to the World Series. He also had a good track record for developing young players, as Grady Sizemore, Travis Hafner, Asdrubal Cabrera, Shin-Soo Choo, and Cliff Lee had all become impact players under his guidance.

This managerial hiring was an important one for Zduriencik. Having already dismissed the first manager he'd hired since taking over, it was critical that Jack get it right this time around, for it wasn't likely the higher ups would let him hire a third manager if the first two didn't work out.

As the end of the year approached, Geoff Baker of the *Seattle Times* spoke with Chuck Armstrong about the budget for 2011. Armstrong revealed that the payroll would be the same as in 2010 and praised ownership for not cutting it.

"I'm really grateful to the ownership for not lowering the player payroll," Armstrong said. "We don't have much flexibility now, so if we had to further reduce the budget, we might have to do some things that might have been damaging in the long run. We're not involved in any kind of salary dump."

Armstrong explained that both he and Zduriencik had made presentations to ownership spelling out why cutting payroll for 2011 wasn't a good idea "since it would lower fan expectations."

Armstrong needn't have worried about Mariner fans having any expectations for 2011. The fans were smarter than that. Coming off a season in which the M's had a historically bad offense, the team's effort to improve its offense was catcher Miguel Olivo and designated hitter Jack Cust. Olivo had played for the Mariners before and had been one of the worst players ever to put on a Seattle uniform, hitting .176 with fourteen passed balls in 104 games in 2004 and 2005. Cust was coming off an off-year with Oakland where he'd spent time in the minors.

With just $5.1 million allocated for free agents ($2.5 million for Olivo and $2.6 million for Cust), that left the M's again without a good solution for left field. Bradley was still around and was guaranteed $13 million, but he'd hit .205 with eight home runs in 2010 and couldn't be counted on to rebound. Saunders hadn't been much better, batting .211 with eighty-four strikeouts in 280 at-bats. Without the funds to pursue a legitimate left-fielder or DH, the M's were left with that meager firepower entering the '11 season.

Fittingly, the team's "Believe Big" slogan was abandoned for 2011, replaced by the less ambitious "Ready to Play."

Zduriencik made a couple of low-profile moves that worked out well, trading for St. Louis shortstop Brendan Ryan and bringing Bedard back on a non-guaranteed contract. Bedard had had shoulder surgery in 2010 and hadn't pitched in the majors since July 2009.

If Zduriencik had been given more money, the M's might have been able to contend in 2011. Seattle had the best starting rotation in the league in the first half of the season, with right-handed phenom Michael Pineda, who made the All-Star team as a rookie, and Bedard solidifying a rotation that already featured Hernandez, improving right-hander Doug Fister, and the underrated Jason Vargas. But once again, the Mariners got the worst production in the league out of their DH and left-fielders. The rest of Seattle's lineup wasn't strong enough to withstand getting so little from positions usually featuring two of the best hitters on a team. Bradley hit .218 with two home runs before being released in May, while Saunders hit .168 before being sent to Tacoma in early June. Cust was allowed to bat 270 times, hitting .213 with three home runs before being released in early August.

With great starting pitching and a stellar bullpen led by closer Brandon League, who was named to the A.L. All-Star team, and capable setup men David Pauley and Jamey Wright, the M's remained competitive for the first three months of the '11 season. After beating Oakland 4-2 in ten innings on July 5, Seattle's record stood at 43-43 and the M's were just two and a half games behind the first-place Texas Rangers.

While the Mariners were in rebuilding mode, the team's close proximity to first place had Seattle abuzz with talk of what kind of mid-season help might be available before the July 31 trading deadline. Veteran switch-hitter Carlos Beltran of the New York Mets was readily available and would have looked good in left field. Several other hitters were available that would have represented upgrades over what Cust was giving the M's in the DH role.

Within days of such trade talk becoming a hot topic on Seattle's two local sports-radio stations, KIRO 710 and KJR 950, KIRO radio reporter Shannon Drayer reported that the Mariners were tapped out on their budget and were unlikely to spend the money needed to add a veteran hitter or two who might help the M's stay in contention in the wide open A.L. West.

While the '11 Mariners managed to hang near first place for the first half of the season and had an opportunity to make a playoff run, just as they did in 2002-03, management refused to authorize an increase in payroll and the team soon fell out of contention.

And boy did they ever! Within days of the pronouncement that midseason help was unlikely to arrive in the form of a bat or two to improve the M's offense, the '11 team embarked on a losing streak of historic proportions. Whether it was a letdown in the clubhouse after the M's players learned of the budget issues or just a mediocre team sinking back to their proper level after months of overachieving, the team lost a franchise record seventeen straight games from July 6 to 26 and landed in last place of the A.L. West, where they'd remain for all but one day of the rest of the '11 season.

Given the M's lack of recent success, opportunities to contend for the postseason should not be easily dismissed. When the team is close to first place, deficiencies in the team should be addressed, especially when those problem areas of the team exist in the first place because of an artificially low budget set by the team's upper-level executives.

While some said that the '11 Mariners weren't ready to win and shouldn't have made trades to improve the offense, that's a losing mentality. There are plenty of recent examples of teams that strengthened themselves at midseason and made the playoffs. Once a team gets to the postseason, anything can happen. The teams that won the World Series in 2010 and 2011, the San Francisco Giants and St. Louis Cardinals, barely made the playoffs, with the '10 Giants winning the N.L. West by two games and the '11 Cardinals edging out Atlanta for the N.L. Wild Card by one game.

With the M's clearly out of contention, Zduriencik set about adding talent to the Mariners organization at the July 31 trade deadline. In two deals with the Tigers and Red Sox, he traded starting-pitchers Fister and Bedard, reliever Pauley, and minor-league reliever Josh Fields. In return, he obtained six young players, including four who would join the major-league club during the summer of 2011.

One young player who stood out in 2011 was Dustin Ackley. Selected by the Mariners with the second overall pick of the '09 draft, he reached the majors in mid-June after just a year and a half in the minor leagues. He stood out immediately as one of the best players on the team and within weeks was installed as the team's No. 3 hitter. While he hit .273

with twenty-nine extra-base hits the rest of the year, he also showed he was a finished product defensively at second base, a position he'd played for little more than a year.

The second half of the season was all about auditioning new players, with right-hander Blake Beavan and left-hander Charlie Furbush filling the rotation spots vacated by Fister and Bedard, while outfielders Casper Wells and Trayvon Robinson, infielder Kyle Seager, and relief-pitchers Tom Wilhelmsen and Chance Ruffin all received significant opportunities to show what they could do.

2011 TOP PERFORMERS

Dustin Ackley, .273, 6 HR, 36 RBI

Mike Carp, .276, 12 HR, 46 RBI

Felix Hernandez, 14-14, 3.47 ERA, 233.2 IP

Michael Pineda, 9-10, 3.74 ERA, 171 IP

Brandon League, 1-5, 2.79 ERA, 37 saves

While several of the rookies were bright spots in 2011 for the Mariners, two players who were not were two of the three highest-paid players on the team, Chone Figgins and Ichiro.

Figgins had gotten off to a poor start in 2010, his first year in Seattle, but he'd rebounded in the second half of that season. Switched back to his familiar third-base position for 2011, he was expected to revert to the player the M's thought they had acquired when they'd signed him away from the Angels. But Figgins was worse in 2011, hitting .186 in the first half, and eventually was demoted to a bench player with fans in Seattle hoping the M's could trade him. Figgins landed on the disabled list in early August with a hip injury. He didn't return the rest of the season and his future remained up in the air, with most thinking he'd played his last game for Seattle.

While Ichiro wasn't nearly as bad as Figgins, he had his worst season as a Mariner in 2011, hitting just .272 after ten consecutive seasons hitting over .300. He missed out on a two-hundred-hit season for the first time and ten-year streaks of All-Star honors and Gold Gloves also came to an end. With just one year remaining on his Mariner contract after

2011, questions about his future were persistent. Would the M's sign the thirty-eight-year-old to a pricey contract extension despite signs he was in serious decline? Clearly he was no longer worth the $18 million a year the M's were paying him, but with Japanese ownership, would the Mariners dare suggest Ichiro take a pay cut in his next contract?

Ichiro's future was one of the key questions facing the Mariners when the '11 season ended. The team had shown significant improvement in several areas, but thanks in large part to the record-setting losing streak, Seattle's final record of 67-95 was just a six-game improvement over the dismal '10 season.

Chapter 35

WILL THE M'S EVER WIN
THE WORLD SERIES?

The question I'm often asked is whether there is hope for the Mariners, whether a franchise that hadn't seriously contended for much of the last decade can turn things around and get to the World Series in the near future.

I believe there is hope because of some of the pieces the Mariners had in place entering the '12 season, most notably General Manager Jack Zduriencik and Scouting Director Tom McNamara. This pair has been charged with resurrecting a farm-system left barren by the previous regime, which traded away several good young prospects and whiffed badly on several high draft picks. Two of Zduriencik and McNamara's draft picks, Ackley and Seager, contributed at the major-league level in 2011 and several more, including James Paxton, Danny Hultzen, Nick Franklin, and Taijuan Walker, should follow in 2012 and 2013.

Zduriencik has a solid plan in place and has displayed good acumen in several key areas — evaluating and developing amateur players, trading creatively, and finding useful talent undervalued by other teams. In his first three years on the job he wasn't given much of an opportunity to spend money because the franchise was still recovering from Bill Bavasi's mistakes, still paying departed players like Silva, Betancourt, and Bradley through the end of the '11 season, more than three years after Bavasi was fired.

That slate has now been wiped clean, with all those players finally off the books and the team able to focus on paying players who are actually contributing to the current Mariner team. The one major free-agent Zduriencik has signed, Figgins, hasn't worked out as planned, but that's part of the game sometimes. I'm of the belief that when all is said and done, Zduriencik's batting average on signings and trades will be well over .500, while it's hard to say that even twenty percent of Bavasi's moves worked out.

The biggest factor in determining if Zduriencik's plan can succeed is whether he'll be able to get the support he'll need from his bosses. The team has been run like a business since Lincoln took over and while the team's owners have made tremendous profits during that time, their approach has caused the team's fortunes on the field to flounder, impacting the bottom line.

The team's ownership group needs to do a better job of balancing baseball with business. Baseball should win out on occasion, because a team that wins a World Series is going to make more money and increase more in value than a team that loses most of the time.

Allowing the club's general manager to make the necessary moves will help them, both in baseball and in business. If Zduriencik needs a few extra millions to sign a slugger or two, he should be handed the checkbook; if the team needs to spend a little extra at the trade deadline to improve its pennant chances and fire up the clubhouse and fan base, it should be willing to listen to the baseball guys.

The task of competing in the American League isn't going to get easier in the years ahead. The Mariners will have to be up to the challenge of keeping up with strong division rivals such as the Los Angeles Angels of Anaheim and the Texas Rangers, both of whom have become more aggressive in spending on talent in recent years.

Additionally, while the American League West has been the only four-team division in baseball since MLB's realignment in 1994, a fifth team, the Houston Astros, will be added to the division in 2013, making the M's task more difficult.

A challenge was issued in December 2011, when the Los Angeles Angels of Anaheim signed slugger Albert Pujols to a ten-year, $254 million contract, luring him away from the St. Louis Cardinals, the team for which he'd played the first eleven seasons of his incredible career. During his time with the Cardinals, the thirty-two-year-old Pujols posted a career average of .328 and averaged forty home runs a season. While Pujols may not be a productive hitter for the entire term of the contract, he makes the Angels a more formidable opponent for the next few seasons. Another of the M's A.L. West rivals, the Texas Rangers, reached the World Series in both 2010 and 2011 and followed up those successes by signing twenty-five-year-old Yu Darvish, said to be the best pitcher ever to come out of Japan, prior to the '12 season for a total outlay of more than $111 million (a $51.7 million posting fee to Darvish's Japanese team, the Nippon Ham Fighters, and a six-year, $60 million contract for the pitcher).

It remains to be seen when and how the Mariners will step to the plate to try to compete with these two powerhouses, but whatever happens, don't believe it if you hear the M's can't afford to contend or don't have the money to go out and sign top free agents.

The team's owners have made more than $100 million dollars in profits in the last decade. In December 2011 the club was appraised at a value of $641 million by the judge in minority owner Chris Larson's divorce case. That meant that the team's value had increased by more than a half a billion dollars since the current ownership group paid $100 million for the team in 1992. Mariners' ownership claims that they hadn't taken any profits out of the team since buying the club, so presumably they're just waiting for the right opportunity to start spending money again to help make the Mariners winners. Hopefully that time will come soon.

Some suggested that the finances of Nintendo, the corporation that owns a majority interest in the team and reported a loss of more than $900 million in 2011, and Larson, who owns thirty percent of the team and reportedly was deep in debt, could affect the ability of Mariner ownership to put a competitive team on the field in the coming seasons.

Those issues shouldn't be a factor for two reasons: The team has significant revenue streams, with $45 million coming into the team's coffers each year from the team's TV contract alone. And despite Nintendo's losses, Yamauchi, the team's primary owner, was identified by *Forbes* magazine in 2011 as the wealthiest owner in baseball, with a net worth of $4.6 billion. However, at this writing Yamauchi was eighty-four, so the possibility of the current owners putting the team up for sale in the near future cannot be ruled out.

While we've got high hopes for the future, we'll be there watching no matter what happens.

INDEX

INDEX

INDEX

INDEX

ABOUT THE AUTHOR

The author interviews Mariner second-baseman Dustin Ackley.

Jon Wells is a baseball writer and publisher who founded *The Grand Salami*, an independent monthly magazine that has covered the Seattle Mariners since 1996. Wells, a former entertainment lawyer, lives in West Seattle with his wife, Michele, and their two dogs.

An avid baseball fan, Jon has been to forty-two different major-league ballparks and also enjoys indie-rock music, NFL football, and red wine.

Despite attending more than one hundred baseball games per year for much of the last two decades, as of the beginning of the 2012 season he still hadn't seen a no-hitter in person. Find Jon Wells on Facebook "ShipwreckedinSeattle."

ACKNOWLEDGEMENTS

Thanks go out to the following people for one reason or many: Dan Levant, Kent Sturgis, Jeff Angus, Dan Raley, Jim Caple, J Michael Kenyon, Pat Thomas, Drew Edwards, Phil Rognier, Herman Sarkowsky, Mike Gastineau, Frank Lee, Tim Harrison, Andy Backlund, Matt Brignall, Mark Aucutt, Patrick Lagreid, Rob Neyer, Deidre Silva, Mark Meyers, Mike Livingston, Ralph Winnie, Bob Condotta, Greg Johns, John Torrance, Laurie Hodges, Bill Wilmot, Mark Thomas, Gary West, Jan Olson, Marilyn Niehaus, Andy Niehaus, Nobu Numamoto, Aaron Bigby, Chipper Wells, the Keller Family, Seth Everett, and Mark Linn.